Praise for *Tales of Times Square*

"Friedman manages to paint a devastating portrait of a culture of vice... *Tales of Times Square* can be read as a brief for action."
— *Washington Times*

"An entertaining obscene postcard of Times Square on the brink."
— *Village Voice*

"Amazing stories!"
— *San Francisco Examiner*

"Short stories that are the best I've ever seen about Times Square. I couldn't put it down. I recommended [Friedman] for a Pulitzer Prize."
— *Show Business*

"Evocative, entertaining, not for the faint-hearted. [Friedman's] no-holds-barred portrait of the porn industry and its workers is intriguing, if a little cold-blooded." — *Chicago Sun-Times*

"Reminiscent of *New Yorker* writing at its best, but with much more humor.... Unforgettable, and good enough to turn Jimmy Breslin or Studs Terkel pale mauve with envy."
— *Ft. Lauderdale Sun-Sentinel*

"A fascinating study of life in New York City's entertainment hub."
— *Variety*

"The most compelling reading to come along since the attorney general's report....This book made me want to shower."
— *Washington Post*

A rainy night in 1923

Courtesy of the New York Historical Society, New York City

By Josh Alan Friedman

Any Similarity to Persons Living Or Dead Is Purely Coincidental
(With Drew Friedman)

Warts And All
(With Drew Friedman)

Tales of Times Square

When Sex Was Dirty

I, Goldstein
(With Al Goldstein)

TALES OF TIMES SQUARE

JOSH ALAN FRIEDMAN

FERAL HOUSE

ISBN: 978-1-932595-28-4

Published by:
Feral House
1240 W. Sims Way, Suite 124
Port Townsend, WA 98368
www.FeralHouse.com

Grateful acknowledgement is made for permission to reprint excerpts from the following: *Carnival Crossroads: The Story of Times Square* by W.G. Rogers and Mildred Weston. © 1960 by W.G. Rogers and Mildred Weston Rogers. Reprinted by permission of Doubleday & Co., Inc. / *Broadway* by Brooks Atkinson. © 1970 by Brooks Atkinson. Reprinted with permission of Macmillan Publishing Co. / *Ladies and Gentlemen, Lenny Bruce!* by Albert Goldman and Lawrence Schiller. © 1971, 1973, 1974 by Alskog, Inc. And Albert Goldman. Reprinted by permission of Random House, Inc. / "Queen of the Gang Bang" originally published under the title "Great American Cream Machine" in *Screw*. © 1979, reprinted by permission of *Screw* / "Pecker Full of Miracles" originally published in *Screw*. © 1981, reprinted by permission of *Screw* / "Season's Greetings from Long Jean Silver" originally published under the title "I Cream of Jeannie" in *Screw*. © 1982, reprinted by permission of *Screw* / "Rave Up" originally published in *Screw*. © 1982, reprinted by permission of *Screw* / "A Schitzy Girl is Like a Melody" originally published in *Live!* © 1982, reprinted by permission of *Live!* / "Tales of Times Square" originally published in *Oui*, and contained the following pieces: "Yesterday's Cheers Have a Very Short Echo"; "The Crystal Ball of 42nd Street"; "In Search of the Longest Stiletto"; and material on Oxuzana (contained in "Inside the Peeps") and material on Bob Anthony (contained in "Old Flesh Agents"). © 1983, reprinted by permission of *Oui* / "Save Our 42nd Street!" originally published in *Soho News*, © 1978.

Tales of Times Square was originally published in a clothbound edition in 1986 by Delacorte Press.

10 9 8 7 6 5 4 3

To My Darling Peg

CONTENTS

AFTER THE DEATH OF BURLESQUE

TELL ALL THE GANG ON 42ND STREET!

LOWDOWN

FOR THE RECORD!

THE SAVIORS

A LONER'S PARADISE

WHEN SEX WAS DIRTY

ACKNOWLEDGEMENTS

Special Thanks:

Al Goldstein, Larry Wichman, John Lombardi,
Richard Brandes, Richard Jaccoma, Larry Sloman,
Gil Reavill, Jeff Goodman, Jay Acton, Susan Moldow,
and Paul McCarthy

B.J.F., G.F. and P.L.B.
for support

FOREWORD

This is a 21st-anniversary edition of *Tales of Times Square*. More than any neighborhood I can imagine, Times Square is a character itself. It occupies a fifth dimension, with its own molecules and voltage, its own history and sex life, and seemingly has a will of its own. A lot has gone down since the first edition. The "New 42nd Street" may be the greatest transformation to hit the streets since—for those who recall—the "New Nixon." I address these events in a new Afterword.

We've also added six chapters from a lesser-known collection, *When Sex Was Dirty*. I wrote these pieces soon after *Tales*, and they seem to fit.

The events in *Tales* took place from 1978–1984. This was the Golden Age of Pornography, when porn was *really* dirty. Mom-and-pimp sex enterprises flourished. All the characters are real, with the exception of Dudley Arnholt, composite Times Square masturbator/Everyman of "Inside the Peeps."

"Save Our 42nd Street" was offered as sheer conjecture. The police officers' names in "Cops and Skells" and "Pross and Pimps" were changed so that they could continue to work in their sensitive positions.

The places are gone; many characters have died. But their ghosts probably still wander 42nd Street, and you never know which face in the crowd might be one of them.

Meanwhile, let us revisit Times Square's nastiest days as a mecca of cheap thrills, ghetto entertainment, and 25-cent fulfillment for our sexually bankrupt masses. Hello, sucker!

Your smart-ass tour guide,
Josh

YESTERDAY'S CHEERS HAVE A VERY SHORT ECHO

Izzy Grove—the "Ghetto Avenger," as he was once known in the twenties as a top middleweight contender—is bracing himself for the street any day now. Loews Corporation, owners of the old show-biz building on 46th Street off Broadway where Izzy's kept a $60-a-month "office" for seventeen years, is giving him the boot. With the market ripe, Loews wants back this little space. And Izzy's become one scared seventy-three-year-old pug.

"I got tears in my eyes just talking about it," says Izzy, dabbing under his box glasses with a hankie. "They cut my phone, they knock down my door. I live right, I behave myself, I'm not a bum. I never been convicted of a crime or felony, I'm no tough guy. People that see me, unnerstand, I don't want them to pity me. People put money in my—looka—" Izzy pulls out a wad of crumpled bills and phone numbers—officials of housing bureaucracy, friends, connections—but none of them do any good. His fingers are twisted, nails fungous; his hands have small lacerations, his ears look like doughy biscuits. "I don't have to cry to ya, it's not pleasant. Sure, if I wanted to I can go ahead and work for fifty bookmakers and ticket hustlers. My wife, Alice, she rest in peace, always told me that instead of being a tough guy, a shylock, a racket guy, a numbers runner or a bookmaker, to go into legitimate business where people will have respect for ya."

Grove scored *the* first knockout at the old Madison Square Garden in the Twenties. He went on to kayo "three out of four former world *champeens*," in bouts at the Polo Grounds, Ebbets Field, Yankee Stadium.

"I got ten columns from Damon Runyon in the *New York American*," he boasts. "But a fella called Dan Parker, sports editor of the *Daily Mirror*, is who made me." In the Thirties, Grove became a Broadway booking agent and a regular of Lindy's society. "I wasn't MCA or General Amusement or the William Morris office—those are the key bookers. The rest is all amateur night in Dixie." Nevertheless, Grove booked Ellington, Cab Calloway, Lionel Hampton, dozens of big bands at dances for some twenty years. "But ya see, truefully, uh, today it ain't here anymore, because people don't want acts." His next career—pasting up fight posters for the Garden, pushing a shopping cart and bucket of glue—began to take precedence. It's been his meal ticket for the past thirty years, but lately they haven't been calling.

Grove is too worried to finish his corned beef at the "new" Lindy's, a failing tourist trap above 42nd Street wallpapered with faces of dead comedians who fraternized at the original landmark on 50th. He wants to get to the Actors' Temple so they can start the prayers. ("Ya gotta have a minyan, nine men—with the rabbi is ten. Ya gotta promise 'em.")

"Hey, Izzy, baby!" shouts a black movie usher outside the RKO National, where *Enigma* is playing. They embrace. "All these people are my friends," says Izzy, knocking on the box office window where an old broad looks up with a wave and a smile. This has been his neighborhood since he took his first job as an errand boy at the I. Miller Shoe Building after World War I. He walks up Broadway to the Gaiety deli, taps the glass, and both counter guys look up from their carving boards, waving.

"I remember when a pastrami sandwich cost thirty-five cents here, now it's five dollars." He crosses the street to True Value. "The locksmiths are my friends," he says.

"Hey, Izzy!" yell both smiths, dropping their tools. The old fighter is making his rounds, reassuring himself that "Everybody knows Izzy Grove," making sure he's still part of the old crowd.

"I know Max Asness, who opened the Stage on Sixth Av'nya. The Colony record shop on 49th, they're in business forty years, unnerstand, wanted to give me downstairs to sleep, but it ain't livable. The owners of

Howard Johnson's, Morris and Jack Rubinstein, I know them forty-odd years, they never let me go hungry.

"I go to the Garden whenever there's a fight. I walk in with pride, with dignity, I wash up before I go, I comb my hair, unnerstand, I have a good name, whaddamy gonna get mixed up with a tough guy? I see the former fighters that I knew from yesteryear, and I have to cry to tell ya, it's pitiful. This is the only sport, that when a boxer retires, he gets nothing. If he's hungry or he needs help, he can't get it because there is no organization. At one time I was a member of the Veteran Boxer Association, but they had no strength, because fighters, they don't come to meetings. But if I do get some real money, I will open up a house for former boxers that need financial assistance, medical supplies."

Izzy can still throw a wallop, and since his seventieth birthday he claims to have kayoed three muggers: "Yeah, well lemme tell ya sompin'. I was ridin' the subway, coming from the St. George Hotel, unnerstand? Coupla guys, one sits next to me here, one over here, and then one that goes through my pockets. I got up, unnerstand. I says, 'Whaddaya doin'?' The first fella I hit a left hook, unnerstand? Down he went. Second guy was a little tougher. It took me three or four punches to belt him out. The cops went through the trains, they couldn't find the guys, unnerstand One's black and one's maybe Spanish. The *Post* found out about it at the police station, they took pictures and all."

Eight bellhops in maroon uniforms surround Izzy as he enters the old Edison Hotel lobby. "How long you know Izzy Grove?" Iz asks the shortest hop, one with a carbuncle on his schnozz.

"Twenty-five, thirty years," answers the hop. "We go back at least that long."

"What fighters have we seen go through this lobby?" another bellhop inquires, then answers himself. "Jack Dempsey, Maxie Baer, Boomer Wilson, Benny Leonard. We seen 'em all."

"What killed Max Kramer?" asks the pimple-nosed hop, "between you and I, now we're gentlemen."

"... Aggravation," answers Izzy.

"No. Too much sex. A chippy over the old Lincoln Hotel. *Boomba*-da-*boomba*-da-*boomba*," goes the little bellhop, smacking his fist.

"This is my family, these are my friends, unnerstand?" says Izzy, a hankie to his eye. "Ge'elmen, you deem me the privilege of being in your company."

Izzy pauses by the Edison Theater where *Oh! Calcutta!* has been in terminal revival. "I ran dances here, boy meets girl, back when it was a ballroom. I made about three hundred fifty marriages through my dances. Lonely Hearts. I'm the one who started the Over-Twenty-eight Singles business."

How does Izzy feel about his beloved neighborhood, Times Square, turning into a porno wasteland?

"I don't bother with that. It's disgraceful, it's distasteful, it is not polite society. I was a family man, I'm still a grandfather, unnerstand, I keep my head up in the air because my self-respect is not for sale."

A little bus driver from the ShortLine depot, where Izzy sits a few hours each day, pokes his head out a bus at Izzy, jokingly: "C'mon, Izzy, ya going uptown, let's go."

"Get lost, ya prick, ya!" yells Izzy, suddenly angry. "I'll drop ya, you ever talk to me again."

"Okay." The little driver shrugs, confused.

"Get outta here," the Ghetto Avenger continues, stalking toward the driver with his fist clenched. "Good-bye, get lost, spadoofa! When ya see me next, ignore me."

"He's a *pal* of yours, Izzy," says another bus man, "take it easy."

"Who needs 'im?" mutters Izzy. "I got my own troubles."

Grove can tell when the temple is open from a block away: "If the lightbulb is on, the rabbi's in." He stops before an In Memoriam wall listing hundreds of Jewish show-biz figures who prayed here. It is only recently that he began any sort of religious ritual. The rabbi offers support, but so far none of his leads for a cheap room have worked out. The courts want Izzy out immediately. Grove can't afford more than the $60 he now pays: "I got relatives, whadda they gonna do. Where are they? I was in the papers. Where are they? Where? When I made money, unnerstand, *hey, yeah*, free tickets, the fights, afterwards somethin' to eat. But I wanna pinpoint one thought. Quote me. *Yesterday's cheers have a very short echo*.... Because when I was making money, it was a different story, I helped people. When I was broke, I didn't have nothin', I starved. All this hullabaloo—you don't get nothin', the world loves a winner. It's one of these odd quirks of happenstance that befall mankind. Wheremy gonna go, howmy gonna live?"

AFTER THE DEATH OF BURLESQUE

A Schitzy Girl Is Like a Melody

Kandi Barbour's June engagement at the Melody Burlesk in Times Square is unique in that she refuses to strip. Several old heterosexuals mutter in chagrin as they amble out of the theater after the five o'clock headline act walked offstage with her dress still on. Some of these gents even hissed—a mild reaction from an audience that hastily applauds each shedding of a major undergarment, culminating in an ovation when crotch is finally splayed.

The Melody girls orchestrate their stripteases over five-song cassette soundtracks; the generous ones reach cunt by the fourth number, while the ones who fancy themselves jazz ballerinas wait till the fifth. In any case, all of them are skilled enough to create a steamy anticipation throughout the audience that can only be relieved when the last piece of cloth magically unveils snatcheroo. But Kandi teased the old dukes by flashing snippets of tit, then hiking her dress up and down. She's taken their blood pressures on a wild-goose chase, and abandoned them with blueballs. As they sang in *Gypsy*, you gotta have a gimmick.

Al Kronish, founder and co-owner of the Melody, makes his way toward the dressing rooms, where women prepare privately to undress in public. "What's wrong?" he asks, taking charge.

"What's wrong?" snarls Kandi Barbour, smashing her head with her hairbrush in a vain attempt to comb it. "Anna friggin' fuckin' Turner, that's what's wrong! Why doesn't she just fuck him right on stage?"

Al steps into the small headliner's dressing room at the Melody. Panty hose, Maybelline lipsticks, and other girlie paraphernalia are scattered about the dresser. "Fuck who on stage?" he inquires.

"My boyfriend, that's who!" she wails in genuine pain, flinging her hairbrush and makeup at the wall, barely missing Kronish. "She's taking him away from me!"

"So why don't you win him back?" advises Al. "Don't act like this." A police siren fades outside the window, two floors below on 48th and Broadway.

The Atlanta-bred Kandi Barbour is behaving like a black-sheep descendant of Scarlett O'Hara. This is the worst fit she's thrown all week according to the old fellow in the audio booth, who circles his finger around his head, cuckoo style. Just that afternoon, she'd gone around announcing she had a brain tumor. And now she huffed and puffed in exasperation, stomping her foot and heaving her breasts into a black brassiere like a demon-possessed Kewpie doll.

"Who're you here to photograph?" she demands of a photographer cautiously stationed outside her door. "Anna Turner?"

"*You*, I'm here to take pictures of *you.* Is that okay?" This seems to calm her for a moment. After all, she is this week's top bill, a veteran centerfold queen and star of X-rated humdingers like *Neon Nights, Centerfold Fever, Screwples.* Anna Turner is merely one of six "Melody Favorites" appearing that week as an undercard to Kandi.

"Are y'all sure there ain't any pictures of that fuckin' Anna Turner in that camera? How do I know you won't take some of her, how do I know you didn't really come for her?"

"Because," soothes Al Kronish, "you're a beautiful woman, and any magazine would want your picture." Al does not pander or condescend to Kandi, but meets her squarely in the mascaraed eye with logic. Besides, the photographer has never even heard of Anna Turner.

"Yeah, okay," she says, agreeing to let him photograph her next set. Then the door to the dressing room slams with Kronish trapped inside, and all hell breaks loose as more of Kandi's girlie products are heard crashing into the wall.

A few doors over, wiry, redheaded stripper Anna Turner is slipping on her black gown and white gloves, about to go on. Anna shrugs off Kandi's tantrum with little concern: "She's a space cadet and I'm a space commander. She fell into a black hole years ago and hasn't found her way out. But if she looks at me wrong, I'll punch her lights out in one second."

Anna chuckles fearlessly, then reveals the root of this current fuss: "I know most major rock stars and music people in New York. So I got Kandi and me a double date with the Dire Straits." As the plot unfolds, Anna explains how Kandi wanted the Straits' lead guitarist, Mark Knopfler, for herself, over drummer Pick Withers. As the English group tours the States, Knopfler weighs in as a heavier catch on the groupie fish scale, what with Steely Dan sessions and his guitar-man-of-the-moment soloing from 1978's "Sultans of Swing." In any case, Kandi was unable to land Knopfler. When she later ran into Anna Turner at a party, Anna was with her own boyfriend who, coincidentally, bore a striking resemblance to Mark Knopfler. To make a case study short, Kandi took Anna Turner's boyfriend for Knopfler, thereby believing that Anna had, in effect, *stolen* the Dire Straits' guitarist from her clutches. And this accounted for the Southern belle's present mental anguish.

Two hours later, Kandi Barbour is back for her 8:20 set, after a respite at Bernard's bar across the street. The profoundly bored emcee in the one-way glass audio booth, who takes charge of the girls' soundtracks, mumbles her entrance through buzzy speakers—"The lovely and exciting Miss . . ." Kronish is out in the aisle, relaxed as usual, but with the slightest trace of anxiety. Kandi prances out on the

T-runway, cute and peppy as ever, sashaying in a floppy maroon gown with black shawl. From the neck up, she has the loveliest face in all the porn parade; an angelic Barbie doll, perfect makeup coordination and waves of black hair that bounce over her eyes. But below the neck is an odd set of hooters that leave some in confusion as she treats the old boys with flashes of them by her second song. They're large, but with imprecise areola borders, appearing to contain too much nipple tissue; although, granted, magazines do receive fan mail from staunch Barbour nipple aficionados.

Onstage, Kandi marches about in circles, dabbing her finger in guys' faces. She's hardly removed a stitch by the third number. "I can't believe it," says Kronish, pacing, in a slow burn. Finally she fishes 'em out, the photog's flashbulb goes off, and she freezes in utter disgust on the T-runway.

"Who the fuck are you?" she demands. As the poor photographer reminds her that she granted permission in her dressing room, some schmuck in the first row decides to play hero. He asks if she'd like him to "take care of the bastard."

"Who are you insulting, me or him?" responds Kandi to the offer. The Protector of Women insists most definitely *him*, and approaches the photographer like a beach bully about to kick sand in someone's face.

"The lady don't want you takin' her pitcher," he says, rolling up a sleeve. At this point, Kronish heads over and the theater's 400-pound bouncer radars in to keep the peace. The guy is about to make a lunge for the camera when he spots the bouncer.

"Say, am *I* gonna be in any of those pitchers?" he asks, changing the nature of his concern. "Are you the manager?"

"Sir, I guarantee you will not be in any of them," says Kronish, "it's just not allowed."

"Well, what the fuck is this, I paid seven dollars to sit here?" The cameraman and the bouncer reassure him his pictures are not being taken. "Well, just leave the little lady alone," he warns. "And no more pitchers." Maybe, just maybe, he'd won himself a date, this middle-aged grease monkey in shining armor, who would steal Kandi Barbour from the Dire Straits.

But Kandi is unaware of his chivalry as he returns to his seat. She dances another minute, then freezes again. Her pain is more comical now—she breaks the "fourth wall," stagewise, once more, by stopping her striptease cold and bellowing for Al Kronish to come over.

"I've got my period," she whispers in his ear when he reaches the stage, and she holds her floppy maroon dress tight between her legs. After a minute of urgent, unheard deliberation, she's back in business, and finally strips, though she hides her puss with the dress. Kronish is reeling a bit from this unusual evening at his theater, where smooth-sailing professionalism is rarely interrupted. It has been a rough week for Kandi Barbour.

"But she draws," says Kronish, with a shrug.

Al Kronish, sixty-four-year-old founder of New York's Melody Burlesk, deals with the caprices, jealousies, phobias, menstrual cycles and successes of a whole generation of strippers, from the fringes to the forefront of the porn industry. And they all seem to adore him, like a good uncle to these girls who have known bad uncles. Ever since Kronish initiated the innovative policy of booking porn stars as strippers—which started with Jennifer Welles in the mid-Seventies—he's attracted every big name in the industry time and time again, only too glad to work for him. And this, balanced against his main profession as a conservative accountant in Westchester, where he also happens to do the tax returns of porn stars.

Kronish was born in The Bronx in 1918, went to De Witt Clinton High, and graduated as an accountant from Pace. He served in artillery for three years during World War II, using his skills in math to direct big guns against the Nazis. He later played shortstop for a semipro army team, and then with the Bronx Shamrocks for "big money."

Al's earliest burlesque memories are of Minskys' Republic and the Apollo, on 42nd Street. "My favorite was a girl named Sherry Britton, a gorgeous beauty, still around today, lives in New York. Another girl by the name of June Marsh, from Chicago. Man, she was *built*... I only tagged along when my friends went. Orchestra, chorus line, strippers, comedians. After the show was over, we'd have a drink and go home." Kronish was nineteen at the time, and dating, even speaking, with one of those strippers seemed beyond possibility. This, in contrast with the modern-day Melody, where fans can munch out on some of the talent.

"Had a lot of hard knocks, too," says Kronish. "Final exams were coming up when I lost my dad, while at the same time, the girl who I was going to marry leaves me. I felt like the world was coming to an end. I got another girl, obviously. My wife and I have been in love for thirty-two years."

In his stark Melody office, Al has two phones, always on the ring. Great quantities of toilet paper and towels line the metal shelves, and a worn couch plays host to small-time Broadway hucksters and elderly Melody hangers-on who mark their racing forms here. A hard-faced stripper pokes her head in. "I'm allergic to this place," she sneezes, sending the old OTB boys into spasms.

Tonight, Al is negotiating a delicate pet project—a three-day, marathon burlesque festival he envisions at the Palladium, a 3,500-seat crumbling rock palace in New York. Never has such an ambitious porn event taken place, and Kronish says there is only a "three percent chance I can pull it off." He is approaching Chuck Traynor, a self-admitted pimp and now manager of Marilyn Chambers, to get her to headline, and Seka's manager/hairdresser, Fred Mark, to acquire her as second bill. Chambers, according to Kronish, is worth "$25,000 more in ticket sales than Seka," who rings in as second in the monstro U.S. wanker marketplace. So far, however, Fred Mark has declined second billing for Seka—"Not for a million," he said. And Traynor has not yet bothered to return Al's calls. Nevertheless, Kronish feels he can secure a lineup of five "top girls" like Annette Haven, Vanessa Del Rio, and Samantha Fox once Seka or Marilyn falls in. Medium-level starlets he plans to book as hostesses, usherettes.

"I'll need to get all the girls together a day in advance to show them the theater. I need a quick turnover—eleven shows in three days. Say the live show goes from noon to one-twenty. At one-twenty you go into the lobby for an hour, rap with your favorite star, get your Polaroid and autographed picture. Each star will have a bridge table and chair. But there are still a lot of imponderables."

Kronish also has designs for a new burlesque house in New York, one that would book porn stars with their current films. But the formula wouldn't stray much from the Melody's. Although he loved old-time burlesque with comics and bump-and-grind bands, he's sure Manhattan couldn't handle a cabaret that would revive it.

"Didn't Ann Corio just try it across the street? I knew she would fail. She wouldn't listen to me, she went out the door and she failed in three weeks. Old-time burlesque? Not in Times Square. People who come to Times Square, they want *raunch.* I told Ann, if you wanna do this, you go to Queens, Westchester, Nassau, get permission. You'll make money there. Couples don't come down here. Also, she tried to charge $25, $30. You can't make it, and she didn't."

How about Broadway theaters?

"That's different. That's been here before we were."

Unlike any other porn establishment in Times Square, the Melody has its own fraternal order. Warming the seats on any given night we might see the likes of someone's Uncle Jack, a contingent of elevator operators, a randy row of young gas-pump jocks from Queens, a drooling paraplegic procession up front, shifty-eyed attorneys, and then, of course, the real royalty—crusty old cadavers brought back to life by the scent of a young, demented girl. The Melody is a living museum for these boys, the only place they'll see 'em.

"A typical Melody fella?" ponders Al. "Far be it for me to try and figure out why they're here... lonely people. They may be old men that never could relate with a woman. They find this is an outlet for what they lacked when they were young. He likes to see a pretty woman, beautiful body, naked, dancing, that's all."

Top stripper and Russ Meyer vixen Raven De La Croix, who headlines the Melody Burlesk twice a year, confirms this theory. She sees the audience as "Guys who just don't seem to be getting any." Especially the legions who show for "Mardi Gras," the notorious weekend program in which up to twenty dollar-a-lick girls cascade through the audience serving economy-priced "box lunch," tit feels, and dry humps. This heavenly, though risky, innovation was begun by Al's partner, Bob Anthony, in 1978.

"I'm sort of astonished at how some of these girls think," quoth the Raven, backstage during her last smash appearance. "Like, it's all right to go out there and serve lunch for a dollar, but the bastard stuck his finger up her butt, ya know? They're out there layin' on those guys like hogs in mud, and their values are hilarious, but it's sad. A lot of them are heavy junkies, real confused. They're broke, they come in, make a couple hundred bucks, get a fix, come back. You know how many guys you gotta hug, bump, and scrub for that money? How many old mouths you gotta kiss? It's heavy. Handi-Wipe city."

"We get a lot of junkies," admits Kronish, who personally books most of the headline acts and hires many of the fifty Mardi Gras girls who work in shifts each week. "You can always recognize a girl who's on something, it's obvious. And when she is, we fire her. But not forever, just until she cools off, for a week, two weeks, maybe a month. When you come back, if you wanna work, you gotta be straight."

About a half-dozen girls associated with the Melody died in its first eight years, according to Kronish. One jumped out of a window, another committed suicide, but none on the theater's premises. One was porn pioneer Tina Russell, who drank herself out. She was, remarkably, the only X-rated star to become completely totaled in the first dozen years of an industry where many live on the edge.

"She and I were very close. She used to call me at home once a week, sometimes just to speak with my wife. We were heartbroken."

Aside from being caught with needles in their rooms, other taboos girls must break to get fired are smoking in the rear, which the fire department bans; habitually coming late or not showing; and attempting to turn a trick on premises. Hiring girls, on the other hand, would seem like your Easy Street dream, but the continual turnover of downhill women becomes monotonous for the personnel department.

"Steve and I," says Al, referring to another in management, "do about ninety-five percent of the bookings, whether they be housegirls or stars." About fifty housegirls do Mardi Gras, working for tips, and some of them are booked as strippers, every eight weeks. Seven or eight different strippers are booked on stage each week, including the star; most stars appear twice a year. Strippers receive a fee, with individual contracts. "Actually, an unlimited number of women come in during Mardi Gras periods," says Al. "If we have, say, forty customers, we'll send about six girls out. If it's a full house, a hundred twenty or more, we'll send out a minimum of fifteen girls.... A lot of girls go on vacations, they work in Europe, Canada, which leaves openings for new girls coming round. But they can come back whenever they want and get booked."

Kronish, in all his admiration for women, is bemused by the instability of the stripping profession: "Even if you have contracts, what are you gonna do if they don't show up? Who you gonna sue?"

Big-chested Raven De La Croix, on the other hand, remembers seeing fierce dedication to the craft that she'll never forget: "It's wild. A girl was sitting around having a miscarriage. She was dragging herself across the stairs, and I asked, 'What the hell's wrong?' I thought she was about to OD. She said, 'I'm losing my baby, I'm losing my baby.' Her doctor ordered her to stay in bed and do nothing, or she'd lose it. Then she stopped hemorrhaging. So she comes to the Melody, pregnant, beboppin' around with all the guys, probably on drugs. I said, 'Why the hell aren't you in bed?' But she insisted she felt good enough to work. Meanwhile, she was trying to get her pants down, bleeding all over the place, ya know? This other chick started screaming, so I told her to get lost. Then I had somebody call her husband in New Jersey, who took her to the hospital."

The Melody management, however, according to one ex-housegirl, is supportive of those women working their way through art college, or trying to enter brokerage firms or become traveling cosmetics executives, which some do. "I was one of their favorites," the ex-housegirl says, her face showing some mileage when she speaks of the Melody. "So they took an interest in how my college was going, and were real pleased when I graduated. They like to see girls make it on the outside in a straight career."

She worked there two years and spent half of her $800 a week on coke. Her worst experiences occurred when, she claims, a psychotic patron would show up in the first row when she came out onstage. He would glare and flash a gun, quietly conveying that he wanted to get her. She declined the management's requests that she point out the idiot so they could "take care of him," for fear of reprisal. Finally, he stopped coming—until the day of her college graduation exercise, when he showed up in the audience, sitting near her parents.

"I freaked out and figured it was time to leave for good." But leaving was like breaking an addiction. Now, a year later, the prospect of a mere visit seems frightful. "They'd all come up to me, say 'Hey, where ya been,' crack jokes. I couldn't handle it, I just wanna keep away."

Last May, four girls were busted on "prostitution" charges, for not wearing panties. Mardi Gras personnel were, for the time being, instructed to dust off their G-strings and put them back on. Marc Lammers, the tall, husky fellow who mans the box office at night, was in the middle: "They put four of us on a chain when they led us out. Then the cops kept me in handcuffs for three and a half hours at Midtown North. They tried to get me on obscenity, but the judge lowered me to disorderly conduct. The system's fucked up. We had to be in court at nine-thirty in the morning. black-ass judge comes in at eleven-thirty then breaks for lunch. We were the last case, at five."

"The safest day at the Melody is St. Paddy's," adds another Mardi Gras girl. "All the cops are out vomiting at the parade."

One of the toughest predicaments from which the Melody seems to have emerged victorious was a sales-tax case brought against them by the state. By law, theaters presenting a drama or comedy must charge sales tax on the ticket; but musical performances are exempt. At stake was a quarter-mil in back taxes.

"The guys at the audit said, 'You're not musical performances, you're pornography,'" explains Kronish. "I said, 'This is the Melody—we can't operate without music, so what the hell do you call it?' I says, 'Who are you to say this is porn, you're a sales-tax man, you can't decide what's naughty or nice.'"

The court decided the major portion of the case in the Melody's favor, due in part to Kronish's expertise in tax law, his profession. He spends most of the workaday week at his accountant's office in Westchester. His clients' first names become familiar when listed together, though he reveals them hesitantly: "I've done tax returns for Veronica, Samantha, Candida, Gloria, Desiree. . . ."

And what do porn stars get to write off? Handi-Wipes?

"Never thought of that, but yeah, Handi-Wipes, if they're dancing. The nature of their deductions are mainly costumes, maintenance of costumes, cosmetics, agents' fees, advertising, taxi fares to work, travel accommodations when they're out of town. It adds up."

Is there anything unique about a porn star's tax form?

"It's a Schedule C. Everyone has to file a 1040 or 1040-A, but in addition to this, since they're self-employed people, they file Schedule C, which indicates gross income and business deductions, winding up with a net profit or a net loss. They have to pay social security on whatever their profit is, which in 1981 was 9.3 percent. They file the same way an unincorporated candy-store owner would."

Anna Turner is completing her last set of the night, and Al Kronish goes out to watch. "What a great ass," he notes, beaming at her performance from the back aisle. Anna practically turns it inside out, leaving the ol' fellers quite breathless. Al stops before a lobby billboard with naked color pix of past strippers.

"You see this girl here? Her parents came from Long Island one night and grabbed her right out of porn. She'd done two films, really liked the business. If a girl is from Long Island, she should go to the Coast to do porn."

Anna crosses over to Bernard's with Al, and God help Kandi Barbour if she gets in Anna's way. "She don't know who she's fuckin' with," warns Anna, like an outlaw gunning for tail. "I'll put her down before the first round." Al decides to enter thirty seconds after Anna. But when he enters the restaurant, the two are chatting amiably, like bosom buddies. The dramatic switch doesn't seem to phase him, he's seen this before. Both girls embrace him, smearing lipstick on his forehead and flirting with his trousers. "Please," Kronish begs off, "my doctor tells me I got only one fuck left in me."

Holding court at Bernard's, where much of the Melody has spilled out after the last set, Kronish appears to be a grandfatherly mentor to every starlet in town. Sultry feline creatures slither from the barstools, asking for his private ear; younger cupcakes, new to the biz, with running tabs here, giggle by with champagne/orange juice cocktails. Al gives any of them his fullest attention. This is the high life, right across the street from the Mardi Gras pigpen. Even fans have the opportunity to mingle, collect autographs, sketch pictures, and shower compliments on their fave starlets. The bouncer is huddled at a table alone, wondering where he'll sleep that night after his mom threw him out of the house.

Amid all these women, Al can pin down his very favorite stripper in a second: "Kristina Fox is probably the most talented girl in burlesque today. Twenty different acts, dozens of gowns and props which she makes herself. Takes a bath onstage with real steam and bubbles all over the theater. Very nice Jewish girl, straight, no porn. Doesn't spread legs, doesn't play with herself or fool around with anybody. It's peculiar, she don't accept tips—if someone throws a dollar onstage she kicks it back. She's very devoted to her profession, in big demand throughout Europe. She's so great, the other girls all take seats and watch each of her moves.

"Just for fun," says Al, calling blond starlet Joey Karson from the bar. "To the best of your knowledge, who's the most talented stripper we've had at the Melody—besides you?"

"Kristina Fox?" answers the blonde.

"That's an extra hundred," says Kronish.

Aside from his theater, Al claims to have no awareness or interest in the rest of Times Square. "I don't patronize anyplace. When I have free time, I spend it at the Melody. Sure, we're part of the whole thing, I don't relate the Melody to anything in Times Square other than X-rated entertainment.... When this location came along in 1973, it just happened to be on 48th Street. The real estate was good, so we took it. A lot of the X-rated theaters, like the Pussycat, the Circus, came after us. But we had a lot of competition when we opened, at least a dozen other burlesque halls. The Mayfair on 47th, two on 42nd Street, the Broadway on 49th, which is now the World Theatre; when Bob Anthony was manager of the Follies, they had a three-piece orchestra, too. Now there's just the Melody."

Rave Up!

Raven De La Croix is set for the big Friday night of her week-long winter booking at the Melody. All I have to do is lug her circus trunk from the Consulate Hotel around the corner, where the Melody management put her up. Along Broadway, black hookers' eyes bug out as they whistle her down, en route to the theater. Raven smiles back modestly, acknowledging one who has been trying to flag her down all week, presumably with romantic intent.

It's those hooters that stop traffic, that make man and hooker alike gasp out wisecracks, which drift past Raven's show-must-go-on, forward-marching step. They jut out cartoon-like, even from within her light-blue jumpsuit, giving the distinct impression that this black-haired vixen of American Indian blood is in a realm of show business in which she earns her living *fishing 'em out.* Raven once confided she was flat-chested until age seventeen, then all of a sudden started to sprout. Her mother took notice of this volcanic development and bragged to neighbors. Raven was embarrassed, the object of sudden adulation. But then, every stripper worth her salt learns to control the tempo, to exercise a power over men that she never had as a kid. Yet Raven achieves this commanding aura without a trace of manipulation.

She lists a jumble of occupations leading up to her reigning tit stardom: real estate agent, nursery school teach, L.A. roofing contractor, record promoter, nurse at Columbia-Presbyterian near The Bronx, where she grew up. She spent years in the Hell's Angels, married one, then broke *into* a prison yard to fuck him, when he did time. She supervised something called "Narconon," a drug rehab program in the California jail system—dressed conservatively, she says, she would mingle with addict prisoners and pit the biggest black guys against the fiercest rednecks in encounter-group staring exercises.

Now in her thirties, Raven has landed dim-witted Hollywood cameos for big-boobed broads, in *The Blues Brothers* and other such rubbish. But she starred in Russ Meyer's *Up!*, which carries a lifetime constituency; she's since had to continually do men's magazine spreads to keep the fans succored. She feels a kinship toward Little Annie Fannie, yet knows how to "walk into a lion's den and survive." With a teenage son, she's come through like a Mack-truck Mary Tyler Moore. And now, clinging to the underside of show biz, bent on bigger movie roles, she commands $2,000 a week, plus accommodations, in what's vaguely defined as the burlesque circuit, here and in Canada.

Once upstairs in the Melody lobby, Raven is instantly surrounded by admirers and tit hounds. A gigantic, jolly black fellow named J.J. is introduced as the "president of her New York fan club." He is nearly seven feet tall and four or five hundred pounds, and his hands are large enough to crush a basketball, which he absentmindedly seems to be trying to do as he shakes mine.

Friends of J.J.'s nudge him in the ribs—"There she is!"—which causes him to burst into giggles. Raven's "Uncle Lou" is here, a more reserved fan she met during her summer 1981 engagement, now elevated to dinner companion. The old cocker in the box office cackles his way out of the booth, complaining jealously because she hasn't invited him to dinner. At every utterance from Raven, the enormous J.J. is reduced to giggles, unable to make conversation with his dream queen. Her pictures, I'm told, wallpaper his entire apartment.

All of these fellers, who act reverent enough before the regular strippers, are downright awestruck in Raven's presence. That such a woman stands before them, living, breathing, greeting them with a wink and a wisecrack, soon to strip off her clothes—which they will witness for a seven-dollar entrance fee—is too good to be true.

"I've always had a really fortunate instinct for picking the safe ones from the Hillside Stranglers," says Raven, both of us settled in the headliner's dressing room, behind a locked door. "Like Lou, for instance. He's like a distant uncle. He's a nervous guy with a stutter; but he's very honest and vulnerable, and I'm the kind of person, it seems, where all of a sudden, a guy feels he can be honest with me."

"Tell me more about Lou," I say.

"He's just a regular guy. I brought him to meet my mother last summer. He'd never try to lay a kiss on me, other than just being sweet.... God, this room smells terrible."

The star's room at the Melody is closet-sized, with exposed heating pipes and a high ceiling. A horizontal mirror hangs across the dressing table, where flowers from Al Kronish and fan cards are stationed. A new, blue paint job, covering old graffiti by strippers, leaves a lingering odor in the air.

"Mind if I get dressed?" asks Raven, with under an hour before her 11:20 show. She opens the trunk, containing six costume changes, each with its own soundtrack cassette. Hers is a self-designed wardrobe of stripperwear, more prestigious than Frederick's. On top lies her trademark Indian costume, which transforms her into "Princess Bursting Feathers."

"What freaks me a bit," says Raven, "are the guys who tremble in their seats with their mouths hanging open." She relates the incident of a pen pal, a lawyer, one of many who persistently write her, and with whom she corresponds. "So the guy came to one of my shows, talked to me a bit in the lobby. But he'd never been here before, and he overreacted to Mardi Gras by pulling down his pants and whacking off in the seat. Someone stopped him before he got tossed out."

Most of the old goats who follow Raven are more than content to be professional fans, incapable of crossing the line. "But who's safe? I never used to trust myself when picking friends from fans, but now I do. I protect myself, though, I don't wanna end up anyplace weird. I'm not a victim.... Most of the guys out there, I would never go out with. They're dear fans, they know what they are, they never expect anything. I'll go across the street to Bernard's with a bunch, but there's no reason to go anyplace else."

These old coots also provide a protective entourage in New York. Raven can deal with wackos in the audience, humor them perfectly. Like the guy out West who falls to his knees and prays to her—she works it into the routine and obliges him with a religious spell. "You'll be the first I'll tell, if I need help," she tells her dukes, who are eager to defend her, "but even if they seem nuts to you, I know how to handle them." It's more dangerous for strippers in Middle America, where folks are more apt to figure her profession qualifies her as rape meat or something. Yet some porn starlets have claimed that they run less risk of being raped because they're perceived as too powerful sexually: the exact opposite of what some idiot bent on rape would seek. When it does happen to a girl in the perimeters of porn, the cops offer no solace.

"Everyone finds the weakness of the other, in this business," says Raven. "I've seen girls forced to give head. If a girl is easily scared or thinks her job is more important than her integrity, the guy'll find out what the weak point is and dive in there. I see thirteen-year-old girls whose parents have put 'em to work in strip clubs."

Raven applies her mineral oil, the better to bounce those light signals off her bosoms into the tit-starved audience. She hates makeup and never uses the traditional Max Factor body pancake many strippers need, which is plastered on with water and alcohol, then buffed like a shoeshine so it doesn't streak. Just this morning, to avoid makeup, Raven spent forty-five minutes under a Silver Solarium sun lamp to maintain her California tan. Only one spot requires the hated pancake: "I had this tattoo on my inner thigh that said 'Forever Damien.' It was removed by a plastic surgeon, so there's a little scar."

Raven does her act barefoot, and never wears heels onstage, since falling and injuring her left bazoom. It almost had to be removed. Russ Meyer recommended a cosmetic surgeon who specialized in Vegas showgirl implants. The surgeon was able to zero in on the swelling from an angle that left the breast intact, and corrected the injury.

"The operation was three and a half hours and I had to come up with $5,000. I figured I might as well have the tattoo carved out too." She dabs the pancake over the faint spot where the good doctor's work was.

"Last time I was on tour for seven weeks straight, my feet were torn and bloody from dancing. I've picked up splinters and glass. The lighting at the Melody isn't too good, but at least their stage is smooth. Stages are all different, and my show changes instinctively with each one. I usually play dinner clubs, cabarets. I was the first stripper ever to play the Playboy Club in L.A. The Melody is still unusual for me."

Friday night's costume turns out to be Wonder Woman; Rave is just snapping on the finishing garters. Before going, I can't resist asking what advice she might offer young, aspiring strippers out there in mental-illness land, who bungle their way into the profession. What brand of sanitary napkins, for instance, should they use?

"Some girls wear Tampax. You have to. You can't wear sanitary pads onstage. Make sure you don't have the string showing. A lot of the audience is real juvenile and they'll point and laugh: 'Haw haw, string!' There are some dreadful stories.

"For instance, this untogether black girl with long, pendulous breasts, a big butt, wild hair. She was onstage and her G-string was black, but she forgot to put it on. This was in Toronto at Zanzibar's, where you have to have your G-string on or it's a $500 fine. No one really noticed at first. She was very black, had a perfect V-shaped you-know-what. Suddenly guys started cracking up, it rolled back through the theater in waves. The girl looked down in the middle of doing a split and there was this little white string hanging out."

A five-minutes-to-showtime knock on the door comes. I leave and pick me a nice old seat in the third row, facing the T-runway head-on. A lot of royalty present; about a hundred old duffers show up for a midnight bosom erection.

Rave moves about the stage in a jazz ballet, an Indian maiden gliding through the woods. She is applauded, however, only after removing each article of clothing, particularly when the Wonder Woman bra comes down. The applause is businesslike, like that which accompanies new elections to a PTA council. J.J. remains bundled in his winter coat in the first row. Only a small portion of him fits over the seat, and he giggles throughout the set, friends slapping him from behind. Uncle Lou makes three separate trips during the set to deposit a one-dollar bill onstage. Rave uses a transparent veil to keep the view of her you-know-what to a minimum. Normally she doesn't remove her G-string, but at the Melody it's a requirement.

"Any questions about Hollywood?" asks Raven during a little Q&A after her last number.

Friends badger J.J. to ask a question, but he breaks up giggling, waving his hand, out of breath.

"You've got God-given talent," declares an admirer.

"Talent? It's just flesh," says Raven.

"How much does a guy need to take you out?" inquires some old Festus.

"I believe in love and magic. Money can't buy that." A few of the old dukes smack their knees over this retort, with a good chuckle at the expense of the wiseass who cracked the question. Rave bids them good night.

When she returns from her dressing room, her contingent is again waiting patiently in the lobby. "Good snakes!" she says, greeting a lineup eager to pose for Polaroids. "I can pay for a daily shiatsu massage at the hotel with these," she tells me—but I don't see her accept one dollar. An assortment of old codgers are lined up like little boys in a candy store, smacking their lips, smiling wide, and shaking their heads in wonder. One grabs her hand, congratulating her on her marvelous pair. Another, who resembles a middle-aged Dennis the Menace, snaps off a few pix, then declares his undying devotion. "I'll be back tomorrow night, Raven," he says, looking up to her as if she were a mommy.

In a few minutes she will make a lonely retreat to her hotel room. She'll remove her sparkles in the bathtub, same as every night on the road, then receive a blabbering phone call from an agent, an old-timer who never gets her any work. She does it all herself.

An old titmouse of a man stands behind the Polaroids, nibbling all his fingernails. "This is my crazy face," says Raven, sticking out her tongue and crossing her eyes. The little gent buckles into a spasm of admiring laughter, his eyes all aglaze. You could barely hear him rasp, under his breath… "What a dame!"

Uncle Lou's Scrapbook

Lou Amber bought his photo album on sale at Woolworth's a few years ago to accommodate some Polaroids. The album now holds over seventy snapshots and glossies, all signed with lipstick kisses and true love. A limo driver by day, Lou is a regular old duke at the Melody Burlesk—one of their up-and-coming resident uncles, a young pup of fifty-one. He's a sad-eyed fan of the porn starlets and a soft-spoken barroom confidant to the Mardi Gras gals. Raven De La Croix, whom he greets in a stretch limousine at the airport whenever she plays New York, is the only stripper he drives for free. Some of the other chauffeurs might mistake her for Lou's girlfriend, but Lou considers himself "part of her family." He's not looking to show off, and keeps the photo album as a private shrine to porn queens who've come to think of him affectionately as "Uncle Lou." And he really does want merely to *uncle* the girls, although, "If I'm attracted to one, and she wants to make the big scene with me, and she's a consenting adult—I won't turn her down."

The first entry in Lou's scrapbook is Raven's poster of *The Lost Empire.* Publicity stills and Polaroids from each of her New York engagements show her arm in arm with a smiling Uncle Lou outside Bernard's and in the Melody lobby. They age together. Polaroids of Hyapatia Lee occupy the next two pages, the Indian squaw leaning fully against her admirer at the opening of *The Young Like It Hot*, her New York debut. "The first time I was just a paying customer who came in and posed for a five-dollar shot," says Lou. "She's like a little Raven."

"Thanks for cumming," reads Lee's inscription on the top photo.

"I came back to the theater a second time and brought her a little bottle of perfume shaped like the Eiffel Tower. Then I came back a third time, when she stripped at Show World, and she remembered me from the perfume." Pictures from his third visit show a stark naked Hyapatia Lee with her tongue jammed down Uncle Lou's throat and her hand upon his crotch. Another shot has Uncle Lou returning the gesture, copping a generous helping of boob and vage. "I'll always remember my favorite New Yorker," says Lee's third inscription. Known for quenching a flaming dildo between her legs, Lee couldn't perform the gimmick due to strict Fire Department regulations at Show World.

On the next page comes Marilyn Chambers' glossy from the opening of *Insatiable*, inscribed "Lou—Love and all my hot, wet licks." Then comes Seka, naked on Lou's lap at the Melody, and being carried off, Clark Gable style. Uncle Lou raises the plastic covering from the page. "The advantage of this book is that you can lift 'em out and put 'em back. People can put their fingers on 'em and not spoil the picture." The back of Seka's snapshot, dated 2-2-80, when she set the all-time attendance record for the Melody, says "Much love and happiness." At that time porn queens charged $3 a Polaroid; within four years they've risen to $5, sometimes $7.

Lou acquired a glossy of Constance Money that she emblazoned with a slutty lipstick smack, during the opening of *A Taste of Money*. Kelly Nichols, who Lou chauffeured to the 1983 Erotic Film Awards, writes "Love and lust to a fan who cares" on her lofty publicity still. "It's very hard to meet these girls for the first time when you're a spectator," says Lou. The next nude portrait is a star who lets no man paw her for photos: "To Lou—Love, Annette Haven. 5-30-82."

"She was in the lobby of the Pussycat when High School Memories opened. I stopped over a few times and spoke with her. She's very intelligent and personable. I understand she went to college and excelled in physics. It was a little hard to chat with five guys surrounding her at once, so I sent a letter. If I express my sentiments through a personal note, they sometimes respond." Untouchable Annette sent Lou a solicitation for her newsletter, which he ordered for "only ten dollars." Two or three issues came out. She also sent the humorless black-and-white study of herself in his album. Haven's penmanship is the finest in the scrapbook.

"You're a great lover," says Juliet Anderson's inscription to the balding Lou.

"But we never made the big scene," he confesses. "Maybe they get vibes that you'd be a great lover, so they put it down." The only lecherous Uncle Lou face is the shot in which he's cupping Annie Sprinkle's bazooms. "Annie encourages that type of behavior," says modest Lou of the golden shower poetess, whose autograph appears in Day-Glo pink.

"They're basically good kids, they just come from a bad situation," Uncle Lou says of these nieces. "The difference between me and some of the other guys is, I don't look at them for what they are, but for what they can be. People fall into three categories: those that make things happen, those that watch things happen, and those that wonder, 'What happened?' The girls in the middle category that can get to the first category are the ones I get involved with, the ones with potential. In a symbolic sense, in the way pimps turn girls out, I try to turn them in."

In the middle of his scrapbook is a coquettish Veronica Hart from her first Show World gig, in the summer of 1981. The newly-wed-mother-to-be hams it up, legs in the air, boobs out, and tongue in Lou's mouth. The Polaroid concession was handled by her teenage brother. Next comes the baton-twirling face of Desiree Cousteau, whose nay-nays are uncle-handled by then-mustachioed Lou at the Melody. The five Polaroids were taken by her husband, *Mr.* Desiree Cousteau. "I understand she's retired from films, going to school in Atlanta," Lou narrates.

"Most guys have this image of porno stars, they see the glitter, costumes, and makeup, they think they're untouchable. After you get to know 'em, you don't look at 'em as sex images, you relate to 'em as everyday people—you get to the nitty-gritty of their everyday problems. Many of these girls never got asked to the senior prom."

The last shot in the book is an out-of-focus though clearly nervous and fully clothed Kandi Barbour at her first Melody appearance. It is also Lou's earliest snapshot.

"Most of the porn stars I've gotten to know had a problem with their fathers or stepfathers. In some cases sexual, in some a communication or emotional problem where they weren't able to relate normally. Most of these girls have been innocent victims of adversity, broken by a fate beyond their control. This brings back my childhood. I lost my parents at an early age, and I grew up in an orphanage from the age of eight to eighteen. A good orphanage, up in Yonkers. We, as young kids, were also innocent victims of adversity. Fortunately, we had people that cared about us, that raised funds and were able to help us establish self-esteem and a positive outlook. Each of the fellas that stayed through high school was instilled with some of the executive director's qualities. He made each boy feel like a son. To me, it's a natural continuity of the principles he gave us. These girls have been either abused, molested, or put down at an early age. Consequently, it's hard for them to get out of that syndrome. Perhaps, in some way, I trigger a positive response.

"I don't come on in a sexual way, I don't force myself on anybody, I lay back. They can let their hair down and not be under any pressure. If a girl wants to do something with me, she does it 'cause she wants to, not because she's obligated."

And how often does this happen, where Uncle Lou becomes a daddy-o?

"Let me put it this way: A gentleman never tells."

Season's Greetings from Long Jean Silver

During the break between her eight and eleven o'clock performances at the Avon 7, I took Long Jean Silver to Bernard's for a couple of cheeseburgers and stiff drinks. The gig coincided with 1982's first serious snowfall, and a wholesome, Christmas spirit had fallen upon 48th Street, in the upper Square. A horse and buggy trotted by the Pussycat Cinema, outside which jolly pedestrians were molding snowballs. Long Jean Silver didn't go for it.

"I hate this shit," she said, clutching my arm.

"A little tighter," I suggested, taking advantage and further remarking that it felt like she was holding *me* up.

"Does it really feel that way?" she whispered, steering us out into traffic as the light changed to green.

Long Jean Silver probably never got to frolic in the snow, skate, or make snowmen when she was a little girl, which wasn't all that long ago. Now, at Bernard's when she removes her new coat—made from "about ten foxes"—she's frightfully gorgeous and I'm tempted to choke on my Adam's apple. She says she needs to join a health spa, tone up her ass and belly. Claims she never exercises and eats like a pig, even though she's in smashing condition. She's got fluffy dirty-blond hair and a majorette face that once earned her extra tips from tricks who thought she was a nice girl and should give up hooking.

Doing four shows a day for a week at the Avon 7 is tiring. The shows she likes, but the three-hour intervals bore her silly: "I wish they'd let me work Mardi Gras at the Melody in between." Mostly, though, she just wishes she could get a new apartment, lie around with her dog, watch TV, fuck—things of that nature. She has to do this porn stuff to make money, and frankly, she hates it.

For the time being, nevertheless, Jeanie says she'd like to drop the "Long" from her title—to make a clean break, I assume, from namesake

Long John Silver, the peg-legged pirate. Likewise, she'll try to play down the stump, which first brought her fame as a special *Cheri* magazine centerfold five years ago.

"Please don't show any pictures of it. I don't want that as my image anymore.... Well, maybe just one."

Do booking agents stipulate that she flash the leg?

"No. I still like to freak people out. But I only do it for a minute onstage, at the end."

Jeanie Silver was raised on an Arizona air force base, and in small, dry towns across that state. Her stepdad is a colonel in the armed forces. She tells me he builds missiles.

"Nuclear ones?"

"Yeah. He may get a job at the Pentagon, in which case I'll quit porn. I don't wanna get kidnapped." The lore of Jean's early years, in a nutshell, goes something like this: She was born with a missing fibula, so doctors amputated the bottom of her leg. Coming home from her twelfth birthday party, she was raped and beaten by five blacks who jumped her in the park. Only one balked when he saw the leg. She learned to walk and dance quite normally on an artificial attachment, even enough to become a professional house burglar. She entered reform school at fifteen, came out a pross, studied child psychology and hitchhiked like mad until ending up happily ever after as a "porn star" in New York.

She pushes a half-eaten cheeseburger aside and starts pouring freshly melted wax from Bernard's candles on her hands. As it hardens, she becomes entranced by the sensation, pouring even more into her hands. Several gals from the Melody Burlesk stop by the table to inquire how she's doing "around the block."

"It sucks," says Jeanie, without looking up or bidding them farewell as they pat her on the back and leave. "All right, so I'm strange," she says, looking up at me lopsidedly, breaking a long silence. Then she retreats back to the wax, molding something with quiet determination. She has a glazed look, like a beautiful blond disturbed child. She's molding a snowman, a one-armed fellow.

The Avon 7 is packed for the late show, rows of horny heads watching *Mistress Electra*, a new film starring the "Unforgiving" Long Jean Silver. The dressing room is a long walk from the stage and it's falling apart. The pink paint is peeling, there are gashes in the walls, and stacks of marquee letters are stored to one side. A sign is posted for the benefit of the "Live Love Teams": ALL TEAMS: PLEASE!! KEEP THIS AREA CLEAN. USE THE GARBAGE CANS. DON'T BE A PIG.

"This gets my vote for worst dressing room," says Jeanie.

The object of her feigned aggression on tonight's program is one David Christopher, Submissive. The theater rented him from Mistress Candice for the week.

"I don't pay for slaves," Jeanie explains.

David is fiddling with his shackles on the bench and assures Jean that he killed some more cockroaches, not to worry. It wasn't easy, considering his own cockroach-like position in life as a pro submissive. But then, he assures me he's appeared in over a hundred regular porn flicks, and remains baffled as to why he hasn't reached star status.

"What you'll see tonight isn't hardcore S&M. I'm into *sensual dominance.* Worshiping. Not receiving pain. Have you ever seen Jeanie as a dominant? She's awfully good."

"This isn't my real gig," says Jeanie. "Next week I'm going to Rhode Island and Pittsburgh to just strip."

I suggest what she does in little theaters like this around the country is a continuation of American vaudeville, but Jeanie's built-in shit-detector won't buy it. David, however, does.

"Long Jean is the first major porn star that the Avon has ever booked," he asserts. "I may have done over a hundred films myself, but they haven't caught on to me yet.... Have you ever seen the movie *Long Jean Silver*?" he asks. "It's a classic!"

Haven't seen it, I say.

"You're lucky," says naked Jeanie, putting on leg warmers. "I hated it."

I ask which, if any, of her films she likes.

"None of them. They all suck... except maybe *House of Sin.* I usually hate working, but I liked *House of Sin* because all I had to do was *watch* sex—and get head from Honey Stevens."

It's getting awfully hot and humid in this dressing room. Jeanie keeps wishing she could take a bath, as the time for the next show approaches. She assembles a tight black spiderweb-type dress around her body, directing her moves in the mirror. She's a knockout now, a blond, peg-legged Vampirella. She shackles up her slave, who trudges out onto the stage ahead of her.

The crowd of fifty sits insanely silent as Jeanie ambles down the aisle. The tortured voice of Marianne Faithfull's comeback record howls dirty words over the PA, ideal for an S&M act. Once onstage, Jeanie captures her slave and descends on him like a spider, but unfortunately only mildly assaults his body during the four-song, twenty-minute set.

She peels off her own clothes along the way. Her tits are champagne-perfect. She straddles his face, disdainfully slaps his pecker, which rages harder the more she tugs it. He groans and grovels under her splendid rump. Then the leg comes off. A few audience members perk up, not yet sure of what they see. She bats her stump against his cock, then has him suck the stump. She quickly reattaches the artificial portion, pulls on a warmer, and that's all she wrote. A solid gig.

The audience responds with quirky applause. Jeanie hobbles off during the clapping, pausing momentarily by my chair to whisper a highly sarcastic "Hooray!"

Old Flesh Agents

The several remaining booking agents for strippers in this country are somewhat bitter, quick-tempered men in their seventies—vaudevillian artifacts who resigned themselves to booking strippers after variety shows perished. They were likewise forced down a notch by representing porn starlets in their old age. Irv Charnoff, who left his Times Square Brill Building office in 1972, continues to book girls into clubs nationally from his Queens apartment, taking time off only when struck by heart attacks, of which he's had a few. Charnoff books the big-tit stars, nonexclusively, including Raven De La Croix, Candy Samples, Chesty Morgan, the aging Tempest Storm, and young stripaholic Hyapatia Lee. "The few that are honorable," he says, referring to those pros who show up at their gigs.

He loves to gab with the gals on the phone when they play the Big Apple, though his services have become less required in their careers. "They all have different riders on their contracts," Charnoff explains. "Like Sammy Davis, you gotta bring him thirteen ice cubes in a bucket, if there's fourteen he gets mad. You're dealing with crazy or temperamental people. They're all insane. The kind of work strippers are doing, they're not in their right mind to begin with. They're not performers like Milton Berle or Henny Youngman that made sacrifices or disciplined themselves to get ahead, with goals to reach, like playing the Palace. All they do is show their body. You don't call that entertainment, do ya?"

Charnoff began with strippers late in his career, having booked variety acts into supper clubs all his life. "When some of my nightclubs started to change over, I didn't know one stripper from another—I still don't and I'm not interested. I wouldn't deal with these girls, I always called an agent who featured strippers whenever a nightclub required them. The variety act went out, the magician went out, the ventriloquist went out. I was forced to use these strippers. I was in a business, I had to stay with it, so I called other agents who had stables of girls. Even then, they were a different kind of stripper. They had continuity, choreography, wardrobe, luggage. The girls today, they have a rug. So they don't get a splinter in their ass when they spread."

Jess Mack, premier strippers' agent in Las Vegas, whose example Charnoff followed, had his original office in Times Square's Paramount Building. Mack began as a burlesque straight man on 42nd Street in 1924. He continued working the out-of-town circuit, nearly a hundred burlesque theaters coast to coast, after La Guardia outlawed burlesque in New York. In the early 1950s he became an agent, explaining that the days of burlesque had ended.

"When the Apollo opened on 42nd Street, we had Gypsy Rose Lee and Georgia Southern as our feature attractions," remembers Mack. "Plus sixteen chorus girls, three comedians, three straight men, and a vaudeville act. That was the backbone of burlesque. You don't see that now, there's no burlesque," he laments, his voice trailing off with irritation. "There are strip shows, but I don't call that burlesque. Now they have what they call 'stripperama.' Strip, strip, strip. That's all."

Both agents profess to being proud family men who never ran casting couches. But Irv Charnoff, with a vaudeville background, tends to dismiss burlesque in comparison: "One was family theater, and the other was just for morons." As for pornography, Charnoff states, "I apply myself to it, but I won't accept it."

"I don't care for pornography," says Mack. "It ruined burlesque, put everybody out of work. How can you enjoy something that hurt you financially, that hurt your career? I don't book 42nd Street—I book coast to coast, Europe, Hong Kong, Singapore. I spoke to Guam today. Agents book wherever they can." Mack feels there are under a half-dozen genuine striptease queens left today. "Stripping is not burlesque. We had burlesque long before we had stripping. But nobody's come close to Ann Corio or Gypsy Rose Lee. If they did, you'd see their name in lights."

By the 1930s, any American town with over 100,000 in population had a burlesque house. In addition to the featured strippers, each theater employed a line of six to eight chorus dancers in skimpy outfits doing risqué material—an easy way for dolls to break into show biz. Geoffrey Gorer, a British critic who'd attended a dozen New York burlesque houses in the mid-Thirties, found "Miss June Glories" to be the typical American stripper of his rather superficial visits. Unlike the state-of-the-art performance set down later by Gypsy, the low-caliber Miss June Glories was not graceful, entering the stage in a backward lean. Her knees remained unflexed as she walked in a goosestep, arms held away from her body. New York State, Gorer assumed, considered it immoral to undress to any light except green or blue; thus spotlights onstage darkened to these colors as garments began to lower.

After the Death of Burlesque

"Give the little lady a hand," repeated each theater's emcee as Miss June walked off in her undergarments, having given a sexless, impersonal performance, like a military drill. The girls of burlesque often came from pious Catholic families and earned only $20 a week for a fourteen-hour day. The show's comedian would often marry one.

Some of the primitive burlesque houses existed in the Bowery, a quarter that was virtually without women. The elevated subway ran down the middle of Third Avenue, which was made up entirely of rooming houses and hotels "For Men Only," where beds cost thirty cents. Here was a melting pot of transient workers—Italians, Poles, Germans, who spoke little English and were too poor to marry. Only at burlesque theaters could they fully view a woman. Every week these lonely guys, hideous with drink, managed to spare twenty-five cents for this sad and solitary female-viewing pleasure, never able to cross the barrier of the footlights.

The Olympic on 14th Street offered your basic low burlesque—installments of sidewalk conversation alternating with the appearance of girls. "I'm in love!" one of the cuties would cry, "I'm in love! I'm gonta jump off the Brooklyn Bridge!"

"Don't do that," said the straight man, "you'll get the water dirty!" The strippers rippled their bellies and peeled to their pasties and G-strings. The forefathers of today's old lobsters watched this sexual exhibition with mute, unsmiling impassivity, only to applaud when they left the stage. Contact with the girls was unthinkable.

In slight contrast to this was the Minsky Brothers' Republic Theater on 42nd, which cost a dollar during the Depression, while Ziegfeld charged six dollars across the street. Laughter echoed through the aisles at sexual "dubble entenders." The Minskys hired buxom girls, not skinny flappers, who earned $25 in the chorus, and betrayed their roles by laughing inappropriately at the jokes. One perennial Minsky routine, "Anthony & Cleopatra," had Caesar in a tin helmet smoking a fat cigar catching Anthony (the Jewish comic) on a divan with Cleopatra (the leading striptease girl).

"Not for Your Aunt from Dubuque," read the *New Yorker* ads for Minskys' in the 1930s. The Republic discovered comics like Red Skelton, Phil

Silvers; they had thirty-two chorus girls, rolling across the stage, posing in silhouette behind a male singer. But the Minsky performers couldn't remove their pasties or point a finger crotchward. Once again, physical contact between audience and strippers was unthinkable.

This thriving, giddy Minsky chain was put to death by Mayor La Guardia, who outlawed burlesque in 1940, closing thirteen theaters in New York. "There was no question it was politically motivated," said surviving brother Morton Minsky during a public conversation at Lincoln Center. "Without this cause célèbre he would not have been reelected. We were denied the use of our name Minsky," said the bald, aging former owner, with a high-pitched Wally Cox-type voice. "If there were no statute of limitations, I for one would sue the city of New York for millions," he declared, forty-four years after the loss of his business. "I am of the opinion that burlesque will return in some form, if young, talented people develop the tradition.... What they call 'burlesque' today is something we would have no part of."

The ringing rebuke to Morton Minsky and the booking agents is Bob Anthony, former day manager of the Melody Burlesk, who became part owner of its new incarnation, the Harmony. The back office at 48th and Broadway remains a salty, sub-show business sanctum striving for legitimacy, a proud alter cocker clubhouse for those never admitted to the Friars. Anthony, who's been in the burlesque game quite a few years, managing various and sundry Broadway theaters before this, is quick to reflect on his early days with Sinatra:

"I was his right-hand man, the early Jilly. I used to be his secretary, belt out guys for him and everything. I once knocked out Buddy Rich in the old days, didn't like what he was sayin' about Frank. We're all good street fighters. We were raised in Hoboken, it was rough and tough, a seaport. He got me my first singing job with Ina Ray Hutton's all-male band in 1944, when I came out of the navy. Now I'm an alter cocker, same age as Frank," says Anthony, with a youthful head of hair and open V-neck shirt, like a Vegas showman. "You'd love Frank. I visit him all the time. He's a mensch."

The Harmony, née Melody, has indeed become the lone Times Square holdout of striptease. The Melody booked a landslide of wild strippers and hot sex queens. There, finally, Anthony let down the drawbridge whereby men could touch, or in fact *lunch out* on the participating strippers, when "Mardi Gras" was first initiated. The typical Harmony gals, however, tend to be the Miss June Glories of today. The dolls' acts are strictly gynecological these days, but Anthony does keep a burlesque aura, what with Doris Day musical interludes between strips, and showcards, the better to keep lawmen away. Apple pie? "Yeah, that's it!" cries Anthony. Ol' fashioned cheesecake? "You got it!" says Anthony. "I give 'em good fuckin' burlesque, we run it clean. Don't kid yourself, there's a depression out there, my friend, they're lucky to be working."

Manny Rosen, confidant of the management, seventy-six, an ex-boxer who came within days of fighting for the lightweight championship, interjects: "I'm very tight with Shecky Green, and I've been on the Carson show twice." Rosen wrote "King Heroin" for James Brown, whom he met while working at the Stage Deli for thirty-two years. He came up with the theater's original name, the Melody, when Al Kronish grabbed the location of the Oasis massage parlor in the early 1970s. He spends much of his time here, holding court with Anthony, keeping a special close watch on the young strippers. "I like to be surrounded by 'em," says Manny.

"Mendel, you bastard you, that's my boy," sings Anthony, a former big-band crooner. "Mendela, you alter cocker. He gives them all a good schtup. Manny's been with me since the Follies Burlesque, my right-hand man."

Some of the crustaceans who linger here are ex-boxers of sorts, an army of old warriors on red alert should any trouble arise. "My day manager is an ex-wrestler," says Anthony. "He'll pin you in a second, throw you a mile. All good people here," he insists. "Stevie and Freddie, that was a bad rap they got. There's no prostitution here, there was never no prostitution, that's terrible," he says, referring to the last crackdown on the Melody, when newspapers revealed an assistant D.A. was co-owner. Hence, the Melody's closure for several months in 1983 and its reopening as the Harmony. "It's a joke, I mean the worst thing we ever did was, they sat in guys' laps and accepted tips. The girls wear G-strings. What was so bad?

"I'd love Mayor Koch to come up here. Rocky Graziano comes up,

Tony Atlas, all the pro wrestlers, fighters come up to visit Manny. I tell ya, priests come up here, rabbis… and all my goombahs from Hoboken come up, Frank's friends."

Has Ol' Blue Eyes ever been up?

Bob Anthony hesitates then seems to recall his coming incognito once to scout a film location. "Straight, clean burlesque is what I run, good, old-fashioned stuff. I guess you could call me Mr. Burlesque."

How do the old flesh agents tell an old stripper when she's ready to be put out to pasture?

"You just stop booking her," says Anthony.

"When she can't get a job," says Jess Mack. "I wouldn't have the nerve to tell anybody that. When they can't get bookings, they know something's wrong."

Irv Charnoff chimes in: "You gotta tell 'em that they're asking for youth, they're not looking for professionalism or wardrobe, they wanna look at skin. I don't wanna recall any incidents, it's sad enough. See, a boxer, he gets punch-drunk. Some of these girls, they feel they're pretty, they're vain and everything, so you cop out, ya tell 'em business is a little quiet, or a little white lie not to hurt their feelings. It's a business where a lot of girls get jealous, envious, they don't know why somebody else does better than them. Some agents, just say 'Go get lost, get yourself a job at Sears and Roebuck.'"

TELL ALL THE GANG ON 42ND STREET!

The Princess of 42nd Street

Fay Gold, an actress who lives on the outskirts of Times Square, has been a Public Library member all her life. When she was a kid, they opened the glass cases in the children's section for her to gaze at original editions. Today, she rides the bus across 42nd Street, since it is unwalkable for a woman in her late seventies. The last time she tried, her purse was snatched, and though some Good Samaritans caught the bandit, a cop snapped at her to shut up when filing a report. She's been mugged six times in the Square, feeling a surreal sensation, as if a film crew were shooting it. But each time she rides the M-106 bus across 42nd to the library, she reconstructs the same panorama from her childhood. "It's still my street, in my mind."

In 1915, at the age of eight, Fay ran her father's newsstand at Eighth Avenue and 42nd Street. It was out on the sidewalk, in front of Jimmy Kelly's Saloon. When school let out at three o'clock, she donned a little change-apron and relieved her father, a stern Russian immigrant, who went back to their tenement on 41st Street to have dinner and sleep. The man in the smokeshop with the wooden Indian outside kept an eye on Fanny, as Fay was then called, but nobody ever stole money from the cashbox. The customers were kindly people from the flourishing theater community who knew Fanny and her father. This was Times Square's aristocratic era, before Prohibition, before honky-tonk emerged out of the Depression, a twenty-five-year epoch, before the grand theaters of 42nd Street converted to B-movie grinders.

Fanny's newsstand customers spilled out of the New Amsterdam, where the Ziegfeld *Follies* of 1915 featured $100,000 worth of costume changes, paraded by a harem of robust glamour girls, giving off an elegant illusion of sin. The Art Nouveau interior of the theater contained boudoirs for ladies, a lavish smoking room for men, carved furniture, a messenger service. Ziegfeld opened the Aerial Gardens on the roof that year, debuting his *Midnight Frolic* show, which ran until 1922. The Candler Theater, a.k.a. Harris, had just opened, managed by George M. Cohan, at 236 West, in the same building as the Coca-Cola Company. The Eltinge, the Liberty, the Lyric, and the Republic were all thriving young theaters on the block, whose audiences Fanny marveled at. Gentry emerged from carriages, autos, and trolley cars in ducktail tuxedos, the ladies dripping jewels. Neon tubing wasn't introduced to Times Square until the 1920s, but a million incandescent light bulbs spelled out the names of stars, formed paintings, ran up and down the façades of theaters, and defined the edges of storefronts in straight rows of dots. Some of the bulbs blinked intermittently on marquees in the sky—the sudden darkness attracted attention more than a solid light glow.

Some of Fanny's trade came from Rector's, the palatial two-story restaurant on Broadway and 43rd, a block below Hammerstein's Olympia. On Rector's opening day in 1899, thousands came for a spin through the first revolving door on Broadway, though none stayed for dinner, throwing the owner into panic. But the joint quickly became a highbrow institution. Suspended over the entrance was the Rector griffin, a creature with devil's tail, lion's body, and eagle's head and wings. The griffin monogram appeared on Rector's linen and silverware. Fanny was too poor to enter this restaurant, where expensive ham-and-eggs dishes were snobbishly monikered *jambon* and *oeufs*, created by chefs with mustaches ear to ear. Diamond Jim Brady could swallow down so many oysters, lobsters, and steaks at a sitting that the owner saluted him as "the best twenty-five customers we had."

Gazing from Broadway and 42nd toward Macy's at 34th, one saw

The Great White Way, the main drag of vaudeville and musical comedy theaters, the medium of the day. This rainbow included the Empire Theater, the Broadway Theater, the Hotel Albany, and the Hotel Continental, with Western Union on the ground floor; Browne's Chop House, the United Cigar Store, Moe Levy and Co., a blazing Budweiser sign, and the Kid McCoy Saloon, named after a fighter who invented the "corkscrew" punch. "Pity the sky with nothing but stars," observed a visiting Frenchman.

Fanny once recognized Enrico Caruso, who stayed at the Knickerbocker Hotel on 42nd and Broadway, serenading crowds from his balcony suite. On a cold night, before a performance at the Metropolitan Opera, he gathered an armful of magazines at Fanny's stand and instructed someone in his retinue to pay for them. Then Caruso personally tipped Fanny five dollars.

She hated delivering papers to the madam of a whorehouse on 43rd Street, part of a route her father sent her on. The madam gawked at her, making her wait while getting change. Then she tipped Fanny a dollar. Her parents, who couldn't even read the English publications they sold, shushed Fanny when she pleaded not to return to the whorehouse. Fanny loved delivering to the Clinton Arms, a five-story brownstone apartment/hotel at 253 West 42nd. She climbed a curved staircase with balconies to the top floor, where a blaze of light from the atrium took her breath away. Here lived painters and performers in artists' studios with skylights.

Fanny Gold herself lived in utter poverty at 306 West 41st Street, off Eighth Avenue, just over the borderline into Hell's Kitchen. Her family used a public outhouse and bath in front of the tenement. Much of the pavement was worn through to cobblestone but would soon be improved during a neighborhood reconstruction in 1918. Her brother was a polio cripple whose name her father put the newsstand under, when the law later established that newsstands were to be run by the disabled. Adjacent to the grimy tenement was an iron works and a blacksmith. Yet, one city block over, a two-minute walk, Fanny could escape this squalor and revel in the brave new fairytale land of vaudeville. Fanny was ushered into several new shows each week.

Herein, she recalls the most magical night of her childhood, with the breathless exuberance of an eight-year-old girl in 1915:

"Eddie was a vaudeville performer who'd just returned from the cross-country circuit, got a job at the Music Hall. He was a hoofer, singer, and dancer. He was around thirty, very nice, always concerned with me—he'd send me off to the Automat across the street for a cup of hot chocolate while he looked after the stand. He came down one day and said, 'Now, listen, Fanny, I want you to come tonight. Be there at seven o'clock. I don't come on till seven-thirty. I don't want to have to look for you, so you get into that seat.'

"When Mama came to take over the stand, I ran home, washed my face, combed my hair, put on my red gown and coat, felt to see if I had my little pouch with the quarters. Then I rushed out to the Automat, pulled out my coins and put them in the slots. Clink, clink, the doors open, it's always so much fun to pull out food with my hands. I stood there at the counter eating fast, the hot chocolate burning, then I rushed out of the Automat, into the American Music Hall, where Benny the usher was waiting red with rage. He took my hand, pulled me down the aisle and threw me across the knees of the people at the very moment that Eddie's music came on. And out he came, dancing with his cane in his left hand, and his bowler up in the air, and when he came center stage, the lights went down, the spotlight came on, and he looked down, saw me, and smiled.

"'Maestro, stop the music!' he said. It was so quiet, you could hear a pin drop. Then he said, 'Ladies and gentlemen, you have a treat coming tonight. I'm going to introduce you to the prettiest, sweetest little lady on 42nd Street. I give you Fanny. Stand up! *The Princess of 42nd Street!*'"

The Crystal Ball of 42nd Street

Times Square's most miserable, ghastly forms simmer in a witches' brew along Eighth Avenue from 39th to 43rd streets. Here are the official dregs of society, the scum of the earth, the lowlife's lowlives whom Mother

Teresa wouldn't bother to save. A Puerto Rican pre-op transsexual stabs a trick in the eye with a sharp fingernail to grab his cabfare before he pays the driver. Brain-damaged evangelists rave aloud to themselves; 300-pound hookers flip out their hooters to stop traffic. Old shoeshine uncles give "spit shines" with more phlegmy bile than polish—though some might look at you as though you were out of your mind if you asked for a shine. Near-dead human vegetation take root in their own excretion in condemned doorways—most of them have slit pockets from scavengers searching for their wine-bottle change. The drug-pitch skells would rather tear off with a wallet than transact an actual exchange, and they make the teenage chicken fags seem like the most discreet commodity on the street. Fifteen ghetto guerrillas wearing Pro-Keds (what transit cops call "felony sneakers") swoop down on a victim, then scatter back into subway oblivion.

Entrenched beneath all of this, at ground zero, on *the* corner, is old Charles Rubenstein, eighty-three, who has been in the penny arcade business for sixty years. The amusement parlor he built and owns at Eighth and 42nd is down a short hop of stairs en route to the subway:

"When I opened up here in 1939, we had all legitimate theaters, beautiful theaters, and people used to come down in tuxedos and evening gowns during intermission. *No one* was there to attack them, to molest them. We had four policemen walking the whole street, and we didn't need that many. I remember that a girl used to go out onstage in a bikini and the patrol wagons were there and locked 'em up. Then all of a sudden I see where they dance nude and nothin' is happening.

"We saw the changes about 1965. Sixty-four, sixty-three, it was still all right. Then we saw that the good people are not coming down here, and I says, well, it's goin' bad. It was a change of neighborhoods, the lower class used to congregate here because it was free.

"If I were to come today, I would never go into business here. But I grew into this here business. I have the experience from way back handling all kinda people. So my experience keeps me going, I'm not a-scared of any individuals that tries to threaten me."

Charlie Rubenstein also owned the Playland Amusement Parlor on 125th

Street in Harlem, which he closed in 1972 after forty years, commenting, a little late, that "the neighborhood ran down." Left with his primary arcade on 42nd Street, his stubbornness in remaining open fading amid unfathomable squalor and ruin, facing legal efforts to remove him—Charlie was suddenly rejuvenated by the coming of video games and decided to stay in biz.

"You have at least ninety-nine percent black that passes this entrance everyday. There isn't such a thing as a white person coming through. You come down here three in the morning, it's impossible to walk on 42nd Street with all the gangs, hoodlums, and riffraff. But there's no trouble in here, no fights, not in forty-four years. We'll have a hundred people playing video games. We may have *one* that'll give us a hard time, or we'll have *none.* That one creates a disturbance with all the rest of the good people around. We don't have any bad people in here. All our help is instructed to immediately get them out. You'll have plenty of lip, arguments, but get 'em outta here. Once they're outta here, I don't care what they do, it's not my business anymore. I see someone even smokin' a reefer, I says, you get the hell outta here!

"You wanna change 42nd Street, you gotta start at 34th going up to 50th, between Seventh and Eighth, and *tear every building down!* Then, *maybe* you could change it. You think you can tear some of those buildings down and have a change? No, sir! So long as you have the low-priced theaters, movies, peep shows, cheap bars and hotels, glamorous lights floatin' around, you're not gonna change this neighborhood for any money. Your bus terminal brings in people from all over the world. This is the dumping grounds of 42nd Street."

Rubenstein won an appellate court decision to remain open until 3 A.M., after the Metropolitan Transit Authority tried to force him to close earlier, making him a "scapegoat for street problems." Three years ago he was ordered to install $10,000 worth of glass partition, which drunks continually break. But on Times Square's most hair-raising corner remains Charlie Rubenstein, the only man to hold out after every other street-level proprietor from the old 42nd Street era had long since disappeared. Bring on the aggravation—Rubenstein's gnarled fingers are forever pointing troublemakers to the exit, and he remains spry and sharp as a razor.

"You talk to those hoodlums, they will not listen. How many summonses a day I see the police give out, but they tear 'em up. They don't care about jail, it's a joke. You have to come back and use that nightstick, and I say let them use it to have discipline and respect. I remember the day they did use it, and I know what's happening now that they don't. The policeman does wanna work, keep law and order, but his hands are tied from higher up. Those men would be rarin' to go, they could clean it up in twenty-four hours, where respectable American people could walk down 42nd Street and not be bothered. Like Theodore Roosevelt said as police commissioner of New York, he says, 'Men, don't make any arrests. There's more law at the end of a nightstick than all your courts put together.'"

Rubenstein's business began with crank-handle penny arcades showing Chaplin and Ben Turpin shorts, Dempsey fights, Ziegfeld girls in bathing trunks or playing basketball—"Not no peeps," he claims, though he does admit to running one of a bikini-clad girl in 1953, which he was "quickly told to remove." He's seen the games he buys go from $35 to $100 in the old days, up to $4,000 for today's largest videos. But one relic stands out amid the Ms. Pac Mans and Breakouts: "I still have the old grandmother with the crystal ball that dispenses a card, tells your fortune. That machine is with me since 1920. It's not making any money, but I have it as an attraction of the old days of the penny arcade. I'm not giving it up."

Dancing on the Frying Pan

A swarm of five black boys, each under ten years old, are trying to break into street-corner show business. They scatter out from the Hotel Carter's new welfare rolls in Times Square, before the Broadway curtains rise. They run alongside pedestrians on 45th and Broadway, the folks headed toward Shubert Alley and a dozen surrounding theaters, and force people to watch them dance. They are fledgling break dancers, executing spontaneous beginner dips and dives and spins, not yet matured into dance steps or acrobatics. But tourists are charmed, and every minute some ticket holder stops to smile, clap, or dance along and toss a coin. Other kids may wash windshields on 42nd Street, but these are minstrels. Street urchins without parental guidance. They have no ghetto blasters, no rap or funk tracks to dance to, which makes them an a cappella dance troupe. All of them wear slum-certified Keds sneakers, and know how to walk on the insides of their ankles, an old comedian's trick that is their most advanced move. The head kid, who whispers instructions to the rest, wears a black cap and carries a cane.

A potbellied, jolly fellow stops to join them, as his wife watches, charmed. He loves little kids, obviously, it makes no difference what kind. He pulls some change from his trousers and has them guess which hand. Making direct eye contact, he matches them step for step, dancing along, belly abounce, a real hoofer. Next he pulls out a dollar bill and throws it in their shoe box. Paper money is a rare and euphoric acquisition, which sets them to yelling and pulling at each other.

"Yo, mister!" shouts one of the breakers, tugging the coat of the potbellied gentleman, now twenty steps down the block with his wife. "Tell 'em it's for me, all right?" The five of them argue over whom the buck was intended for, but then scurry off to another corner, as if they'd already milked this corner for its spoils. Wow!

Next to the Orange Morris (formerly Julius) on Seventh and 46th, the four best break dancers in Times Square are passing the collection plate to a dozen spirited passersby. "Pay up, pay up!" demands the collector with the box. "If you watched, you gotta throw in at least a penny!" Only three or four cough up. The collector hams about in a duck walk, an ankle walk, but nothing so tricky as to spill over the coin box. On a warm spring night such as this, they might get $15 apiece. These are the big boys, about sixteen years old—though the fourth member is eight. They have a high-volume JVC blaster with plenty of rap cassettes. They wear uniforms, or at least their own cultivated personal dress. Two of them have windbreaker jackets and pants, the fat one named Jelly wears a brown stocking over his head, and the small fry just wears corduroys. They are joined by friends who come and go, subwaying down from Harlem, but basically they are known as the Fantastic Four; they were once picked by Pee Wee Herman to do a guest set during his engagement at Caroline's Comedy Club.

When the five undomesticated street urchins arrive before the Fantastic Four, they are too intimidated to speak and merely take their place among other spectators on the sidewalk. In fact, they're treated with disdain by the Four, who keep yelling for them to make room "so the people can see." None of the urchins would dare break dance in such presence, but they study the motions with mouths agape, especially the little member of the Fantastic Four, whom they follow enviously. This little fellow is advanced, born into rap and backbeat funk tracks, knowing no other music before this electronic genre—not Motown, not James Brown, not Bach.

The Four's rival breaker group, Float Committee, spills past Orange Morris. The pavement heats up now, the Four breaking harder, screaming louder, pushing back the five little squirts, who can't seem to stay out of the way. Someone yells for a face-off—Fantastic Four versus Float Committee. This is dance gang war!

The fat guy with stockinged head glides out to face Float Committee's fat guy. They dance off. The first fat guy falls to the ground in a seal imitation, rocking like a seesaw, flapping his fins. He maneuvers his hands over his torso, simulating quivering belly flab. His rival merely holds out his arms, as though electricity is snaking through them, then falls to the sidewalk, ending in a hand pirouette. One of the little urchins dares to try a back spin, but is shoved off by the big boys. "Get the fuck back!"

The next cat from Float has his routine interrupted by a Four who wears a tanktop T-shirt and toothpick far back in his mouth. "This be you," says Tanktop, mocking his opponent, a sluggish, bulky dancer in a windbreaker. Tanktop executes some cliched robot moves, à la James Brown ten years ago, to demonstrate his point. Then he starts to do his own moves, his nostrils flaring angrily. Spastic, jerky muscle twitches, quick-changing face contortions. He measures his challenger's head between his hands, then prances about, as though still holding the head. This is Tanktop's take on Japanese electronics, robots, computers, and video games, all coming back at you on the street corner.

"Okay, we through," announces the collector, flatly and suddenly, without any flourish. The partying stops on a dime, the crowd disperses, and they're finished on this block.

Pee Wee Is Not a Happy Man

The short-tempered black midget, a Times Square novelty since 1943, paces at the doorway of Hawaii-Kai like Napoleon. He's been serving time here since 1960, greeting folks with his cane, pointing the way upstairs at the schlock tourist restaurant next to the Winter Garden. His domain resembles a tropical Hawaiian Disneyland exhibit with a coat check and rest rooms. Business is terrible. If you grease his palm, he'll sit you down by the mock waterfall and tell you his life story:

"I'm Pee Wee, been on Broadway almost fifty years. I come up from Nashville in August 1943. I was singing and dancing with the late Frances Craig, owned a white band down South who had a black man performin'. After he gave his band up during the war days, he give me a hundred dollars, ticket, and letter of introduction.

"I had met the great Billy Eckstein down in Nashville, gave me his Harlem address, told me whenever I come to New York City I could stay with him till I got something to do—" A personage interrupts him at the door. "Don't come over here 'n' bother me now, this *my* b'niss!" Pee Wee shouts, lording over the Hawaiian forest like a Cornish hen. Upstairs, the Hawaiian revue of hula girls and singers are starting their chant on the dining stage, which Pee Wee has no part in. Pee Wee performed at the Three Deuces Club on 52nd Street during his first few years in the city. "Ballads, jazz, rhythm, that was my act. But I stopped singing in the nightclub b'niss after '44. They made me greeter and host. I preferred that to singing, because so much red tape getting started. I had more fun as emcee. Did that for 'bout twenty-five, thirty years."

Pee Wee worked Times Square joints like the Royal Roost, and Zanzibar's at 49th and Broadway, his favorite because of its old-time mobsters and decor. But it was at Birdland that he became a fixture: "I introduced onstage Miles Davis, Teddy Wilson, the late Charlie "Yardbird" Parker, late Fats Navarro, late Bud Powell.... Never went to their funerals, always wanted to remember them as I saw them."

Pee Wee dresses in an old-fashioned blue-and-gray doorman's uniform that he "messes up" with a rose in his lapel, a police button, an American flag, two religious emblems, a diamond stickpin under his bowtie, and gold jewelry, making him look like a tiny, decorated general.

"I lived in Harlem, the Hotel Theresa. That's when Harlem was Harlem. It was clean, weren't no muggin', nobody think about stickin' ya up, everybody was beautiful. Times Square was so clean in those days, you could eat off the sidewalk. When you get offa your job, you'd go to the *all-night* movies in Times Square. I don't mean no bad, ugly movies. Legit movies, reg'lar, clean. Then I'd go down to Romeo Restaurant with a friend for spaghetti and meatball, prices were right."

Pee Wee cites the closures of the Strand, the Capitol, the Roxy, and the Paramount, "where the great Frank Sinatra performed," as the "beginning of the downfall of Broadway. It used to be a Great White Way, everybody was dressed up, tuxedos, gowns, no overalls, no short pants, no khakis, none of that mess. They had cops on the beat all night long, kept the peace, nobody mad at nobody. Walked anywhere I want anytime, never look back. Now? I can't get home fast enough." Though he lives around the corner from Hawaii-Kai, Pee Wee takes a cab home. "Thank God, I haven't been mugged, because the man upstairs always takes care of me, so I don't worry 'bout nothin'."

After Birdland closed, Pee Wee "wanted to be with the people on the street." Characters of questionable deeds continually wander in from the avenue to whisper in the midget's ear, then dart back out. "Sometime I enjoy working here, sometime I don't. These crazy nuts off the streets walks in and I straighten 'em out, tell 'em, 'I'm sorry, you can't come in, you in the wrong place.'" The four-foot-eight, sixty-eight-year-old midget carries a metal cane: "And know how to use it, too. First their legs; when they bend down, their stomach, then their head. That's it."

Was The Pee ever married?

"Never got hung up with nothin' like that. They got a big mouth. All women got a big mouth, gettin' in people's b'niss. Not one of 'em I know today I would trust goin' 'cross the street. Don't get me wrong, I had my girls, crazy 'bout beautiful women, sexy, decent, clean women.

"Hey, baby, how you doin'?" booms the Broadway greeter into the street—where rumor has it he's really a woman in drag. He remembers Police Commissioner Ben Ward walking a Harlem beat ("He was tougher then than he is now"), and scolds the governor for not putting criminals in the electric chair. It was the sixties assassinations that first messed everything up in the country. He then admits having been scared to death last night during an electrical storm, the likes of which he never before saw strike the Broadway pavement: "The signs of the time. All over Broadway, b'niss is terrible. In the next few years, all hell will break loose over the world. The battle of Armageddon is already started. People minds is boggled on pornography, all that ugly filth and stuff. They all dope addicts, their minds turn to ugliness. We in the last days."

Pee Wee looks far above his prison perch at the schlock Broadway waterfall and breaks into hymn:

When your bod-y
Suffer pain
And your health you can't regain
Take your troubles to the Lord
And leave it there.

LOWDOWN

Inside the Peeps

The scene is a crowded weekday lunch hour at a modern Times Square sex emporium in the late 1970s. Outside stands "Dudley Arnholt," commodities broker, tough guy with a tax form, mid-forties, divorced, paranoid neurotic, Times Square Everyman at the moment. He's so horny that the crack of dawn ain't safe—he followed the direction of his erection all the way here, like a donkey following a carrot. But he freezes near the entrance—passersby are onto his game, he fears. Checking all directions to make sure the coast is clear of any clients, neighbors, or nieces, he sighs woefully and steps briskly through the door. Arnholt is home free in an evil candy store of gaping fuck holes, lassoed bazooms, twelve-inch cannons of shooting manhood, electrifying hardcore sound loops, and a blatant subculture of fetishes, all arranged in McDonald's-style elegance. But the pang in his gut leads him past all this to an even greater spectacle—the fantastic, featured "Live Nude Girl" peep show.

There are twenty occupied booths, each with a glowing red bulb that indicates a quarter has been inserted, giving the viewer his thirty seconds. Cocks of every age, race, and size are being drawn out in the booths. Some will spurt onto the walls, some into Kleenex, some will even discharge into fifty-cent French-tickler condoms from the store's vending machine. These will be discarded on the floor.

Arnholt waits his turn, careful to avoid the jolt of eye contact. A crowd of gawkers stare aimlessly at the women on display in the "one-on-one" booths. An Eisenhower dollar buys a minute on the phone with one of these broads—but a full-length glass partition, dripping with ejaculate, keeps you at bay. Arnholt never springs for the telephone gimmick—what if the peep girl spots him later at a debutante ball?

Roving quarter-cashiers double as barkers, trying to perpetuate some cosmic momentum of flowing cash. "C'mon, fellas, keep those quarters comin', take a booth or clear the aisle, get your change here for live sexy girls, four for a quarter." Every ten minutes, one of the four sexy girls is replaced. A hidden female emcee announces each new entry, guaranteeing they'll love her.

"Foxy Bertha joining the sexy girls now, big daddy, all for a quarter, love to love you, baby, come in your pants, yeah, right now!" A fat man, barely able to stuff his huge belly into the narrow booth, responds to the mating call. Unsatisfied customers linger in the aisle, checking at each interval until they find a girl worthy of their jizz. They've come in blue jeans, in cowboy hats, on crutches; there are even palsied spastics. But this being the workaday lunch hour, the business community prevails in suit and tie. After all, this is a commercialized form of voyeurism, a modern way to go girl-watching, you might say.

Arnholt regrets missing the "Boy-Girl Duos"—Cuban refugees who fuck on a revolving platform (which switches off with "Lesbian Love Teams" on weekends). Current disco Top 40 shakes the walls; Arnholt knows of this only as peep show music. *Two black guys are about to tear into each other with Afro picks, but the cashier spots something more distressing—some nitwit peering into the crack of an occupied stall for a free peek. This unfortunate is verbally assaulted the hell out. Arnholt doesn't dare interfere. He's humiliated to find himself here, straining not to draw attention, eyes downcast to the floor.*

A central booth opens and Arnholt makes his move. The soles of his Oxfords skid for a moment like ice skates and he notices a sopping Kleenex contemptuously wedged into a crevice. The management expects this, it's part of the operation. The adjacent booth is being mopped by professional scum-scrubbers; mop-and-pail Leroys, urban descendants of dung-shoveling *stable jockeys. They work their roll mops like dance partners, soaked in Fast & Easy ammonia, which they slide into unoccupied booths in sync with the disco backbeat. With the outward boogie-oogie-oogie sweep comes a trail of used Kleenex. Arnholt takes a freshened booth. He hangs his coat and briefcase on the hook and flips the lock. In the womblike confines of his own private stall, Arnholt stands like a horse in heat. A hefty supply of quarters jingles in his pocket and he knows he better keep 'em comin' or the management will slam on his door. This is a peak turnover hour and others are anxious for Arnholt's booth. He has seen certain customers try to settle down and make the booth their permanent living quarters. But the management is fast to catch on and charge them 25¢ per minute rent (or $10,800 a month, according to Arnholt's quick mathematical brain). He flips a quarter into the slot, which triggers an ascending metal curtain. The partition slowly rises to reveal a naked Times Square maiden writhing about on a rotating platform. Spread-eagled twats and hind ends float by the window, ecstatic aquarium fish with ghetto-girl faces. The booths form a semicircle around this naked parade and he can see the shadowy faces of other masturbators peeping out across from him. Fortunately, the blaring disco drowns out any cries of passion from neighboring booths.*

After a forty-second introductory peek the curtain crawls back down. Arnholt has spotted the object of his desire. He pops in another quarter and fixes his stare on Foxy Bertha. She twists and grinds, her enormous buttocks protruding upward like a gigantic brown hen freaked out on disco. Dudley Arnholt, midlevel juggler of soybean certificates, is entering the point of no return. He knows nothing of silver futures now, he can't quote you today's copper closings or tomorrow's can't-miss capital ventures. His life, business, and hemorrhoids are far away from the world of Foxy Bertha and her fat, jiving, juicy black ass in the sky.

"Calling all men, calling all pussy inspectors. We got chocolate clitty onstage for ya now. Come warm your bones, warm your main bone, gonna race into space, yeah, big daddy!"

The intermittent drone of the emcee is inaudible as our hero's eyes roll up in passion. It's time to whip it out. With trembling fingers, he fumbles his pecker through the slit of his boxer shorts. His adrenaline is coursing as he strokes up a storm, but he pauses to keep feeding that slot or the Bertha of his dreams will disappear. Mirrors line the walls, so she's never out of view. But now she's coming closer, pumping her snatch right into Arnholt's window, her crooked smile revealing two missing choppers. Juicy Jane and her jagged cesarean scar is revolving on a platform behind in a spread-eagled Quaalude stupor. Arnholt's building a furious pud callus, all the more unbearable as Bertha's eyes meet his in a conspiratorial wink. She presses her labes into his window and the commodities broker flicks out his tongue, lathering the funky glass with spittle. He has reached his own Times Square heaven, lost in a nirvana of sleaze. . . .

Oxuzana Brown, four-year veteran of Show World, always claims she's going to leave her post at Times Square's biggest sex circus and head for Europe. She plans to live there a long while, but can't seem to get going. This big-bosomed Harlem child, of "French and Nigerian background," who still possesses a soft glow in her face, is ready to retire.

"I've had my fill," asserts Oxuzana, but with a lack of bitterness. "I've learned to do sex shows, to simulate lesbian and S&M acts, developed basic booth skills—like getting guys to spend money. I've seen enough come to last a lifetime. I'm tired of guys who look like dogs tellin' me what they wanna do over the booth phone. You know you may not be a beauty queen, but you know you doin' better than them. I've seen the strangest cocks in the world. Saw a tiny Chinese with a huge monster cock. Then I saw this giant, muscular black guy whip out the tiniest dick I ever saw. Wanted to introduce the both of them so they could get an operation and switch."

After a hard double shift, Oxuzana stabilizes at the Blarney Stone across the street with a white wine, though last night she was robbed coming out of this bar by two dykes. And last week, she finally switched from the downstairs booths to the upstairs concession: "A lot of pressure's been building up downstairs. My manager accused me of taking time off from my booth to talk with someone because he was white. There was a meeting to reduce the queens [pre-op transsexuals] to no more than three per shift. And a customer had a gun two weeks ago, threatened to shoot the manager."

Oxuzana began in 1979 at "Lee's Baby Doll Revue," a live peep downstairs at the complex. Times Square had just been forced to put glass back in the partitions after a year of frivolous open-window encounters between patrons and dancers. "I would not have taken the job if the windows were open," she claims. "But back then you really had to dance and sweat, and hit each of the fifteen windows, even though there were no tips." Starting salary for peep show girls in 1979 was three dollars per shift in the "Peep-Alive," plus a forty percent cut of the newly installed silver dollar one-on-one booths. The split increased to fifty-fifty with management, then returned to forty-sixty. Though Oxuzana only averaged $175 after a week of dancing back then, she has a higher regard for days past. "The tightness is gone. A few years ago, if there was a fight, everyone jumped in, we were more reliable. Today, you can pull $200 in the booths in a night, but the change man can screw you up. If he's not right there with silver dollars, customers'll leave."

As a matter of course, Oxuzana learned how to avoid the pimps, who generally zero in on the dumber girls. "But they *never* spend any money. They might have an old lady who works here, and they'll get their girl to pull another. If one comes in my booth, I'll just leave, say I gotta dance. Look at the way they dress and act. You get one of them by themselves, unprotected, and they are chicken shit."

Oxuzana's customers at Show World divide up into three general categories. Some guys practically live there, masturbatory junkies, in for a daily fix. Then there are curiosity seekers, occasional visitors to Times Square who might even bring their wives. And "juniors"—young men or teens in for a worldly thrill with a Live Nude Girl. "But I have seen, in my four years, a lot of straight guys fall from simple fantasies into mental illness. A lot of customers have gotten sicker. One guy can't orgasm unless I pretend I'm drowning in quicksand over the phone. Every night, there are guys who creep in and lick come off the windows. And one customer was a slasher. I saw him arrested on TV. I have no respect for these men. But I also met a famous conductor in my booth, real nice guy, and a soap opera star from *Days of Our Lives*."

The girls can't show too much that's legal these days in the peeps. They can technically get busted for touching their tits or opening their legs. "As long as you don't show too much coochie," Oxuzana says. "One way you can spot undercover cops is, they don't look like they want to be here. They don't even look horny. But new girls don't know any better, they're the first to get busted. With a clean record, you're out in hours. Slap on the hand, makes the city look good, cops look efficient.

"My biggest fear about Show World," reveals Oxuzana, "are the mops. You got AIDS, herpes, gonorrhea, and syph out there—and guys come and come and come. There's not enough detergent in the world for me. I'm terrified to get touched by a floor mop. They skeeve me out. You can't rinse them enough."

What have the battlefields of Times Square done to her own libido, seeing man at his worst?

"I'm more into women now than men," says Oxuzana. "Although I do still prefer tall men, hairy men, European men. I won't let Show World disturb my sex life."

The Peep Machine

In his fourth-floor technical lab at 42nd and Eighth, Roger Kirschner is mulling over the conversion of all peep-machine coin slots to a more sophisticated system. Show World boss Richard Basciano's twenty-eight-year-old mechanical wiz has nearly made his decision: to remove the conventional $4 "Coin Mech" and go with the advanced $40 "Coin Comparator Mech." As he is chief of operations, Roger's decision will convert many hundreds of peep machines throughout Show World's reigning empire of Times Square emporiums by 1985. A lot of research went into acquiring the new gizmo, including two trips to Chicago. "We deal with companies all over the country that supply coin mechanisms to all types of vending machines, from candy and cigarette to slot machines for Bally, in Atlantic City, Vegas, and video arcades."

Roger's work deals with computerized electronics, his office filled with logic circuits, microprocessors, "mother" PC boards for the video peeps. He also cuts and edits loops and videotapes here, for all the main locations: Show World, Show Follies, Show Place de Paris, Les Gals, Joy, and the Pussycat Showcase. Boxes labeled COIN MECHANISMS and COIN ACCEPTORS—two of the biggest such firms—lie around the lab. Roger has an affable manner, very much absorbed in the electro-mechanical aspects of peeps.

Roger picks up a $4 Coin Mech, now used in all peeps. Each is manufactured to take one coin forever; in this instance, a Susan B. Anthony silver dollar. The paperback-size gizmo says "SBA" on its gut. In an ironic feminist slight, all locations had to change their one-on-one booth mechs when the smaller Susan B. Anthony dollars replaced Ike. The old coin mechs are 80 percent foolproof against slugs. But the new $40 Coin Comparator is 100 percent foolproof—their slots won't take slugs, small change, or washers—"Sometimes guys even tie a quarter onto a string and try to drop it through." Measuring conductivity like a metal detector, the Comparator will gauge weight, thickness, and metallic composition of a coin. Any coin that doesn't match perfectly will be caught on a magnet and rejected. It can be instantly readjusted to any price or token change. "Although it's $40, it'll save money in the long run, and you'll have 'em forever. If we went back to quarters from tokens, all's you do is stick a quarter in, from then on that's all she'll accept."

Show World, the U.S. Steel of porn palaces, switched to its own monetary system of tokens by 1980, now in all locations. Bags of them lie on the main-floor manager's desk, like sacks of Wells Fargo gold, spilling over at the brim. "Give them tokens," the floor manager might instruct one of his boys, when visiting pornographers enter his office. And then, amazingly, they'll fill the guests' hands with jingling, octagonal twenty-five-cent tokens, both silver- and copper-colored. Each has the inscription *Worlds Greatest Show Place.*

Show World switched to tokens for security reasons. "Before," says Roger, "Show World booths had cash in the boxes. People tried everything to break into machines. Nine times out of ten, they did more damage trying to get at the money, even when never getting it. People won't break in for tokens, they can't refund them. Unless they have someone on the inside to cash 'em in." Show World tokens can be found in taxi ashtrays, scattered across Times Square parking lots and train tracks—incriminating evidence fellows don't want their wives in suburbia to see. At one time Les Gals used to refund them—a detail of black boys went to the train tracks nightly to round up littered tokens and cash them in. "The tokens are also a gimmick. They don't cost twenty-five cents to make—maybe four or five cents. If those tokens walk, you've profited."

There are thirty people in management at all of Show World's locations, not including endless girls, quarter cashiers, mop-ups. They handle everyday shit. "We have guys that come in and just go around all day taking pieces of paper and stuffing up the coin chutes. They get their kicks on that. We figure it's an older gentleman who doesn't have anything to do, who gets off on seeing us go crazy after they stuff up all the chutes." Roger has nine mechanics working three shifts, between the stores. "They handle breakdowns. Bent coins people put in that jam up. If they know a little about physics, people take wax impressions, then make a lead impression for a slug."

Show World alone gets about $100 a week in slugs, or four hundred. "But if they get slugs past the dollar one-on-ones, you're not talking about twenty-five cents anymore. If someone hits on the right size, shape, and weight, this guy can save a lot. When the machines are dumped every week, there's a meter reading taken to help us see what's popular and change the loops. If we have pennies in that booth, they're recorded also. That tells me the mech's not adjusted right, or the guy who's making the slug is getting over on us. We've caught people plugging up or breaking into machines. All's it winds up to be is a lawsuit if somebody gets hurt; you don't want the confrontation."

Roger flips over his newest design—a huge two-dollar Show World token with silver finish. It will buy extended time in the one-on-ones, currently standardized throughout Times Square at forty seconds per dollar. "Some customers will take their pants off in the booth before they even drop their money. They get ready so they'll save that dollar, they know it's only forty seconds."

Touring the live peep, Roger unscrews the electronics of a booth. The Peep-Alive mechanism—now commonplace throughout Times Square and perhaps the world—was developed by Roger, who worked nights with a New Jersey electronics company. Yesterday's more rickety system, by a company called Textoil, used compressed ball bearings. Roger's sleek innovation is "a very simple circuit," utilizing a "worm gear" to raise the shade: A quarter activates a timer and sends voltage up to a motor that turns a threaded "worm gear." The shade climbs up on a nut, like a screwgun. A microswitch stops it at the top. When the timer's off, it unlatches a relay and the partition comes back down. And thus, in the interim, are the thrills and chills of "Live Nude Girls," the neon-community catchphrase.

Show World gradually incorporated safety precautions for dancers. "Girls used to get their hair caught in the worm gear. We put a cover over it. They used to hang on the pipes and pull out the electrical wires. We put handles on, so they can pose before windows. We don't rotate the tables anymore. A girl would lay there, she wouldn't get up and dance." The company recently installed full-circle Peep-Alives instead of semicircles, where all the money would come into the center booths. New peeps, nine feet in diameter, take up less space and give each window an equal view, though the peep queens appear to be trapped in a cage. These eighteen-booth circles operate at Show Follies, while Show World's remain with fourteen booths but a panoramic runway.

"In New York, space is money, every square foot is worth something," says Roger, surveying the film peeps. "If I can fit fifteen machines in this aisle, compared to ten, that's good business." The film-peep booths are seventy-nine inches deep, but the video booths, honed by Roger, are only fifty-nine inches deep. "Video now does four-to-one over film peeps."

Show World introduced video peeps in January 1981. "We started with ten multiple-choice selections. It was very complicated, people weren't yet geared to computer-type operations, we were ahead of our time. They just wanna drop the money, not get involved." Roger videotaped clothed porn stars Lisa DeLeeuw and Desiree Cousteau reciting instructions, which each booth ran on a promo channel when you entered—how to drop in a token and key a program from 01 through 10 on the computerized touch-tone pad. "But guys would come in and jerk off to the instructions." Furthermore, the wear and tear on ten machines, which funneled porn to each booth's TV monitor continuously, broke the machines in a month. Twenty-minute loops would unload and rewind three times an hour, on customer's token time (unlike the film loop, which *loops* around nonstop).

"We were complicating simplicity. I learned this from my boss. Guys were geared to the quarter, they walk in and drop it in either A or B side, it would come on. I used to stand downstairs and watch, customers couldn't understand how it worked. I fought with everybody here, insisted video loops could make money. So I worked with an engineer night and day for eighteen weeks to develop the A and B video system in 1983. Eighteen weeks of hell."

Roger enters a video base room, the fruits of his labors. Forty-two VCRs are in operation twenty-four hours, playing features now, though they only run when a token triggers their tape. A *Please Stand By* message appears during rewind, with scenes from Side B—the customer's token freezes till Side A returns. "I have people trying to send me airline tickets to fly out and help 'em develop systems." Roger compares notes with peep show engineers from all over the country twice a year at the X-rated industry's consumer electronics show, held in Vegas and Chicago.

"Fuckin' heat," laments the main-floor manager, over poor peep show attendance during a heat wave. "Nobody can get it up in this weather." All cash boxes from booths are emptied at the end of the week, with amounts varying drastically—this week's haul sucks. A box might contain anywhere from zero to a hundred and fifty tokens, which registers on meters. "When I get the sheets at the end of the week," says Roger, "I average all the machines. If one is below fifty plays, we pull it. If a loop does great, we'll put another copy on the floor. A feature like *Behind the Green Door* will play forever."

Fresh porn shipments come in weekly, with video making film loops obsolete. Roger monitors all machines at more than a half-dozen locations; he wants to program a computer to take in all the meter readings from more than three hundred peep show booths in the empire, by direct feed into a microprocessor terminal. He will gauge weather conditions and seasons into his computer printout, which he'll check without leaving his office.

"I studied electronics at a vocational school. If you went to college, you were a good kid at that time, whereas if you went to Votech, you were a troublemaker. But when I got out, people started to realize that anybody who went there was gonna be somebody. It's satisfying to know you're pioneering a field. When I started here ten years ago, everyone was working under the gun, you never knew if you were gonna get locked up—though I was only an electrician." Roger has friends at NBC who try to lure him out of the smut biz to work in their corporate world, but he was miserable when he tried another job for several months. Show World's boss, Richard Basciano, he says, gave him room to stretch out electronically, to innovate every incarnation of the peeps, setting Times Square's standard. What other company, he asks, would encourage such freedom, even after large, costly mistakes were made? His parents now acknowledge that Show World's action keeps their son happiest. Roger plans to incorporate video discs in the future for all peeps, eliminating the wear and tear of current equipment, and he is experimenting with holographic porn.

"I worked as a laborer/electrician when they began building Show World in 1974. This was a hardware store and a Chemical Bank. We did everything the opposite of what anybody would have done in the business. Guys thought we were crazy, nuts." The complex was built behind closed doors for about $400,000, with eighteen months of construction. The store opened with twenty-four telephone-booth film peeps and a dozen live-peep booths, nothing special. But two years later, a newfangled McDonald's-like porn center began replacing the sawdust floor "scumatoriums" of Times Square; Show World broke in their slick design at the Pussycat in 1977. Supermarket aisles, everything steel, Formica, tile floors for simple swabbing, no more linoleum that became rotted with discharge. That old-time 42nd Street squalor, thought to be a crucial environment for the self-degradation of customers, waned; Show World's stores *upgraded* the neighborhood from the "Hell's Bedroom" nightmare parlors they replaced, in the view of many.

"I tell ya the truth—I don't go into any of those other places in Times Square," says Roger. "I'm afraid to, I have no reason to. If they know who I am, they may take offense—what am I lookin' for? I hear about drugs, who's gettin' their heads broke, who's havin' a shoot-out. You gotta be on guard even walking past those places. A lotta these guys are on ninety-nine-year leases, they're not payin' the high rent a new tenant would. They're more of a nuisance than competition, they're giving us a bad name. We've spent a lot of time and money to run an up-and-up joint, a clean-cut place, well lit, so you don't worry about losing your wallet or your life. The smaller operations don't care if they're gone tomorrow, they're in for the fast buck, I would say. They'll be condemned. We feel we're runnin' a cleaner business."

Peep History

Pornography was as dirty as its name when it first came to Times Square, reared by bad guys from other rackets. According to journalist William Sherman, the notorious Martin Hodas made his fortune introducing the first Times Square peep shows. Hodas managed a vending machine route in Brooklyn till 1966. "One day," he claimed, "I was talking to this repair guy over on Tenth Avenue near 42nd, and the guy says, 'I bet you could do something with these old film machines.' They were like nickelodeons. So you could say, the modern peep show was born by accident."

At the end of 1966, he bought thirteen of the old machines, offering fifty-fifty splits to the several existing risqué bookshops, whose most extreme material were under-the-counter nudist volumes, girlie playing cards (French Decks), and Times Square standards like urinating rubber statues and colored photos of nudes. Hodas threaded the machines with California stag films of dancing broads flashing tit and cunt, images never exhibited publicly. Store owners said no, fearing the law—but after a few weeks the owner of 259 West 42nd (still in business, featuring books, peeps, and knives) went for the sales pitch, placing the first machines. To everyone's surprise, the quarters wouldn't quit—the other stores wanted some, so Hodas custom-ordered machines from Kentucky, placing them at 113 and 210 West 42nd (Blackjack), and 1498 Broadway. Customers who flocked to the stores in 1967 allegedly asked for more explicit mags and loops. The neighborhood saw rapid conversions to porn, which replaced small merchants around Times Square. Major realtors who owned property cashed in on the phenom, as Hodas and other newly christened smut peddlers bought up leases, paying up to five grand for six hundred square feet. West Coast distributors took the lead in churning out films, while Hodas opted to shoot his own grainy, pimple-assed loops, such as "Flesh Party" and "Elevator Orgy." Gradually the G-strings disappeared and out danced loops like "Sucky Fucky." In 1970, the Mine-Cine, in the Wurlitzer Building on 42nd, presented Times Square's first live cock-in-cunt routine before spectators, in the guise of "studio tours" of fuck loops being filmed in progress.

The mob made their thrust into Times Square porn shops in 1968. They opened their own joints and muscled in on others, maintaining a legendary grip on the area's vices, which stemmed back to bootlegging and gambling in the Roaring Twenties. Here was a semilegal "gray area," a flowering industry where owners couldn't exactly run to the cops when they were leaned on. In March 1968, Hodas was competing with John "Sonny" Franceze, a family boss who'd backed a rash of peeps. Hodas paid $150,000 in mob protection from 1968 to 1971, but the returns were large—other cities opened up for him, strong-arm assistance was provided. By the end of 1968 he either owned or leased peeps in more than thirty Manhattan locations.

Hodas' main man was a powerfully built ex-airplane mechanic who twice a week wheeled a large steamer trunk from store to store to collect the quarters. He also lugged a balance scale that he dumped each location's spoils onto until they evened out for the half-and-half split. Once it was full, Hodas and his collector wheeled the trunk to one of four Times Square banks where Hodas kept accounts. The Chemical Bank at Eighth and 42nd (where Show World now stands) counted $15,000 in quarters one afternoon from Hodas. During the first two months of 1969, eighty-five percent of the quarters shipped to Chemical's main branch, according to a vice-prez, were brought in from Hodas' peeps.

By 1970, four hundred film peep machines were scattered about New York City, according to Senator Everett Dirksen's alarming anti-smut exposé in the *Reader's Digest.* The Organized Crime Control Bureau estimated more than a thousand by 1972. They were in dark backrooms of porn bookstores, which reeked of urine and old orgasms, shown by nickelodeon or projected in curtained-off booths. Viewing time in the good old days was two minutes for a quarter; inflation would drop this to thirty seconds in just a dozen years.

Martin Hodas, by 1970, owned two Lincoln Continentals, a swimming pool, and a forty-foot cabin cruiser, and raised a large family on Long Island. He commuted to his office, East Coast Cinematics at 113 West 42nd, listed in the phone book, unlike other porn store bosses who still ran business from backrooms of Little Italy social clubs at that time. According to a police raid of Hodas' office in January 1972, the Poppa of the Peeps was taking in twenty grand a week. He served a year in the slam for income-tax evasion, then returned to the Square, where his stores began to pale next to the newer ones.

Peeps became the meat-and-potatoes attraction, as common to Times Square as slot machines are to Las Vegas. Perhaps the most remarkable aspect of Times Square is the boundless variety of sexual nightmares and sweet dreams depicted in thousands of ten-minute loops. Loops were the tough, heartless training ground for the first generation of porn stars, a fifteen-year phenomenon made obsolete by video. This was pornography's strongest medium, in which one could pick his favorite female creature, crystallized into a perfect 8mm, ten-minute rhapsody, and pop one's cookies. After a preview in the booth, a washed-out color reel could be obtained up front for $18.

Some of the first, true to cliché, were ground out by hardened criminals in grungy basements on 42nd Street, with syphilitic junkies fucking for a $50 fix. Before professionals entered the field, any moron could pose behind camera as a director, for his personal perversions. Bobby Surretsky, a short, fat con man of many crimes and aliases, pushed gay hardcore into his newly acquired Midtown Books in 1967, at 138 West 42nd. He filmed his own primitive loops across the street, much of it S&M and kiddie porn. By 1969, he was moving 2,500 reels for ten grand each week. The pimp who supplied little boys for his films turned him in to the FBI, who discovered Surretsky had recently cashed $400,000 in bogus police paychecks. Surretsky turned informer, served two years in jail on a murder conspiracy, and was last reported to be in the coin business.

There were good pornographers and bad pornographers, same as in any field. Toby Ross, one of the early pros who was beloved by some of his actors, was the only black director in porn. Having made hundreds of flicks by the mid-1970s, he stated his own strategy of directing to Marc Stevens: "You can be used… but not misused."

The earliest loops—the first pornos produced by organized companies with ongoing series—went by the brand names of Kiss, Pretty Girl, Color Climax, and Lasse Braun (from Europe). Stars of Sex presented Tina Russell, a reigning loop queen of the early seventies, while the Collection series introduced Candy Samples. Young John Holmes, out of rural Ohio in the early 1970s, looked like a monkey, with a lantern jaw and greasy crewcut—he began his career in endless loops for Playmate, Kama Sutra, and Limited Edition. The Diamond Collection was the raunchiest of the straight loops, each ending with an ugly female specimen blubbering under a harsh facial come shot. Club International (not the mag) tapped even more misogynous territory, like "Maternity Ward Sex," featuring lovely Susaye London in her ninth month of pregnancy, taking on the obstetrician and black hospital attendant. Joys of Erotica presented stripper Veri Knotty with a four-foot co-star in "Anal Dwarf." But even the less frequent S&M material, or obscure rape loop, acted out its psychodrama bloodlessly, or with little authority.

Most standard loops portrayed suck and fuck. America's favorite "fourteen-inch" son, John Holmes, starred in 150 Swedish Erotica loops alone, ubiquitous in the Square, while Vanessa Del Rio popped up in every other booth, with Seka gaining.

Any public traces of highly illegal kiddie porn disappeared for good by the mid-1970s from Times Square. But the kook loops remained in the rear ends of several scumatoriums. A dive called Exotic Circus, at 140 West 42nd, contained familiar Swedish Erotica loops up front, but those with the courage to walk to the back found loops of menstruation-vampires, bowel movements unloading, girls fucking horses, Great Danes getting their peckers sucked. The slicker Peepland, former locale of Hubert's Museum, opened in January 1978, its downstairs sanctum harboring a hundred blue assembly-line booths. Here were strange and unnatural acts from German distributors, a Disneyland in hell, as quoted from showcards: "Two wild girls shove live eels up snatch and asshole!"; "Fish-fucking!"; "Farmboy fucks cow"; "Man fucks a hen"; "Woman sticks arm up cow's ass!"; "Man licks 400-lb. pig's asshole!"; "Girl takes on dog, horse, and pig simultaneously." Though these were supposedly novelty loops, a browsing patron might just have easily spotted a wad plopped across the screen of "Two Nuns and a Donkey" as he would in a John Holmes loop, romantic by comparison. "Mice Torture" depicted two men pumping live mice through a tube that was inserted up a bound woman's vage—before the viewer could get hot over the mice, the two guys started blowing each other. In retrospect, none of these poor animals ever fucked their way to the top, becoming the first Lassie, Flipper, or Mighty Mouse of porn.

Times Square's "Live Nude Girls" surfaced at 109 West 42nd in 1972. Customers gazed through a mail slot, and the girls raced into bikinis during police raids. Around the corner at the Paradise on Sixth Avenue, one flight over the 11-11 bookstore, attractive models rotated on a platform, spreading their legs so wide, gents in the curtained stalls could almost see China. This, at a time when mere pubic hair had hardly surfaced on newsstands. Both peeps smelled like subway urinals and were short-lived.

The peeps had glass partitions dividing the Live Nude Girls from the voyeurs, whose hot breath smeared across the windows like that of rabid paupers at a toy store window. The girls reciprocated by smudging their flanks against the cloudy divider. In mid-1978, these glass partitions shrewdly began to disappear, one by one, as vice-squad policies seemed to relax with Mayor Beame's retirement. Stores hung OPEN WINDOW signs over the newly christened booths, which offered an "even closer view" of Live Nude Girls. Naturally, the course of human nature drew these two opposite species together—the cages were finally opened. The girls began to offer quick feels for a dollar, and as customers grew more demanding, tit-sucking and cunt-lapping soon became routine. Within months, all peep stall windows throughout the Square were removed. The crowds were as never before. Bathrooms opened at the Pussycat and Adulterama where customers gargled afterward.

Show World's peeps had metal risers that were like guillotines—previously, girls could lift up the shade. Girls commonly got caught halfway through the windows. "Guy'd give 'em ten dollars for a blowjob," remembers chief engineer Roger K., who rescued dozens. "They'd go through the booth, hang there, the shade would come down, they would get pinched. You couldn't reverse the type of mechanism we were using, it had to go all the way down before it went up."

A peep show patron could summon a naked, willing stranger to his window with the wave of a dirty dollar bill. He could request tit, twat, hind end, have a leg hoisted into his booth, a boot in his face. Starving octopus hands grabbed over girls' bodies, trying to wangle a finger into paydirt. In this peculiar mating dance, ghetto girls paraded booth to booth, fondling their wares and twitching their fingers in a *pay up* gesture. Dollars were stuffed into shoulder purses and stockings. Some couldn't quite decide whether they belonged in this racket, standing back haughtily while a customer craned his horny neck out the window, lips grasping for a nip. More enthusiastic girls, often black and Hispanic, propped a wide-spread ass over the window ledge to be sucked heartily. A grizzled old Festus might pay ten dollars for a soul kiss, while a younger guy might have his hair petted romantically as he sucked a boob.

In their workaday world the girls faced a wall of windows which opened and closed on a humorless gallery of zombie faces. "All you see is a hand, you don't see a face," remembers Candy Staton, an Amazonian Peep Queen whose bod made her $150 a night during the open-window days. "I started as one of the girls who'd rather wear panties and keep the guys above my waist. I didn't want just anyone to touch me down there. But after I saw how much money you could make, I did it. It drove me crazy, I couldn't handle it. But I did it."

Candy "graduated from Syracuse with a major in physical therapy." She had an ugly-duckling childhood, then turned stunning at eighteen. She felt a calling to parade herself in Times Square by night, but worked as a children's therapist by day. For one year at Blackjack, the most squalid of peeps, where junkies grapple desperately for tips, she ground her pussy into the middle fingers of anonymous menfolk with more passion than any other Live Nude Girl on 42nd Street. "Everybody was in one untidy dressing room, all the girls, the janitors, constant traffic streaming through, pimps hitting on you—you didn't know who was who. I knew two junkies who died, both young women with children. The management was nasty to the customers. But the money was there, and I met some good people who I stay in touch with."

The live peeps were the straight man's closest equivalent to the underside of gay nightlife—wandering into a dark booth to mouth the slimy genitals of strange women, whose breasts were coated with the slobber of fifty previous tit-biters and whose sucked-out cunts glistened at premium rates. Underage black youths snuck in, having a high old time making the girls cringe with embarrassment ("I see yo' titty, ha, ha!"). Eugene, a twenty-two-year-old employee at Barking Fish, the Cajun fast-food joint across from Show World, recalls his bemusement when he began waiting on peep girls: "I recognized about six of them from high school in Queens, I even went to junior high with some—Jamaica High, Andrew Jackson. They try to stay away from me, they don't want people to know what they doin'. Girls from Queens, they all act the same. Real quiet, but when they come into the city, they become nymphs. Girls from The Bronx or Manhattan would think twice about working a peep show, but a girl from Queens thinks nobody from out there will see her. A lot are also from the South, you can tell by their accents."

In January 1980, Show World chief Richard Basciano ordered windows reinstalled in all locations. "We closed windows in the Peep-Alive 'cause we felt it was getting carried away," says Roger. "Girls were makin' all kinds of deals with the customers—in fact, we were threatened that we'd be shut down for prostitution. We made a lot of money, but he chose to shut the windows. Now, we got hurt, we really took a beating in profits, our business almost went down the tubes, we shut down Peep-Alives at two locations."

The cops keep a steady pressure on Show World, whose personnel take it in stride. There are periodic roundups of girls, inspections for electrical codes and health department violations. Even Candy Samples was carted off in handcuffs after her grandmotherly striptease on the Triple Treat stage. "But what upsets my boss," says Roger, "is how these other stores can still have their windows open. We took busts and harassment for prostitution left and right."

Blackjack, one of two Times Square peeps to defiantly continue the open-window tradition, toned down the contact with its harlots to no more than breasts. A scrawled ultimatum by the runway lays the final responsibility on Live Nude Girls: *No finger in crack of ass. If caught, you will be fired.*

. . . In the darkness of his booth, Dudley Arnholt senses a disturbance. On the brink of climax, he glances down from Foxy Bertha to see what looks like a tiny Martian spacecraft hovering at the bottom of his booth. But then his eyes adjust on a hand-held camera, which suddenly clicks off a round of

flashes. Some fag pervert is snapping pictures of Arnholt's balls from under the divider! He zips up, eyes blinded, and kicks at the outrage rather effeminately. His worst fear has been realized. Was it some blackmail attempt? He storms out of the booth stuttering, but quickly pulls himself in check. Back among the horny assemblage, everything normal, nothing out of the ordinary going on. Arnholt makes it to the cashier, whose fingers are dishing out grubby coins in spurts of four. The masturbators make easy targets for shortchanging.

"How many?" the barker demands, oblivious to Arnholt the Man. His bare arms are cut like stone; Arnholt's are like macaroni. Arnholt steps up his courage, about to utter the first words he has ever spoken in a Times Square sex joint. His outrage comes out weak-voiced, but he gets across the urgent matter. "Get'cha kwaters here, live women on stage!" answers the barker. Arnholt feels like a rape victim, but he can't identify exactly which booth it was. The cashier is finally distracted by Arnholt's charge, and points to a sign that states, sure enough, that picture-taking within the premises is forbidden and dangerous to your health. If they catch the culprit, "we'll fuck him up," says the cashier. But whoever did it has disappeared into the wild blue yonder.

A cold sweat forms over Arnholt's forehead as he trudges helplessly toward the exit. Somebody, somewhere, has photos of Arnholt smacking his beef. He is afraid if he comes back he'll find his cock being marketed on a deck of cards. Worse yet, what if he pops a quarter in a film peep and sees his own celluloid image masturbating back at him? He starts to dream about returning with a tube of Krazy Glue to gum up all the quarter slots.

In Search of the Longest Stiletto

The Paradise Bootery opened at 1586 Broadway in 1925. Twenty years later, the store was acquired by Harry Weller, a double-chinned, rotund sultan of slut pumps whose supply of high heels came from a Hungarian named Alex Kaufman. An old-world shoe artisan, Kaufman acquired the store himself in the mid-1970s. Kaufman has outsmarted the trendy commercial shoe industry—he lines the walls and ceilings of his little shop with pumps, button-downs, slut platforms, and raw materials that he will soon mold around the finely turned ankles of Broadway's slickest chicks and highfalutin broads. Though he says he owns nine shoe stores, Kaufman can be found every evening at the Paradise. Almost every hooker in Times Square shops here, every peep show girl and topless dancer who saves her tips, and certainly any stripper worth her salt. The Radio City Rockettes from around the block drop by; stars of Broadway stage and screen have been customers for fifty-eight years. But business will never equal the days before the Latin Quarter closed, in the late sixties, when the Paradise stayed open twenty-four hours.

"Fox Studios just ordered two hundred pairs of high platform forties shoes," says Kaufman, stapling shoe boxes together after hours. "We can either duplicate them or pull them out of stock." The secret behind this Times Square establishment is that Kaufman has been holding sixty thousand pairs of shoes in stock for years—thousands of new unsold shoes from each decade. When they come back in fashion, like forties platforms, he pulls the originals out. "Workers who made these shoes are dead; they don't make these anymore."

Kaufman also makes periodic trips to Bloomingdale's, then duplicates designer brands "with even better materials." The same pair of Charles Jourdan pumps, which cost $175 at Bloomie's, are $40 in the Kaufman label. "Alligator shoes that sell for $700, I sell for $150." They duplicate famous designers on premises, at 40 percent off designer cost, sans the bullshit. Kaufman remembers Liz Taylor going for one of his sandal styles: "She bought twelve pairs in each color, and we make about ten colors."

Kaufman makes shoes from customers' scrawled illustrations, pulling out orders from Tokyo, Paris, and the Midwest. He used to make them by hand until he grew too old, and now employs assistants to keep up with mail orders.

Gonzales, a college kid on the Paradise night shift, admits he is in a dream position, servicing the whims of hot dames who strut through the shop. "It's a museum here, they make a fuss over the stock. If Kaufman doesn't stop me, it's great, you meet the kind of hookers who pick *you* up!"

"I had one girl from Atlanta yesterday," says Kaufman. "She was beautiful, and she lifts up her skirt, asks me to take measurements. I was embarrassed. They come in here braless, their shirts open."

At night the store is empty, and Kaufman and his Hispanic assistant are resigned to stapling shoe boxes. "You wanna do it the way you did in 1920?" whines Gonzales over his boss' instructions. "I do it 1983. With all due respect." But Kaufman, more than fifty years his senior, has the kid beaten with more finished shoe boxes.

"I have customers who steal two right shoes, they come and ask for money back," says Kaufman, relating the most common scam in the shoe game. The walls are lined with thousands of right shoes, and only rights, so thieves can't make off with pairs. "But every day we have at least five single shoes stolen."

City planners have been coming in frequently to measure the basement for a projected Broadway mall. But Alex Kaufman's most vexing problem at the moment is where to find a six-inch stiletto heel. The shoes, ordered by a local hooker, are otherwise finished. "The leg looks much better in a high heel. Very big difference between low heel. But for this heel, I look all over the world. They want higher all the time so they can be spotted more. But this high a heel I will never find.

"We also have a lot of homosexuals looking for women's sizes," says Mr. Kaufman, with a sly twinkle. "Nice men, executives, go in corner and try on shoes. More now than years ago. They say they're here for their wife, she wears the same size. . . ."

FOR THE RECORD!

Queen of the Gang-Bang

They called it the "Spermathon," and by evening's end the score of media reps and toweled studs were euphorically certain they'd witnessed a true-blue episode of sexual history. Not a drop of blood was shed as Tara Alexandar, the heroine of the night, successfully balled, sucked, and jerked off eighty-two strange men and her husband for a gang-bang total of eighty-three. This was not a gang*rape*, mind you, as the event was fully sponsored at Plato's Retreat by *Midnight Blue/Screw*, with all involved having avidly volunteered. Especially voluptuous young Tara, whose adolescent dreams of taking on football teams and army platoons reached some sort of fruition.

In her dressing room an hour prior to scum time, Tara was applying little dabs of makeup and brushing her brunette waves like any honest secretary on a coffee break. She was concerned about her hair holding up, things of that nature. In fact, this twenty-four-year-old lass, who went to Washington Irving High in Manhattan, was so cheerfully confident and appeared in such good mental health that all our psycho-hooker preconceptions were quickly dispelled. Her face, with just a trace of mileage closing in, still took on a lovely expression as she tilted her head in the dim light. Her perfectly upturned nose may or may not have been the work of a plastic surgeon. Slipping out of her street clothes, Tara proved to be bustier and more curvaceous than her photos, with smooth white flesh that would soon be ravaged by an onslaught of sexual volunteers. How did she feel?

"I've been thinking about this for weeks. I hope all the guys have. I haven't been training, but I've abstained from sex for four days to stay horny. For me that's a lot. Got plenty of rest.... I suppose I do have exhibitionistic tendencies."

If she was looking for man trouble, the poor girl may have gotten in over her head. Over 1,200 responses arrived after Tara's declaration to produce at least 75 male orgasms was announced in the press. Invitations to 750 were henceforth sent out. Tara was expecting "200 to 300 fellows" to show, but it had been raining all day. And there was no telling who she'd have to face, be they scuzzoids from the Orange Julius sector, nose-bleeding derelicts, or Iranians with Islamic BO. It seemed an almost nightmarish sexual feat to attempt.

She would delegate her body to four at once, the anatomical accommodations consisting of her vage, her mouth, and two unmistakably feminine hands. In other words, she'd be blowing, fucking, and handjobbing four guys simultaneously, an act that would make her Queen of the Gang-Bang. Her hind end remained off-limits.

A gallon jug of "Olde Country" lay on the table, a Plato's Retreat brand of diluted mouthwash. Her husband, John, walked in with the see-through robe in which she'd be making her grand entrance. She was entitled to some degree of anxiety, and by God, it was evident with each deep inhalation from her cigarette.

"I feel that most women cannot do what I'm about to. Not many would have the guts to try in the first place. You have to be extremely hot... and enduring. I know I'll do as many as I can and I'm sure the number will be satisfactory to me. If any girl tops it, fine. I might have an annual rerun of the event."

Even when grilled about SALT II and the Iranian crisis, Tara was feisty, willing to shoot over and fight as a woman soldier: "I would have started the war a long time ago. I feel that America should not stand for this, the hostages have been held for too long. I'm serious."

One aspect was serious for sure. This Tara Alexandar, local kid, who ran away from home to become a topless dancer at the Lucky Lounge in

Queens, spread her legs in a loop or two, which catapulted her into two obscure roles on the silver porn screen… this lady was looking to get discovered.

Meanwhile, the formation outside Plato's was shaping up better than a Salvation Army bread line. One of the attending Plato's officials was impressed. It was a quick, unofficial demographic survey of the *Screw* readership: poker-faced elevator men, veteran "swingers," young cabbies, businessmen in smart raincoats, middle-class blacks, artists, and several studs recognizable from their work in loops on 42nd Street—all to be Tara's faceless lovers. If any magazine wants to get a fix on "their guys," all they have to do is throw a massive "Spermathon."

As they increased in numbers, so did their desire increase. Some were there to be "part of a record, a big goof." Others were just yearning for sex, and Tara had become a celebrity dream-fuck. The horniest in line had arrived at five-thirty, while the elevator man who was second stood at a loss for words, shaking in his pants under the rain. None of them bothered to draw lots for how they would divvy up Tara's charms. Al Goldstein arrived to rousing applause from the crowd, which realized it wouldn't be long before they could stick it in. Countdown to ecstasy.

A formal press conference was held at 8 P.M. Sex-rag correspondents were buzzing about. "Hi, I'm covering for *Partner*," resounded one voice, along with other more abashed introductions between *Genesis, Swank*, and *High Society*.

"The owners are sinking a lot of bread into upgrading the magazine," confided the man from *Pub*. "We're going from a third-rater to a real second-class slick." *The Village Voice* was present, and even a rep from Hefner's publication. Photographers elbowed for space at the dais. It was requested that strategic priority be given to the *Screw* cameras, and "to that slob over there covering the event for *Screw*." Gossip passed that *The New York Times* had sneaked a man in—perhaps in the event of an obituary.

Tara was escorted to the dais by Plato's owner, Larry Levenson. The electronic flash of cameras was reminiscent of King Kong's historic Broadway press unveiling in the film.

"The guys from *Playboy* are jerking off," noted Al Goldstein the moment Tara's robe dropped. Can miracles be real? Hot shots of actual tits, ass, and snatch! Porn starlet Vanessa Del Rio, who had left tongues hanging as she passed the line outside, gave a dumbstruck *no* when asked if she would fill in for Tara.

Enter the motley gang-bangers. Each is given a number. All are instructed to proceed to the lockers and remove their clothes. Towels are given out, along with a rule sheet, from which the following is reprinted in part, permission granted: "Thank you for coming to help Tara establish her world's record.... We ask that in the spirit of the occasion, you take as little time as possible with her. The faster you can be, the more you will be helping her.... After you are through, we ask that you please leave the premises. If you wish to shower first, please be our guest.... Sorry for so many rules, but you can well understand that this is an unusual situation and we will try to make it as pleasant as possible."

Indeed, what was so unusual about the situation? Cleopatra, Catherine the Great, and the empress Messalina of Rome had staged similar events. And, more recently, rumor had it that a major rock star's stomach was pumped to the tune of sixteen ounces of semen at an L.A. hospital, which would indicate that he sucked off about thirty faggots. But unlike the aforementioned, whose sexual shenanigans were more mythical than documented, this lady had chosen to establish an official public record in modern America. And one Gary G. was the first number called to commence the action.

Young, cherubic Gary broke into a sweepstake winner's smile as the entire crowd gave him an ovation. Naturally, he thought he'd be getting the first clean shot at Tara's fresh snatch. Not so. Larry Levenson had already spoiled Tara's virginity for the evening in the dressing room.

With Gary at the helm, the first four were led into the orgy room of Plato's Retreat. A king-size, elevated mat was centered in the room, and on it lay the lady of the night.

Larry Levenson, the "King of Swing," momentarily lowered his head with fatherly remorse and wondered aloud, "How could such a nice young girl...?"

Tara had employed a nurse for assistance. Danielle, a professional RN in transparent leotard, was busily attending to the next four cocks in line. As soon as one popped, another would be ushered in. Awaiting cocks were swabbed with alcohol, and those entering Tara vaginally were fitted with a Trojan rubber. How did Danielle feel about being here, or was she professionally detached?

"All I know is, I've got a reliable baby-sitter minding my kids. I have to be up at eight tomorrow morning for medical classes. Would *I* attempt to break a record for fucking? I'd think about it, you bet."

"Danielle," called Tara in her soft-spoken voice. "More lubrication, please!" The nurse marched over with a tube of Ortho Personal Lubricant. The gang-bangers were rotating round the orifices, musical chairs-like, and one fellow had trouble fitting limp member in twat.

Next in line was an overexcited black fellow who heckled his crony on the mat. "Come on, fuck dat bitch, you can do it, Charlie!" It was obviously his first upcoming taste of a white woman. The cheers continued as the next quartet of studs took up positions. From every open nook and cranny leading to the orgy room was a peering face, a horny craned neck, the beady, glow-in-the-dark eyes of a sex journalist.

Tara's husband, John Alexandar, a co-organizer of the event, looked as worried as any man would be whose wife was about to be gang-banged by a hundred men. He stood by the doorway, calling out numbers.

"Sixteen, seventeen, eighteen… come on up!" he hollered, with his coffee-stained detective's voice. He's built lean, with a pot belly and a Fu Manchu mustache, but tough as nails—the kind of guy you somehow wouldn't want to tangle with, much less mess with his woman. His eyes were wells of anxiety.

"I had to take a tranquilizer, I'm so anxious. I want her to perform; I know she can pull this off. Last night I had a dream—everything went perfectly. She was just reaching out, touching dicks like a magic wand, and they were popping off, one after another. She produced two hundred orgasms. Tonight she'll prove she can do it."

And proving it she was—meeting the great challenge of making these sultry troops climax in front of lights, cameras, and Larry Levenson. One cabdriver was stopped on the brink of orgasm by Larry, who had the harsh responsibility of timing everyone (five minutes and out). The guy ran off, hard-on in hand, to slap ham in the lockers.

Husband John was chalking up the victories on a pad. His eyes darted furtively at the action from a sideways angle. "She's great at French," he continued. "Anyone'll come when she Frenches. The hottest scene I ever saw was Tara and this other chick going down on each other. These guys started to crowd around and join in. By the time the other chick finished fucking one of 'em, Tara had sucked off five."

John enjoys telling stories about his wife, as befits an enormously proud fellow. What can you say to such a remarkable man, whose unselfish display of generosity had rescued the sexually deprived. (Hey, bud, that's your *wife* in there, your goddamn *wife.* Holy wedlock!)

"What should I do?" asked a rather dumbstruck fellow, next at bat. Nurse Danielle was there to instruct, getting hornier as she warmed up to the job.

"She's got two hands, a mouth, and a vagina. Stick it in whichever of those becomes available."

"She joins in," said John, with an unamused gaze at Nurse, "and I'll shoot her."

One of the black guys was nearly demanding a warm-up, some contrivance to stiffen his Johnson before the main event. Perhaps the nurse would oblige? "No *fluffers*," screamed someone—the rule sheet strictly forbade it. This was an important factor for future "Spermathons," as John stressed the point: "Anyone who tries to break Tara's record *can't use a fluffer.*"

A momentary cease-fire was declared after an hour or so. Confused participants worried whether irate feminists had stormed the barricades, or a Hare Krishna procession was on its way through. No such luck, for it was, in fact, the *Midnight Blue* camera team and a cluster of photographers entering the orgy room to shoot some live action. Reporters' heads were popping through the window to inquire what number she was up to and how our lady fared.

"Twenty-five guys so far," came some official word.

"I'm feeling fine," said Tara in her most vixenish tone, "but I haven't come yet. I could use a hamburger or something, but make it *very* rare. On second thought, make it raw meat."

Tara seemed more interested in how everyone *else* was holding up. It was time to catch her breath and reach for a Miller.

After signing model releases, the four cocksmen about to be filmed congregated outside. One was wearing a paper bag over his head. "I own a restaurant and I'm afraid I'll lose customers if they find out," said the mystery fucker.

"Do you have a bag on your dick also?" I asked.

"No."

After the cameras had finished up, directing both hardcore and softcore poses for the different markets, Tara was off to her dressing room to reenergize with a Philly steak, french fries, and a Milky Way. A group of pornographers were sitting cross-legged in the orgy room talking about guns. John Holmes was apparently busted with a .44, or some such news. Mobs of unfucked men were milling about in the lounges and getting restless. Some had been waiting for hours. One fatso was straining to keep his towel on, but there was no way it would reach around his flanks. Would Tara emerge fresh as a daisy?

"It doesn't matter, I'd stick it in a snake," said the next in line. Some were reclining on Plato's Retreat lounge chairs while others were starting to proposition the female guests. This only seemed to enrage John Alexandar with some phobic form of reverse jealousy (Hold on, not *without my wife*, you don't).

The long wait had set one of the old boys hopping mad. He wanted to get his rocks off sans delay. When Tara returned, her husband was biting his nails, irritated. "Hurry up, Tara, there's a million guys waiting—soon there'll be a riot!"

Tara was collected and as lovely as ever. A porn movie director was tending to her nose. She shed her robe and kicked off her heels. At this point, emboldened by snort to new heights of sexual expression, she hopped back on the mat, spread-eagled, mouth agape, fingers itchy for more and more! Extraordinary.

The guys were getting more time with Tara now. Larry Levenson had left, there was no longer any need for a referee. Tara would occasionally surface from the mass of naked bodies on top of her with a soft smile. She actually took on a softer glow with each new foursome. After fifty guys she was "really starting to get loose," according to John, who sighed with relief.

"I'm starting to calm down now," John said. "You know, when I was in the army I took pictures of B-52 bombers. They come down the runway looking like they're going to crash into the canvas fence. But the suckers always took off. That's what tonight is like. After fifty guys, she's really starting to take off."

"I'll be back next week, har, har," said one satisfied customer, winding up his orgasm.

"Bring your friends," said John, marking his scorecard. Yes, sir, here was the unsung story of the evening. "*Push push in the bush*," he sang absentmindedly, reaching down to readjust his balls. "Number sixty-five, come on up!" His partner in holy matrimony was throwing it up to a Sydney Greenstreet clone. The man kept missing the vaginal target, then had to grapple for his pecker under the folds of his great belly and try again.

"God bless her," commented one bystander. "There should be a million like her in the world."

"I give her a lot of credit for trying," uttered one guy who didn't pop.

"I'm in love," came another starry-eyed participant, after he *did* pop.

By the time Tara had polished off eighty-two fellows, she had used up more than sixty rubbers, four tubes of lubricant, and six pints of alcohol (source: Nurse Danielle). Trojan wrappers, cotton swabs, and cigarette butts littered the floor. A heaping pile of towels in the corner smelled like hell. And what should lie at the bottom of this pile but the favorite dinner jacket of yours truly. But these were the signs of victory. Tara had achieved her fantasy and shot past the minimum goal of seventy-five—her name was destined to appear in lights on 42nd Street. Her nipples were swollen; her hair disheveled.

"I'm still not satisfied," she said to the interviewers. "I want a hundred more." But her tired eyes told a different story. Besides, there were no more participants left. Many had departed during the long wait. She claimed that she herself had experienced approximately twenty-four orgasms. What gave her so many was "the feeling of so many guys coming inside me. It was a powerful experience."

Her longest blow and fuck was yet to come. It was almost as though they had rigged the whole thing for this moment, the only way they could get off on each other. For Tara's husband, John, number eighty-three in succession, was slowly, solemnly removing his clothes. His wife lay on the mat alone, finally prepared for him; she had fulfilled the prerequisites of their lovemaking. He began by kissing her upturned nose, which turned her into a mass of girlish giggles. But then her eyes turned to fire and she descended on his cock with a hunger like never before. The hushed media at large watched on as though it were the culmination of a royal circumcision. Tara was true to her man at last.

Pecker Full of Miracles

It was publisher Al Goldstein who wanted to see if Larry Levenson could shoot off his pecker the way he could his mouth.

"I can come eighteen times in one day, easily," Levenson bragged to Al while visiting the *Screw* executive offices. Al declared this was impossible. "Look, why would I lie?" Levenson sputtered. "I've done it many times. Can't you?"

Levenson would do an Edgar Kennedy slow burn whenever anyone doubted his claim. His time was wasted by merely stating such an obvious fact. When Goldstein finally bet $500 that he couldn't do it—couldn't even come *fifteen* times in one day—Levenson set aside a Friday night at his club, Plato's Retreat, to prove his prowess. And on that night, the King of Swing could find not one woman amid the vast vaginal resources of Plato's to participate. The bet was called off for a week; Goldstein laughed his way home.

Meanwhile, an odd series of events set the innocent little bet snowballing.

Candy Samples and her legendary jugs were booked on 42nd Street. The Roxy Burlesk, in a bid for respectability, had solicited her services from California. Candy's drawing power was worth a $3,000-a-week salary, and a limo with bodyguards to usher her back and forth from the Plaza Hotel, where they'd put her up.

I arrived at Candy's dressing room one night to make arrangements for a *Midnight Blue* shoot—we'd interview her in a champagne bubble bath. Candy graciously agreed to meet our video cameras in her hotel room the next day.

But, back at the *Screw* office, I got this call from a certain "Butch Katz." Butch said he owned the Roxy as well as several other Times Square establishments, and would I be interested in doing the Candy Samples shoot at his posh new ultra-modern swing club in Jersey? They might not let video cameras into the Plaza, he said, and besides, the "super-sized, luxurious hot tub would be a knockout setting for Miss Samples." I agreed that it would. Unfortunately, though, it was already the night of the interview, too late to switch plans.

"No problem," said Butch. "It's only ninety minutes by car, and the club is *beeyoodyful.* Even Larry Levenson would flip if he saw it." In fact, Butch persisted, "Why don't you plan on doing the interview there, and bring Levenson with you. Okay, pal?"

Levenson, I explained, was preparing for a bet against Al Goldstein, and wouldn't be able to make it. I filled in the details.

"No man can come fifteen times," Butch declared flatly. "Will Al be there?"

"Yeah."

Butch asked me to hold, then came back. "I'm a gambler," he said, "I bet horse races, football games. I can't resist a good bet. My partner and I would like to bet $10,000 cash that Larry can't do it. And if he does, I'd be honored to lose."

I quickly relayed this information to Levenson by phone.

"Tell those fuckin' greaseballs they're on! Get the cash, bring it here for proof, and I'll start coming on the spot—right in their fuckin' face. I need the money bad.... Now I gotta go, I'm busy fuckin'." [phone slam].

The principals of this bet finally connected, and a date was set for Friday 9 P.M. The paydirt between Larry and Butch diminished to a neighborly $5,000, while Larry took an extra $1,600 in side bets. Butch said that he consulted with his live-sex performers, all of whom assured him it was impossible to come fifteen times in one day. And Goldstein's sex doctors from institutes—he has loads of them—cried no way. Maybe a freak sixteen-year-old with souped-up hormones could come close, but not a forty-five-year-old, potbellied bullshit artist who just got sentenced to eight years for tax evasion.

Larry indeed grew cockier next time he phoned me: "Tell those assholes to come down at four o'clock and watch me start fucking. Baseball players need batting practice, right? Well, I'll be warming up all day, hours before the event. Oughta come six times before nine o'clock, and I want those assholes to come and watch me spurt. I'll even shoot some in their face for 'em."

I delicately reworded Larry's request to the 42nd Street boys.

"What, is he, nuts?" asked Butch. "He's gonna fuck all day *before* the contest? I know a good bet when I see one."

It's the night before the contest, and I'm now in this bet up to my neck. Butch calls me to insist that the rules state Lev will have to produce each of his orgasms with a woman. Lev is not allowed to palm it; if he runs out of women, he loses by default.

"I wanna see him come with girls, either fuckin' or blowin'. I don't care if he fucks 'em in the ass, between the tits, so long as he pulls out before coming. But no jerkin' off."

Butch confides that in a few weeks he has to "go away for a year." He isn't sure which prison they're sending him to, but shit, he wants "more than just the memory of Larry Levenson jerking off to take along."

Friday, 9 P.M.: A screeching cab deposits me at Plato's Retreat. Sitting at the liquorless Plato's bar is Mark Lee Smith, Illinois blues musician and Master of Barbecue, who once actually did some time in medical school. Butch has requested an "official judge" in case of jismic disagreements—someone not connected with him, the newspaper, or Levenson. I'd spotted Mark on the street that morning and asked if he'd like the $200 gig—officiating Levenson's orgasms.

"I got this great new girlfriend who I'd hate to miss a Friday night with," he said. "But I could buy her a new dress and a coupla bottles of Roderer Cristal with the two bills."

Mark always has a great girlfriend by his side, but tonight he sits alone on a stool, long and lanky, black hair bending into a perfect duck's ass behind his neck—a Conrad Birdie of sorts.

"I don't wanna fuck no one up with a bad call," he worries. "You sure these mobsters won't bash my brains in?"

I reassure Mark, then stroll with him past a DO NOT ENTER sign, through two closed doors, into a hard-boiled lair that looks like it was decorated by a bookie. A few cluttered desks with all sorts of telephones, bare walls and floor, harsh lightbulb, a refrig here, an ashtray there—Levenson's inner sanctum is as cozy as an underground parking lot's office. This must be where the King of Swing conducts business, takes phone calls, dresses, does the books, clips his toenails, and, no doubt, finds time to fuck. There are a half-dozen unhappy people frozen in place. Something is not right.

A short, fat man with puffy eyes and cheeks stands up from reading tonight's rule sheet, extending a hand.

"Hi, I'm Butch. It's good to meet at last." Several teeth are missing up front, and I sense a hushed strain in his voice, like that of a child holding back tears. "This is Dave," Butch continues, "the best stud on 42nd Street. He worked my sex show all day, but I brought him down to watch a shift. He knows orgasms."

A skinny, long-haired kid with tattoos covering his arms, snaps out of a bored daze to shake my hand. Each of his tattoos is an indistinct illustration, as though they were all botched. Somewhere near his shoulder is the inscription *Born to Raise Hell.* He is too marred for porn films, and thus has opted for a 42nd Street career.

I announce Mark Lee Smith as tonight's official judge of jizz. Mark shrinks off onto a corner stool, playing it cool, low-profile. A close brunette companion of Larry's is propped up on a chair with a headache, and an attendant secures the door shut. Butch and Larry are in a tizzy, it seems, and the air feels thick with disagreement.

Butch directs me to #7 on the rule sheet, which states that "Larry may utilize flutters, watermelons, strokebooks, or harems of women to summon forth the gop. If no women show, however, his palm must suffice."

"I crossed out everything but *women*," says Butch. "I told him no masturbation, no tricks—just women, that's all I care about."

This had been a shady criterion all along, and I have spent the day fearing the whole event will be called off over it. Just two weeks ago, the King of Swing had pathetically canceled his $500 Goldstein bet because he couldn't find a female soul to ball. Butch looks at me like a timid puppy, a well of doubt in his eyes.

"I told him I got fuckin' broads all over the place who'll get me off!" snaps Levenson, storming toward me. "But the rule sheet says I can use watermelons!" He fumbles his finger across the page, breathing heavily, sinuses swollen. "Right here, watermelons, it says, that means I can use anything."

Larry and Butch don't appear to be on speaking terms. For the moment, at least, they don't face each other while talking.

"It's gotta be women only," states Butch, gazing at me for clarification with a stubborn, koala bear expression.

"You don't really plan to use watermelons?" I ask Larry.

"No, of course not. But I don't see what difference it makes what the hell I use—an orgasm's an orgasm.... Sure, I'll use women only, if he wants. I got lots of 'em here tonight. But I don't know what you need a rule sheet for, I'm just gonna come fifteen times, period, over and out."

Butch takes me aside and further confides his fear that Lev may have some cunning tricks—perhaps the girls have "sperm capsules"—something along the lines of what John Wayne's opponent would have bit and spit out for a bloody jaw, after a punch. Or maybe he was crazy enough to have some sort of sperm bank implanted?

"I don't care how many broads he uses at once," states Butch to the room at large, "or how he fucks 'em, as long as he pulls outta their mouth or cunt before he shoots, so we can see it."

Levenson's black hair is slicked back, his bared teeth look like the work of a mediocre dentist, and his bushy eyebrows become cross. "Don't worry," he says, "I pull out before coming and move my hands clear away, all right?" He throws up his hands, thrusts out his pelvis, and gyrates like Ralph Kramden, irritably mocking his future orgasms. "All right?"

Which brings us to the second order of uncertainty—the consistency of orgasm; the visibility of a "*certifiable, milky-white, spunky, funky orgasm, capable of impregnating a woman. No dry spasms, piss or clear drops of 'dog water,'*" according to the glib rule sheet, concocted several days before at the *Screw* offices.

Lev's response: "I don't know what the fuck color it comes out, so don't give me this dog-water bullshit. Of course the consistency changes after a few times, becomes clearer. When I come, you'll know it, you'll see it shoot out. I don't know how far it'll shoot. Gimme a break; when you come, you come."

Furthermore, Levenson balks over having more than one judge in the room, even though at least two are necessary for impartiality and protection of interests. "Let's let Al decide," threatens one party to the other as they continue disagreeing over rules.

Thankfully, Goldstein chooses this very moment to arrive with a small group. His golden presence relieves me, and drains out a pressure cooker of tension in the room. Finally at ease with the rules, Levenson dons his King of Swing robe. Butch lounges against a wall, a gambler, gentleman, and self-proclaimed "good loser."

"I just hope Levenson is too. That's the only thing I worry about," he tells me.

And so, at nine-fifteen, our sporting little entourage spills out of Larry's back office and treks through 23,000 square feet of Plato's Retreat—past the "Famous Hot & Cold Buffet," the "Arabian Tent Fit for a Sheik," the thickening crowd on the disco floor, and the locker room area, where mountains of fresh towels await their pick to absorb the glandular discharges of a thousand swingers strong. I follow in procession as we walk through mazelike corridors of lounge rooms. I can't resist yanking up curtains, many of which reveal a boff scene in progress—a long landscape of naked swingers, as oblivious as museum exhibits in a Pentagon of poon. Levenson confidently leads the way through his kingdom, pausing to settle a question here, instruct an attendant there, and pick up his women.

In the very back corner of Plato's, last in the line of curtained cubicles, sits Levenson's private swing area—the "King-of-Swing room." Its black wooden door is presumably kept shut when the King bangs through a nightly procession of dames who come to test his mettle. The swing room is elevated by several concrete steps and a rail. Tonight, a guard is stationed outside.

The entire Goldstein-Levenson entourage squeezes in to christen the event. The floor is entirely cushioned, with huge pillows along the sides. A stained-glass mirror lines the back wall, and a master phone bank emits muffled beeps, like some exotic bird. It is an economy-size, middle-class, bastardization of an Arabian sultan's orgy room—perfect for Larry Levenson. The unusual adornment to this quarters, however, is a monstro six-foot airbrushed blowup of Al Goldstein's face—retouched and prettified like a *Playboy* centerfold—which stares over the whole room from its perch, angled so that its reflection fills the mirror across from it.

The Boss of *Screw* beams at his portrait, more confident that Lev will not win—after all, Al's image curses the room like some god of impotence, and will stare Larry down before each orgasm, unless he closes his eyes.

But Lev is unaffected. His fifteenth jizzing, he announces, sinking into a cushion and kicking off his slippers, will be on Al's poster. "Right in your fuckin' face!" he spits at my boss. The poster is a good twelve feet from the center of action, so it'd be quite a hot spurt.

Butch takes a corner and reflects on the nature of the entire porno industry as he sizes up the Goldstein poster: "We all eat today because of that man."

I hear this as a prayer, a modified grace before Lev's squack supper, to be eaten under the imposing image of The Great Pornographer, which looms overhead as a testament to sexual failure.

"I oughta have this wrapped up by ten tomorrow morning," says Lev, while one of his cheerleaders boasts that the night will make history.

Larry's first milkmaid, an eighteen-year-old blonde with big tits, seems restless to start. "I'm not in the business," she insists. "I'm really a singer, getting my shit together." Even Larry confides he's flabbergasted to have her on the team. How she journeyed to Plato's is beyond him.

"Are you ready, faggot?" Goldstein asks. Lev seemingly develops a stomach cramp, like Roberto Duran, and lies on his back.

"Naw, let's wait awhile," he answers. I figure he's finally about to chicken out.

The Woolworth's candelabras in the King-of-Swing room flicker low. Mark examines the flashlight he and Butch will use to distinguish each orgasm in the barely lit room, when Lev does his "money shot." Evereadys inside, lots of battery life to spare, and the smart choice for a $6,600 twenty-four-hour jism contest, when you count on your batteries for your life.

At nine-thirty, the entourage files out, save for the principals. Butch and Mark station themselves in opposite corners, and the blond singer begins removing her clothes. Lev is on his back, his robe draped open, penis exposed, appearing unconscious.

Butch and Mark appear in the buffet area a half hour later. "He came twice," says Butch, unimpressed. This seems right on schedule. Many guys could come twice in a half hour, if they were horny and engaged the help of a good woman. "And you shoulda seen this broad," adds Butch. "She ain't much with her clothes on, but underneath, jeez, she was *beeyoodyful.*"

The eighteen-year-old blonde blew Lev to his first pop, reports

Mark, and then was replaced by a short-haired brunette, who brought Larry to number two in under thirty minutes. Not a bad start, but so what? Butch notes the difference in odds, which sound a little more in Lev's favor now: He has twenty-three and a half hours to come thirteen times. After four or five, he'll be through, Butch says, reassuring himself. Nothing will come out.

Al Goldstein, stationed in a nearby cubicle, also considers it par for the course when a newsflash of the first two orgasms is relayed (The sonofabitch—not bad). Among Goldstein's several guests is a guy named Nat, who once supplied thousands of stock-photo fuck shots to *Screw.* Nat has thrown $100 in the pot against Lev. Lisa Be, on her way to a stripping gig at a dyke bar in Brooklyn, is offering foot massages, but cautions those with questionable socks to refrain. Nat, with a look of great worry, curls his legs back into a fetal position, opting to pass, but Al thrusts his out proudly, having just received a pedicure that afternoon. Lisa zeros in on his feet.

I can only wonder, during this break, what kind of man goes for a pedicure. Businessmen who simultaneously own beauty parlors and whorehouses, maybe? Manicured pornographers who hide behind a polished handshake are one thing, but what kind of pornographer gets pedicures? Goldstein is into one of his monologues:

"I'm the publisher of *Screw*, right, I come to Plato's and all I get is a massage. Never have I gotten laid here, just massages. Maybe when Larry goes to prison, I'll take over as manager, and then, finally, I'll get laid. I'm forty-five years old and still inept. Friedman, look at him. How old are you? Twenty-five? Just a kid, but he thrives on sleaze, lives in Times Square. It's okay for him to be inept, but at my age there's no excuse for it."

I usher Al out to a buffet table where a contingent from 42nd Street—Butch's pals and partners—wait to meet him. This is what they really came for, it seems, what they staked out five G's for—to join The Great Pornographer as comrades in sport—to bet with Al Goldstein himself on a world-record jism jamboree. Al captivates those boys, all smiles and natural-born charm as he greets the lineup. ("I love these guys and why shouldn't I?

We're all in the same business. Besides, maybe I can hustle some ads.") But after everyone settles into sandwiches and jabber, a terrible problem arises.

Lev, it seems, went ahead and had his third orgasm of the contest with only one judge present—Mark Lee Smith. No witnesses from Butch's end, a clear violation of the rules.

"Whadda we do now?" Butch asks me, perfectly entitled to have the alleged orgasm scratched from the record. Jizz disputes erupt between Larry and Butch's sides, and a dozen pornographers hunch over a table, spitting morsels of cold cuts and potato salad. I explain to Larry that a gambler cannot take his opponent's word.

"Why would I lie about such a thing?" says Lev, missing the point. "I came, I pulled out and spurted right on her. I know when I come. Ask the judge, he was there."

The judge (Mark) was acquired by me, and though empowered with final say for an orgasm of questionable value, he was a total stranger to Butch, who wanted his own rep witnessing the scum evidence. Mark, who's honest as the day he was born, described the third time as such: Lev ate her shaved cunt, she came, then they fucked. He sort of matter-of-factly removed his dork, pressed the length of it sideways against her, and jizzed on her ass—like a robot.

"I felt it hit me, and smeared it over myself to make sure," asserts Lev's female accomplice of the Third Coming. "I've seen Larry come many times, and this was legit!"

"Look," says Lev, being a sport, "I'll give you that one for nothin', I enjoyed it so much. Discount it from the record, I'll keep it for myself...."

Lev was starting to look like he meant business. Three jizzes within one hour was pretty good, everyone agreed, and the sonofabitch was willing to discount one of them.

"Okay," says Butch, with a handshake, "that one counts, but from now on there *must* be two judges." Agreed. Amen.

By 11 P.M., Plato's is really starting to show its Friday night stuff. Swinging is big business. People, mobs of them, actually walk around buck-ass naked, thinking it's perfectly okay. Healthy sexual expression. The atmosphere condones this behavior, and it's all legal here in Swingland, U.S.A.

But this is no mere nudist colony. I see heterosexuals fucking in huge circle-jerks in one orgy room after another. Tourists, horny suburbanites, city folk, and swingers of all ages and creeds file in at $50-per-couple for the swingin'est setting anywhere. You can hear Lev's own pitch from his cable-TV commercial come alive in that grease-monkey, heavily sinused voice: "Come down and fulfill your most fantastic fantasies and stimulate your wildest dreams. The new Plato's will have everything...."

I stumble into the main orgy room in my regular L'il Abner getup, about to stampede over the writhing bodies. But a guard yanks me back.

"Sorry, sir, you have to be naked and with a woman to enter."

MAT ROOM RULES
No one admitted fully dressed
Couples and single women only
No drinks, food, or smoking on mats
When female leaves, the male must also leave
Respect thy neighbor

Lev's philosophy toward females—an alleged reverence—is surely reflected in Plato's policy. Women who come down solo are allowed in for ten dollars. Single men are barred, made to feel extra miserable by the fact that they have no woman in their life. But what Plato's philosophy really reflects are plain old middle-class values, gone a bit haywire. I see poolside furniture, mirrored walls, Advent TV screens playing hardcore loops, a pool table, video games, and a live, blaring disco, the equivalent of any suburb, except the bodies are toweled or starkers. The disco here even contains that most despicable, newfangled breed of half-assed celebrity—the live disco DJ, spinning his platters of shit while "rapping" along. At this moment he's mumbling something about the King of Swing having had three orgasms, on his way to glory by setting a world record of fifteen in twenty-four hours. The voice is garbled, no one pays attention.

People do, however, pay attention to Levenson. This is his turf, and he is the star. He saunters through crowds in his beach togs and maroon bathrobe, flashing that mediocre King-of-Swing smile. Ladies flock to kiss him, pay respects, and, in some cases, hope for a little boff.

"I'll fuccch whoever comes by, then mix outside a little," says our gentle captain of the Plato's ship, on a breather. The attendants and bouncers will attest that on any given night, their boss shoots his wad about eleven times. But how can they know? Is he really the swing champ of all times, like his moniker? Who would care to argue?

An eighteen-year-old black kid takes over outside the King-of-Swing room in a sort of changing of the guard. There is no one inside at the moment, but he sits there dutifully guarding the sexual quarters of his boss, whom he probably doesn't even know. It's his first evening on the job at Plato's.

"I be getting $30 a night. That's all my momma care about, she don't need to know what go on here. It's a *job.* I come here three times last week to see how it work, then mah fren get me in."

He seems undaunted by the task he will inevitably perform later in the evening, this being his novice night—that of collecting a Mount Everest of scummed towels.

A brunette glamour queen comes into Plato's looking like she just stepped out of *Hollywood Babylon*, all effervescent, made up, dressed to kill, and a little lopsided. She swings an arm around Lev's neck, smacks his lips, and cackles in a throaty rasp. I don't know who she is, but my blood boils when I find out she is scheduled to be Lev's next jizz date. In fact, she was brought in, I hear say, as Lev's ace in the hole, in case of an emergency. According to Lev, she could chew fifteen orgasms out of any man's cock. But why save her for the clutch at the end of the contest? This feisty little dame, in fact, is about to become Miss Orgasm number four, five, six, and seven. This I have to see.

"I can make him come the fastest 'cause I treat him like shit," announces Patrice Trudeau, the first words out of her mouth. She unstraps her heels, shakes her exhaustion, and kicks into a second wind. Patrice has just arrived fresh from the set of *Prisoner of Pleasure*, her first "big movie role."

"I've been fucking all day. Now I need some *love.*"

This is all Lev needs to hear to get his cock ready for number four. Mark Lee Smith is summoned from the pool table, and Butch from the buffet, by virtual royal escort to assure their dual presence in the King-of-Swing room before Lev's arrival: no slip-ups this time. In the arms of Patrice, Lev won't even respond when patted good luck. He only has pussy on the brain.

"It was a pretty good squirt for the fourth time," says Butch afterward, scratching the side of his head. "I'm surprised, she didn't look as great up close. . . . She talked dirty, insulted the shit outta him, musta turned him on. But I don't care what the fuck she *said*—he *came*, that's all I care about. Pretty big squirt."

Four times, and it's not even midnight yet. Butch and his cronies, tattooed superstud Dave included, are starting to feel impressed. They're reassuring themselves that fifteen is still an impossibility. Mark, a Casanova himself, reports Patrice's blowjob technique to be so passionate, he almost jizzed his pants watching.

Two old delivery boys, both little guys with tomato-stained aprons, steer themselves through mobs of naked flesh, their arms piled with steaming pizza boxes—this is surely the highlight of their Friday night rounds. Goldstein, glued to the phone by the pool table, rolls his eyes as news of Org Four is relayed.

Larry Levenson disappears into his office to break for half an hour, do a little bookkeeping. A no-nonsense Plato's official, emerging from the private room, informs me Lev is getting a blowjob.

The sexual union of Larry Levenson and Patrice Trudeau is one blessed event I'd hate to miss. Lev is starting to let down his guard and relax. I'm eager to see the dark-haired Patrice in action and nonchalantly neglect to leave the King-of-Swing room as its doors shut before orgasm number five begins.

Stationed below the steps, I peer through the railing as Butch and Mark take their respective pillows at opposite corners, like bored tennis referees. Above me is the huge, prettified Goldstein poster, beaming out into the mirror. I notice a roll of flypaper hanging parallel to the poster, covered with dead houseflies—a symbolic insult on Lev's part, no doubt, yet necessary to repel insects from the room, which stinks of old orgies.

Patrice removes her towel, unveiling two firm little bouncers, well-exercised legs and stomach, and a black-haired pussy as nice as you'd want. She spots me through the rail, an unmistakable representative of *Screw.*

"Al Goldstein wants me. Will he call, or do I arrange it through you?"

I tell her I can probably arrange it.

"I'll charge him $500," she says, spreading open her legs. "He's a Jew, so I'll settle for $400. I know he's an asshole. I can talk to you one way, but I have to talk to him another because he's a rich asshole. Besides, I want his digital watch."

Her voice is sultry and hoarse. Levenson lies there, his flaccid, overworked cock waiting to be pumped up so he can ram it down that raspy throat of hers.

"It's a beautiful watch," she continues, her voice getting hoarser. "Like a Piaget. That's what I would really like… a Piaget watch."

Patrice is the only woman so far whom Lev's face registers some sort of adolescent desire toward, even fear, and certainly a willingness to let her take charge. Maybe he loves her in some weird Larry Levenson way.

Patrice pulls Lev's elastic dick into her mouth, slurping away, working it up to hard-on consistency, which after four forty-five-year-old orgasms, is amazing. The King of Swing's pecker looks a mere five to seven inches at full mast, or so it appears in the murky light. Once he reaches this equilibrium, Larry lies on top of his woman, his soft, large belly spilling over the sides of her body. He doesn't move much while he fucks. He closes his eyes and just sort of lies there like a small beached whale, occasionally giving a buck or two. In short, the King of Swing is a lousy lay.

On the night of the big contest, however, it is up to the women to do most of the work. Patrice is a four-star pro, and she whispers sweet nothings into his ear. Her gravelly voice becomes louder: "Fuck me… Fuck me, you bastard, I love it, I love it…. No one makes me come as hard as you."

First, we hear Lev's initial groan, which resonates once from his chest, cuing up the judges' alertness. Then, a buildup of grunts from his throat, and his face scrunches up, turning red.

"Fuck me!" she yells, bucking like crazy, digging her heels in his back. "Bounce off my feet!" She has been announcing her own "multiple orgasms" throughout, even though Lev does virtually nothing to cause them. Furthermore, she sucks his tongue, digs a finger up his ass, then starts to panic.

"I'm gonna come again! I want you to come with me, baby, I want every last drop, please, *please*, Larry, fuck me so it shoots right up to my throat. Oh, God, come for me, I want to feel it shoot up my throat. I'm not finished with you. I wanna feel your orgasm in my throat. Now, I'm gonna come, and you better too!"

The final warning from Lev is the buildup of *Ohhhs*—it appears he may be having a heart attack. Then the most amazing thing happens. Lev yanks dork from squack, dropping it on her belly while, from out of nowhere, Mark and Butch are fired out of a cannon, landing directly over the spot with flashlight. But it is Butch who holds the flashlight, defying the laws of obesity with his leopard-like moves. My own eyes, peering from between the rail, see the flashlight click on simultaneous with the first spurt, followed by three more spasms of jism onto milady's belly. Hallelujah.

"Bull's-eye," Mark declares, looking up at Butch for confirmation.

"It's good," says Butch, on his knees, flashlight held out like an elegantly poised surgeon's, with an inquiring koala bear expression. These guys have it down to a science.

Lev is out of breath, his heart attack having reversed to light-hearted laughter, and some modest proclamation of victory. (That was the best fuck so far—lemme keep it for myself, haw haw!)

And so it goes throughout the night. Larry pulls out of the female assembly line a moment before ecstasy, half machine and half animal, a spunk-splashing Zorro unleashing his sword—and then, *voilà*, proof of manhood on belly of woman, gushing forth in disgustingly frightening amounts. The ease and precision with which he displays each "money shot" for the flashlight under the adrenalated eyes of the judges defies enjoyment. But the amazing thing is that he genuinely is having a great time, loving each boff.

This is what overwhelms men like Goldstein, who celebrate for a week after having had one successful orgasm.

"Write me up!" demands Patrice, cleaning herself off in the room. In the porn game, it's always up to the gal to clean off the jizz. "I want coverage! My man is a soul brother with a thirteen-inch cock, and I can swallow all of it.

"Here," she says, grabbing my hand, "put your fingers down my throat. Go on, try it, and I'll show you how it's done."

I comply and Patrice goes through a skilled set of maneuvers involving great amounts of saliva, acrobatics with her tongue and suction technique.

"You see, I could teach any woman how to be a great whore. I'm a born whore. Not a slut. There's a big difference between the two, you know. The other girls are sluts. They're doin' it cause he's the King of Swing, and they'll fuck anything with a dick, some money, and a name.

"I'll make Larry come seven or eight times tonight, and I'm the only one gettin' paid for it," claims Patrice, hitting her thumb between her breasts. "A whore does it for money, for power. A slut does it for free. So don't you dare think of me as a slut."

I'm not quite sure what to think at this point as Patrice leads me out into the crowds.

"My sixteen-year-old brother had me blowin' him when I was four," she admits. "He taught me how to suck cock by practicin' on his. And my mother was a French prostitute. So, it runs in the family.

"French women have less hair than any other nationality. Here, look carefully at my pussy," she says, lifting her towel. Sure enough I notice a neat, natural black triangle, not a single hair of peach fuzz surrounding it.

"I don't even have to shave my legs," she adds, "or my armpits. Feel." She runs my hand along these parts, and Lord have mercy, they sure are smooth. Who cares whether she has to shave or not?

"Not only that," says Patrice, "but I'm a gymnast. Feel how tight my muscles are. I'm an expert at keeping muscles tight, believe me. Me and my soul man—that black guy over there's my husband, you know—have to fuck thirteen times a day at the Avon 7 in Times Square. So you gotta be a health nut to keep in shape for that. His cock is so big, he can fuck me up to my wall, and he ain't in all the way. So I let him have other women."

My shirt is off at this point, trying to get into the *swing of things*, here at Plato's, in between Lev's orgasms. Patrice notices a particular pimple on my back while professionally inspecting my musculature.

"That's ready to pop," she says. Nice to know, I answer.

"Lemme do it!" she insists, moving into some sort of karate position. "I'm trained at this from when I used to be a nurse in France. I'm an expert at popping zits."

"That's okay, really, I'd prefer you didn't bother," I say. Her husband ambles over at this point, a black man wrapped in a towel.

"Look, Rick, isn't this ready to pop? Aren't I an expert at it?"

Rick glances over my back somewhat irritably, humoring his wife along, and shrugs. Before I know it, she's pinched me.

"Look!" she screams, shoving her black thumbnail under her husband's nose. There's a little speck of pus on it.

"Didn't I tell you, Rick?"

Rick is unamused. I back off, biting my lip.

"Say, man…" he says, losing his cordiality. "Didn't you bring your own woman down here tonight?"

Al Goldstein leaves for his summer home at twelve-thirty, telling Butch to "watch my bet. We're in this together and we're still gonna win. He'll dry after six."

At 1 A.M., Levenson unleashes his sixth orgasm.

Butch and his prize bull from 42nd Street are deliberating at the buffet. "He's got it," says the tattooed stud, a pro sideline commentator. "Six in three and a half hours—all's he gotta do is one every two hours, and he's got till nine-thirty tomorrow night to glide on home."

Levenson cruises by sucking on a joint, his fat belly hanging out of the bathrobe. Butch's eyes fill with woe. His own pro had sized up the situation and declared Lev the winner. Five grand is five grand.

"Jeez, when I come, I'm exhausted," says Butch. "When I was younger, maybe two, t'ree times in a night. My stud Dave, here, he sticks it nine times a day on stage, and I'd pit him against anybody. But this guy… if he comes fifteen times tonight, I'll double the bet to ten grand that he can't do it tomorrow. And if he does, I'll bet him triple that he can't repeat it the third day."

I relay this information to Levenson, who merely shrugs and exhales a chestful of pot smoke.

"I could come till I'm dead… but why press myself?"

Lev's seventh orgasm occurs at one forty-five. Mark and Dave, who officiated over the payload, claim it barely qualifies: "Just two tiny drops."

Larry claims the first two spurts were in her cunt: "I just didn't pull out in time." When Patrice leaves the room, he elaborates.

"I need a looser pussy now. Patrice is too tight. My hard-on isn't hard enough when I penetrate, and she's too tight for me to pull out fast. I'll use Vickie next." Just like changing golf clubs.

Butch feels a spark of hope after the two measly drops of semen are described to him: "We haven't lost yet. The well's gotta go dry sometime…."

I guess your time is numbered at Plato's, because sure enough, by around 2 A.M., I become a "swinger." Stripped down to a towel, feeling somewhat like a moron, I dive into the Jacuzzi with Lisa Be, both of us buckass naked. It goes against the sex journalist's ethical code to actually *participate.* We don't usually fuck before porn cameras, or even show our precious cocks in public—we've got families, you know. The Jacuzzi is not designed to accommodate the breast stroke, which I casually attempt through annoyed swingers, while choking down a mouthful of warm dick-and-cunt water.

"Wasn't that water chlorinated?" *Screw* editor Richie Jaccoma asks later.

"Couldn't taste a trace of chlorine," I answer.

"But they're supposed to, it's the law."

"They're supposed to pay taxes, too."

When I traipse back toward the round table where our sporting members are centered, I am dumbfounded to see we have all become swingers. Butch, of 42nd Street, is unnaturally draped in two white towels, Roman-toga style; rockabilly Mark is in a towel that barely fits his waist, on the hunt, but always nearby so's not to disappoint his buddy by missing a Jizz Call. Plato's apparently turns down the air-conditioning at about 2 A.M. to make things hot—much in the same fashion a bar serves salted peanuts to make folks thirsty. The holdouts in clothes break under the heat.

"I figured I might as well try and get laid," says Butch, swaying a pudgy leg back and forth on the barstool. "Jeez, lookit that one, she's *becyoodyful.* I wish she'd toin around, I can't see the face."

Patrice's hubby, Rick Lucas, is clad in a towel, finally at peace after the pimple episode. He'd also put in an honest day's work fucking onstage in Times Square. While his wife helped Levenson establish a world record, Rick held firm to his manhood.

"Levenson's no threat. Fifteen times is only two inches more than my dick. No big deal. I come from eight to twelve times onstage every day. You gotta learn to hold back your orgasm at two to three drops. But Levenson don't know what he's doin'. He's throwin' his balls to the wall."

"If he wasn't Larry Levenson, owner of Plato's," adds Patrice, "I'd charge him a million dollars." I learn that the happy couple crash in a sex cubicle in the rear of Plato's—their own little nest.

"Look," continues Rick, "if he'd only drink a malt with three raw eggs, he'd have it wrapped." Rick divulges his own stud recipe—the Breakfast of 42nd Street Champions: Helth Malpotane vitamins, a swig of Geritol, and a malt with two raw eggs.

"Here, have a Malpotane," he says, emptying one into my hand. "It'll grease your prostate gland. You'll shoot off like you were sixteen, hitting the fence from ten feet." I tuck the vitamin away for future use.

Levenson joins in, swearing he has no secret formulas, uses no vitamins. "All I gotta do is take a nap, for two, three hours. I wake up horny as a bastard, with a piss hard-on."

Butch's stud, Dave, having just awoke from a nap himself, relates to this wholeheartedly, a young pro acknowledging an old miracle man. "No matter how much I been fuckin'," says Dave, "I can come immediately after waking up."

"Yeah," says Lev, "but do you have wet dreams?"

Levenson jizzes for the eighth time at 3 A.M. "I really hope the guy don't have a heart attack," says Butch. "Maybe we should have a doctor in the house."

Plato's still jumps between 3 and 4 A.M., possibly the hottest hour on this swelteringly jammed summer night. The dancing, fucking, sucking, scoring, striking out, eating, and barfing—otherwise known as "swinging"—reaches its apex. But on this particular Friday night there's been a little too much hanky-panky for even the likes of Larry Levenson.

"One of the judges fucked me up!" Lev complains, barging into the King-of-Swing room. "I think it was your man," he bitches to Butch, who rubs his confused eyes awake, a puppy being scolded. Butch has abandoned his towel ensemble, sporting instead a pair of baggy-assed white underpants. Mark Lee Smith looks up worriedly, waiting for the Ninth Go, but he is not to blame for the trouble.

Tattooed superstud Dave, the varmint, has gotten into Larry's coop and *schtupped* his two best broads—broads Lev had painstakingly procured for this high-risk, cash-on-the-barrel contest. And the eighteen-year-old blonde, the one Lev was counting on for some "loose" pussy for his next jizzing, now suffered on the sidelines, holding her vagina. Wanting to test the mettle of Dave's 42nd Street schlong, she bit off more than her little box could chew. An innocent matter of girlish enthusiasm. Dave's professional putz was just too big. Larry had found her lying in this overfucked condition in the makeshift team room for his girls. The blonde mumbled that she wouldn't be able to fuck for a few hours; maybe she'd just blow him.

"I'm worried that he hurt her," cries Lev, standing over Butch for an explanation. Dave lies beside Butch, sunk into a cushion, his face lost in a savagely peaceful sleep, and his long pecker uncoiled on his waist.

"I know she shouldn't have done it," Lev adds, "but she's only eighteen, and *he's* a fuckin' judge!" Lev storms away to tend to his wounded girls, and Butch turns my way, nodding his head with disappointment.

"Dave's built like a racehorse," he explains through missing teeth. "He's the best in the business. Gets hard like a fuckin' rocket. Fucks eight, nine times a day...." He glances sourly over his stud, a stuffed coyote in slumber. "So why the hell did ya have to go and fuck that little blond goil, Dave? It don't make any sense."

Two fresh troupers who have remained out of Dave's grasp—one, a brunette looker about to debut for the evening—enter the King-of-Swing room. They work Lev to the mat, sucking his tits as he smokes a joint to calm down. As I lean on the railing, the door bursts open and a stray woman waddles in.

"What's the big sex secret?" she drunkenly demands. Two apologetic bouncers dash in after her. Her sexually frustrated face bobs up and down, and her naked breasts flail about as she's carted out backward, begging to be let in on the fun.

Lev is oblivious to this racket, his only vital signs being the smoke signals that rise from a twisted pile of fem flesh on top of him. The young blonde has even returned, making it a foursome. I detect Lev's hand emerging to discard a burned-out roach in the ashtray. The three bimbos work their mouths all over his flabby body, but he appears to be limp and stoned. Lev is in big troubs. He's so pathetic, he can't even stick it in, as he takes a stab at each twat.

"I shouldn't have gone to the office for a blowjob," he gasps.

The girls begin a valiant job of fellatio, managing to get his cock half erect. Butch and his flashlight are ready to shoot over with each groan. Lev is trying to come, his face grimacing as though he can force it out. Shortly after four-thirty, he succeeds for the ninth time.

A hundred or so swingers remain at Plato's in various stages of orgy at 6 A.M. DJ makes his last announcement: Lev is up to nine. Then the disco music pouring out of the blurry PA scratches to a halt, some spotlights readjust, and Larry Levenson steps out center stage on the disco floor in his maroon robe and slippers. It's time to close shop, and the perfect host with the most stands before his throngs, microphone in hand. His black hair is neatly slicked back with fresh grease. He extends a hand to the audience, assuming the classic pose of the crooner. A dramatic orchestral intro segues over the PA and Lev starts singing "Goodnight My Love" at ear-shattering volume. His face is unflinchingly sincere, lost in the rapture of his operatic wail, a cross between Como and Caruso. My own reaction is one of amazement, if not confusion, and I'm slightly reassured to see Mark Lee Smith across the room with his jaw hanging down, and Richard Jaccoma also frozen in his tracks.

Levenson snaps into "The Wonder of You" next as swingers file into locker rooms, discarding their towels in pungent piles. Women douche themselves in the johns, toilets flush, and the last of the gallon jugs of "Olde Country" diluted mouthwash are gargled up. People actually start emerging in clothing, bidding each other *hasta la vista.*

I assume Lev has been lip-synching to records, but at this point anything's feasible. The two DJs, whacked out of their skulls, swear Lev has been doubling to his own records, released only in Europe. But they padlock their area when I reach for the record labels. Anyway, this is how Larry closes the club.

Only the Plato's elite remain, mingling tiredly around the liquorless bar sipping Italian ices. Fresh bottles of milk, juice, ice, and mineral water are set out.

Patrice breezes Lev through orgasms number ten and eleven at 7:30 and 8:30 respectively. Lev has, of course, made a believer out of everyone; nobody doubts his greatness or his ability to win before noon. Both 42nd Street champions, Rick and Dave, begrudgingly admit that this man, twenty years their senior, is the king. What especially impresses them are the *amounts* of jism Levenson contains—the last two times, he came cats and dogs.

More people depart at 8:30, leaving only the principal elements of the contest. I'm the only rep from *Screw*, sipping a glass of milk at the bar. Everyone else breaks for a nap. Lev had threatened to take his wonder nap, wake up, and bang off the last four. Instead, he emerges from his office restlessly, and pulls up a barstool.

"I had no doubts," he says. "I knew I'd win this contest. I don't gamble. I don't go to Vegas. But in this case, I'd have bet thirty grand—they're the ones who lowered it.

"This club runs itself," he continues. "I'm in the back fuckin' all night. Anyone with half a brain can run a club. I wish they said I was a genius for thinking up Plato's Retreat, but it just happened. No great idea, nothing brilliant, I just happened to be the first one to go public with swinging. Swinging shot through the roof. Now I'm riding the crest. I'm a fat, middle-aged guy. These chicks only want me 'cause I'm the owner of Plato's, ya think I don't know that?

"You know what I used to do? I was general manager of a McDonald's in Brooklyn. After that, I cashed unemployment checks for years. This place could have been started by anybody. I'm thrilled it was me."

Lev thanks his lucky stars with few regrets. With an eight-year jail sentence for tax evasion on his back, he must be some kind of cunt-crazed animal to do what he's done tonight. Or maybe he's storing up memories for his trip upriver, like Butch. He's convinced of his innocence and amazed at how hard the law came down on him.

"A quarter-million bail? C'mon, now, really. They hate me 'cause I'm in the sex business," he says, looking out at his "Jungle Habitat"—a waterless swimming pool filled with shrubbery, just one of his many hassles with the city. "People can fuck here but they can't swim. Can you believe it?" He talks about how Goldstein offered to put up his house to make the bail. "You never forget that your whole life.... I love Al Goldstein."

With that said, Lev stands up, sighs sorrowfully, and proceeds to the mat room where he knocks off number twelve shortly after nine o'clock.

On Saturday morning, the King-of-Swing room is littered with casualties of the night before. I lay there, one tired eye cocked on this smelly family, half of them wasted from performing sex all night, the other half wasted from watching. There is Mark Lee Smith, six foot three bluesman/bartender, his duck's-ass hairdo still holding perfect. Butch and his racehorse, Dave, are sleeping close as kittens. Butch is still decked out in his tent-size Fruit of the Looms in pursuit of a lay. Mark and I have given up swinging for normal dress. Lev is sprawled out on the highest mat, a bemused smile on his come-drunk face, chain lighting cigarettes that he allows to burn out in ashtrays.

A double dose of Quaaludes hits Patrice and she starts moaning for a Valium to "mellow me out." Spread-eagling herself, she begins to whine hoarsely to her husband. "C'mere and eat me out." Rick won't budge, dog-tired against the wall. "Goddamnit, suck me!" she demands, drifting in and out of sleep, and farting rather loudly. She crawls over and snatches Dave's waist towel to blow her nose. Mark exits before getting in her warpath.

"When's the last time you saw me eat pussy?" she asks her husband. Her next move is toward the brunette girl, resting near Lev. "Two years, right? Two and a half years. Well, I'm gonna eat some now!"

The brunette is wide awake, fidgeting. "I've gotta piss," she says, in a beeline toward the door. Patrice coaxes her back, wanting to perform for the men at large, who are too zonked out to give a shit. She runs her tongue along the slimy mat and then up into the brunette's snatch, commanding that everyone watch, like a bullfrog-voiced child on a diving board. The Woolworth's candelabras on the wall flicker on morning current. Butch looks up through bloodshot eyes—was the lezzie scene worth losing five grand for?—apparently not, and he drops back to sleep.

"We need lubrication," says Patrice, fingering her prey, "our pussies are sore."

I spot a container labeled SLIDE super skin lubricant—some sleazy swinger shit.

The gals lube each other up and lock tongues. The eighteen-year-old blond girl grows disgusted by this excess. She'll lick Levenson's perineum, but she scruples at lez cunt-sucking. Clearly, there's been a rivalry between the blonde and Patrice all night over popping Lev's cookies. The blonde considers Patrice's style crude and phony, and tells Patrice to fuck off at every opportunity.

Lev rolls himself into the action, and the blonde storms out in a huff, having seen enough. Within seconds, he springs a hard-on.

"This guy's way outta my league," says Butch, rubbing his puffy eyes and nudging Dave for the flashlight. "I hope his prostate don't give out, or his dick don't fall off."

Mark is shooting pool when I run out to warn him that Lev is eating pussy. Within seconds after we dash in, Lucky Thirteen occurs at 9:45.

Levenson is a horny son of a bitch now, and keeps the momentum going with Patrice. His cock is on a riff, springing to full erection only moments after his thirteenth official splat. Butch and Dave are asleep, their hands folded neatly under their heads like nursery rhyme images. Mark's face droops between his knees, and I'm about to go under, until the loud, sweaty slap of Lev's haunches against Patrice's thighs calls us to attention. There she is, legs in the air, being pounded into by Levenson, his beet-red face gasping once again.

"Oh, Larry, fuck me so it shoots right up to my throat!"

Mark and I snap our fingers to arouse Butch across the room, who in turn elbows Dave awake just in time to click on the flashlight for number fourteen, at 10:30. This one's received with no fanfare or congrats. Just standard procedure, observed for the record. Lev seeks no official receipt for his scum.

"I seen enough, I know he can do it," says Butch, finally putting his pants back on. "I'll just leave the money with Dave."

But he assists in the ceremony of removing the huge Goldstein poster from the wall and laying it out on the floor. I feel somewhat like a traitor helping in this, but then again, I'd been rooting for Larry all along, even though I had $50 down against him. Butch repeats what a pleasure it will be to lose five grand to such a feat, anxious to get the hell out. I remind him he still hasn't lost.

Lev voices concern for his guests, wanting to send us home early. But first, he must call his doctor, as though asking permission to do one more. When he strolls back into the King-of-Swing room, he appears absolutely fresh as a daisy. Wide awake, horny as a dog, and looking like he just stepped out of a barber shop, he even dares to be a little philosophical, lighting up a smoke.

"I never fuck girls for more than twenty minutes. There are so many women, it's not worth it to spend that much time with *one*. But I'll tell ya, I idolize women. I know professional studs who hate women, they're in it just for money. But I genuinely love them."

He turns my way, instructing me as if I plan to follow in his footsteps.

"You need *good* women for a thing like this, you can't do it without the best. These girls were the most important thing in the world. They stuck it out. And they really kept me horny the whole time.... Of course, I'm paying them $50 per orgasm."

"Who the fuck would believe it, huh, Larry?" says Butch. "Only thing that can stop you now is if they pinch this joint and don't let us out till ten tonight."

Designated to go last, the blonde takes her natural place beside the Jizz Maestro. A tough broad for eighteen, she loudly insists that a certain party leave the room, and Patrice obliges without a word.

"I like to take my time, baby!" shouts the blonde slut to the departing whore.

At 11:55 A.M.—fourteen hours and twenty-five minutes after the start—Levenson pulls out, rolls over like a fat dog, and dumps the motherload on Goldstein's pretty poster face. He aims for Al's mouth, but misses. A few droplets hit the chin, while the bulk of the discharge ends up on Al's shoulder.

Lev sits behind his desk in his robe, five rubber-banded rolls of money laid out before him. Each bundle contains a thou in peep show bills—grubby fives and tens, fresh from the hands of 42nd Street masturbators, Butch's receipts from a night at one of his peeps. Butch has shaken his hand and called him a god. A real gentleman gambler, that Butch.

Lev is a happy man now, a great, satisfied victor, as he takes care of Mark and tips others $50 apiece. I call Goldstein, whose voice jumps to falsetto in disbelief. ("What is he, some kind of cockroach who farts on cue?")

I think back several years, when Larry Levenson was found in a deserted Queens parking lot, both legs and arms broken, left for dead. Within a week, he had finessed his way out of the hospital, backed an electric wheelchair into his private chamber, and fucked all night. Coming from lawside, Larry was convicted in July 1981 for "tax fraud." Goldstein, who had peered into the eyes of a hundred judges, received the dirtiest look he'd ever gotten from Lev's judge. This judge was out for blood, handing down an eight-year sentence over an easily correctable mix-up of tax forms. But even this shattering act hadn't put a dent in his dick.

Tonight, Larry proved he is an honest man.

He continues thumbing out payments for his girls, at $50 per org. "Let's see... Victoria went first, Rose second, Barbie was third. Patrice fourth –I couldn't have done it without her. I think she did seven. Then Mary.... They were all so beautiful...."

THE SAVIORS

Father Rappleyea's Parish

The only house of God to survive 42nd Street—where churches once flourished across the same strip that would fester with peeps and kung-fu attractions—is Holy Cross. Its parish, founded in 1852, erected the red church in 1870 as a stabilizing influence in the Hell's Kitchen shantytown. Holy Cross witnessed from a block away the birth of Broadway and theatrical opulence after 1900; it cast a reproachful eye on the honky-tonk debauchery that crept in after the Depression. Holy Cross became surrounded again by a ghetto of massage parlors and hookers in the "Hell's Bedroom" years of the 1970s. It is the oldest building on 42nd Street, with an interior of marble, stained glass, soaring ceilings with clerestory windows, mosaics designed by Tiffany, and a rare Skinner organ.

The priests of Holy Cross are fighters of legend. Father Francis P. Duffy, chaplain of the "Fighting Irish" 69th Division in the trenches of France during World War I, became pastor in 1921. Beloved by the theater community, he was a force in busting up the Hell's Kitchen gangs. Braced behind a Celtic cross, his statue stands opposite George M. Cohan's, the only two fellows bronzed in Times Square. He was succeeded upon his death in 1932 by Monsignor Joseph A. McCaffrey, a Fordam football star, World War I hero, and NYPD chaplain, who wrote the following:

"Adjacent to America's amusement center on 42nd Street stands a Roman Catholic church older than Times Square itself. More than a century ago, it was a parish of farmlands, uncultivated property, dirt roads and horse cars. Its spires towered above everything around it, but now they are dwarfed by the surrounding skyscrapers. In contrast to the pleasure and amusements and hurlyburly of the rest of Times Square, it is an oasis of peace and quiet and prayer."

In the late 1950s, Father McCaffrey wished aloud for the return of *Abie's Irish Rose* (the show lasted 2,327 performances at the Republic Theater; the location then swiftly converted to Minskys', with huge billboards of sneering strippers outside). Say what you will about La Guardia, he told interviewer W.G. Rogers, but at least he got rid of burlesque. He surveyed the marquees over 42nd Street, with titles like *Super Sonic Hell Creature, Fiend Without a Face, Valley of Nudes*, and the latest Elvis and Boris Karloff flicks, and lamented: "I don't know how it could get much worse."

Twenty-five years later, Father Robert Rappleyea, sitting in his rectory at Holy Cross, reflects on his predecessor. "Father McCaffrey used to refer to this as 'The parish of parking lots.' When he began, this whole area was filled with tenements, teeming with people." Much of his parish was lost to the Lincoln Tunnel and Port Authority Bus Terminal, which troubled the priest, particularly when they kept adding parking lots. "He tried to fight these things and he was all alone. If the trend continued, he couldn't imagine what would take place on 42nd Street." A major transformation did begin in 1968, when Eighth Avenue harbored more than a thousand hookers. "I had breakfast with him about a month before he died in 1970," remembers Father Rappleyea. "He was depressed and discouraged about the whole thing and felt helpless. He didn't know what would become of the parish—in his time, there were over nine hundred children behind the church on 43rd Street. When I first came, we had around four hundred and fifty kids; it's now down to two hundred and fifty."

Raised in small-town Poughkeepsie, Father Rappleyea had been stationed at an East Side church and was totally unaware of what Times Square held in store. "I have no idea what was in Cardinal Cooke's mind, he just asked if I would go to Holy Cross as pastor." In January 1973 the priest wore civilian clothes to survey his new neighborhood: "Your immediate reaction is one of depression. The whole area was negative, there was a lot of cynicism, crime, rampant prostitution, massage parlors were all over. The parking lots were being used by street prostitutes. There was no Manhattan Plaza, just a huge parking lot, McGraw-Hill was empty, there were fleabag hotels and unsavory bars. I used to visit the bus terminal, the fire houses, get a feel of the whole parish. Many times you had to fight your way through the prostitutes.... Even today, when you dress in your clerical outfit, you can't walk a block without being accosted by derelicts and unsavory people who ask for money."

Father Rappleyea has never once entered a sex joint, explaining that "the marquees are bad enough." He sits in the rectory, a cane in each hand. He is currently battling a disease that affects his ability to walk—"With the help of God, I wanna get back on a pair of skis." The illness does not affect his work, as he remains instantly available to his parish, generous with his time, without the pomp and circumstance of Father Ritter, head of the nearby Covenant House.

Father Rappleyea says he felt an obligation to the local working-class families, thus becoming an activist in many Times Square civic organizations. He spent six years at St. Agnes in a luxury area: "It was lackluster, no community action, no family life. I have never in my life gone to so many meetings or belonged to so many different groups since coming to Holy Cross. Without families or children, you don't have a real solid community. I have a devotion to the children, who I felt were being harmed most. That was one of the hardest things that we had to get across to the city fathers and the police department—in this area lived families. We began pressing for the observance of the law, because most of the stuff out there was illegal." The priest formed a three-way alliance between his parish of poor, noninfluential residents, the Broadway theater, and local business, who all met for the first time in his rectory. In 1975 the parish took stock of their homes after years of helplessness. "By pure vigilance, we became successful in keeping massage parlors off Ninth Avenue. Any time we saw an empty store, we always made sure what was coming in. Once a massage parlor opened its doors, they could fight in court and stay open a year, which is all they wanted."

Father Rappleyea looks out of his rectory to see a vast redevelopment that he helped lobby for—not a single sex establishment remains west of Eighth Avenue, massage parlors are nonexistent, and fewer than a dozen whores cruise the mythical "Minnesota Strip." The huge Royal Manhattan Hotel, suffocated out of business by hookers, has reopened as the Milford Plaza. "The police did excellent work in the early days," remembers Father Rappleyea, "they were the only ones to turn to. But it was like the little boy with his finger in the dike. Then Mayor Beame started the Office of Mid-town Enforcement (OME), and it was made stronger and more vital by Mayor Koch. They are excellent in terms of knowing the law, of shutting down these places, handling street prostitution. "The only negative factor we are working on now is that the real estate vultures have swooped down on the area because of its improvement, trying to drive out the poor, hard-working people. They give out eviction notices, harass them, no heat or hot water. We have one instance where they put transvestites and drug addicts in the building to force them out. We have established our own parish housing committee."

But Father Rappleyea's sworn enemy, the big one that refuses to give, is Show World, a hop away from Holy Cross. "It's degrading and dehumanizing," he told the *Daily News* in 1982, adding that mothers of students are subjected to taunts from Show World's human spillage. "We're going to fight him [Richard Basciano] any way we can," he warned, including a "parents' war against the smut belt." "We'll picket. We'll march. We'll do anything we can to get him out of here.... It's a disgrace. Our forefathers never intended that the First Amendment protect perversion."

"I'm not an angel," countered the graying, curly-haired, fifty-seven-year-old Basciano, who had earlier made the papers when it turned out the government granted a $65,000 loan for improvements in his porn empire. "I'm not sprouting wings, but I'll argue that this business is not a detriment to the community."

Show World owns all the property from 42nd to 43rd on Eighth, except the bank, and most of their Times Square land parcels are not slated for redevelopment. Clenching his canes, in frail health, the priest seems less feisty than he was two years ago, when he vowed to win the war, even if Show World won the battles:

"We're trying to get it in on the redevelopment, though I don't know if we'll be successful. It's been alleged and fairly well substantiated that organized crime is behind it. But they have tough lawyers and they are astute enough to stay just on the borderline.... The attitude of the judges is that it's still harmless and victimless. But people who live here can testify that wherever there are sex-related activities, there has been a comparable increase in crimes of assault, muggings, break-ins, we've had so many. It's open twenty-four hours, seven days a week. When Mayor Beame completely closed Show World for two weeks under a city ordinance, that corner took on an entirely different scene. It became a hundred percent better.... Midtown Enforcement is still actively trying to do away with it, they've been very successful in getting ordinances passed to close the places down. So we are watching Show World very carefully. In all likelihood, this fall, we'll have a demonstration out in Long Island where these people have big estates. Finally, these people tend to trip up themselves. . . ."

The pastor does acknowledge that Show World is more troublesome because of what takes place around it than what goes on inside. "There have been rumors, which I'm trying to nail down, that there is some kind of organized gang trying to pick up young boys," he points out, as though all roads lead to kiddie porn. He is opposed, "as a Catholic priest," to designating a red-light district anywhere in New York, even as a compromise.

"Holy Cross stands out like a sign of contradiction to everything around it. Half a block away we have some of the greatest evils in our society. We still have all of the social problems besetting our country—the homeless, the discharged mental patient, the drug addict." The priest absorbs threats with a smile, in this neighborhood consumed by transients. Total nutcases, arrested after "causing a disturbance in church," sometimes return: "Out of the blue, one day, a fella shakes hands with me and smiles and says, 'You're my good friend, but I'm gonna kill ya.' I said, 'You're gonna kill me? For what?' He says, 'Because you killed my cats.'"

Holy Cross feeds 450 homeless every Saturday and takes in bag ladies during the winter. "After eleven o'clock at night on 42nd Street, ninety-five percent of the people are there for no good. You have the strata of prostitute and transvestite involved in drugs. Most of your transvestites are involved in assault and robbery. I'd say eighty percent of whoever their customers are get mugged. They rarely get a complaint against them, because the person who was mugged is so embarrassed. The police tell me if they had the opportunity to search, ninety percent would be armed. After eleven, I wouldn't venture out without a police escort."

Father Rappleyea always emphasizes the decent, church-going citizens of his neighborhood: "I think this is the most unique parish in the world. We have people from Colombia, Ecuador, Argentina, Puerto Rico, the Islands. Yugoslavians, Irish, German, Italian. It's much more provincial than people realize. An awful lot of people refuse to move. The Poseidon Bakery, they've been here for generations, Alps Drug Store. This is why we have the Ninth Avenue Festival every year, it's considered one of the greatest ethnic mixes in the whole city. Down the block is Manhattan Plaza, where seventy percent are in the performing arts, many of whom are our parishioners, and we want to see them succeed. Hopefully, we have brought them God.... I feel it's a great honor and privilege to serve this area as pastor. There's only one Broadway. When I was in Poughkeepsie High School, the big thing was to visit Times Square by bus—the Paramount to see Frank Sinatra, Joe E. Lewis. We had no fears. I hope and pray that 42nd Street becomes a place the city is proud of again."

Cops and Skells

"All the losers who can't make it in their neighborhoods come to be losers here," states Officer Skeeter, cruising his patrol down 42nd on an August Thursday night, windows rolled up, air-conditioning cool, and the Beach Boys surfin' over the FM dial. The police radio crackles at a lower volume, but no matter what's on WCBS, Officers Skeeter and Parillo can hear when their car is summoned, even in the midst of philosophizing.

"Asshole Alley," Skeeter calls the lineup of shoeshines along the Eighth Avenue parking lot between 41st and 42nd. A half-dozen bulky stands, portable with wheels underneath, are open twenty-four hours to Port Authority bus travelers who brave a nerve-racking shine here. Athens liquor store on 40th Street helps bottle-feed a whole scuzz industry of loud-faced winos. "If they closed that liquor shop, most of it would disappear," posits Skeeter. "But when it's closed, the shoeshine stands sell it. We removed ninety bottles of wine from under that stand there Sunday morning."

"You don't have to be a brain surgeon to figure that out," adds Parillo, "just follow where the winos are goin'." Their beloved Terminal Bar, the lowlife's shrine on this energized skid row, was closed a year back, while the adjacent Terminal Hotel, home of the ugliest five-dollar whores in the U.S.A., was converted to a legal haven for bag ladies. Yet another firm on 39th designates more Thunderbird and Night Train shelf space than anywhere on the Bowery itself.

"You better find a cab fast, honey," warns Skeeter under his breath. Three young stewardesses stupidly try to hail a cab from the shoeshine side of the street. "They'll get your suitcases, they'll get your bra and you won't know it... if you're even wearin' one."

Fresh-scrubbed, freckle-faced boys wearing grown-up policemen's uniforms are stationed across 42nd. "Anyone can be a cop now, they'll take anything," laments Skeeter, who's husky himself, with blond hair, large arms, and six years on the force. "Look at the size of some of those cops," he says in wonder, pointing out the foot patrols. A tiny blond woman in blue soberly stands between a condemned doorway by herself, looking more like some pervert's fantasy than a police officer.

"They put these rookies from East Cupcake, Long Island, out on 42nd Street," says the wizened Parillo, a tall, gray-haired seventeen-year vet. "They aren't streetwise at all, and the skells love it, they eat it up."

"Females haven't been tested, they're still new," says Skeeter. "There hasn't been a female cop killed on the job yet, knock on wood. Once it happens, then maybe they'll take 'em off 42nd Street. And it'll happen from her own gun taken away."

"When I joined the force," says Parillo, "they checked my whole background, they even traced my grandparents' fingerprints for criminal records. Now they take you if you have a record. Some of the black cops don't know who their parents are, the department won't trace it. I had a partner once who was a black cop, when I joined, up in the Thirty-second Precinct in Harlem. Turned out he was doing hits for the mob on the side. He's doing time in an Arizona jail."

The Midtown South patrol car zigzags through Times Square traffic, passing red lights, making U-turns, free from the laws of traffic in order to make sure others obey. Tonight's tour of duty is from 34th to 44th streets between Sixth and Ninth avenues, the four-to-midnight shift. Skeeter stops at a roadside-repair police van, where a mechanic quickly fixes a faulty window-handle roller, essential for times when someone approaches the window. The two officers trade seats, relieving Skeeter at the wheel.

"Wasn't that pretty," says another cop, stopping his squad when the officers get out. "Would you do that again so I can take a picture?"

"When I was in the Thirty-second on 135th," recalls Parillo of his early years, "we stopped a car filled with blacks that had a 'Wallace for President' sticker. Dead giveaway it was stolen. I asked 'em, 'Who did you vote for?'" Parillo moved out of the 32nd when the 14th precinct became Midtown South, a "super precinct" in 1972, needing volunteers. "I remember about ten years ago, three security guards were shot to death at Nathan's Hot Dog during a robbery. Next day, I saw this ad in the *Times*: 'Three security guards wanted, inquire at Nathan's.'"

Parillo left the 32nd for Times Square to escape the drug wars that were killing three cops per year at his Harlem precinct. He's somewhat fed up with the area, can't wait to collect his pension and retire to another job. "The orientals come outta them restaurants every night drinkin' that saki before they drive. Their driver's licenses must come in a bottle of saki. We fought 'em in three wars, now they're takin' over the city."

Last week Parillo collared four out of eleven black boys who crowbarred into the metal gate of a 42nd Street camera/electronics store at 4 A.M., a current fad. It was a hard chase for the graying officer. "Four virgins, never been locked up, it's before the court now." Next door to the camera shop is 259 West 42nd, specializing in men's mag overstock returns. "That guy's the worst," he says of this joint, which was the first to install peeps in 1966. A sparkling display counter of knives, handcuffs, fake badges, and the like make this the only weapons-pornography hybrid in the Square. "You can see 'em buying that shit from the car," says Parillo, slowing the squad out front. "I busted a guy who bought a gun holster inside. Now, whaddaya assume he's gonna put in it? Judge threw it out, said 'You're *assuming* too much.'"

The squad passes the Holland Hotel, one of the midtown hotels now accepting welfare cases at $70 per night. Little kids spill onto the street at all hours. "Those mothers blame Reagan for making them poor," says Skeeter. "They oughta try closing their legs for a while, and learn to read books." Other welfare families trail out of the larger Hotel Carter on 43rd, across from the *Times*, where arson fires occur weekly.

"If they don't like it, they light it," says Parillo. An elderly white couple carrying four suitcases have left Port Authority through a wrong exit onto 40th Street. The man drops his baggage and asks the patrol where to hail a taxi. If either cop is concerned about the couple's welfare, he doesn't particularly show it, passing up a Boy Scout opportunity. The old man and his wife are about to walk through a scaffold filled with black junkies vegetating in various stages of consciousness. The cop car just happens to be stalled in traffic, right along the scaffold; none of the junkies budge. The cops get paid whether they stay in the car clocking time, or get out and mix. But without the police presence, the old folks would have been goners, or at least their luggage.

A bearded, blond-haired man with bloodshot eyes hails the patrol car. Parillo rolls down the newly repaired window.

"I'm from Texas, ah was robbed three days ago and I'm at the end of my rope. Ah haven't eaten in three days, I've never been in a city before, ah just don't know how to get back home."

"Did you try Travelers Aid on 43rd?" asks Parillo, staring past the man.

"Ah *tried* Travelers Aid!"

Parillo shrugs. The reek of liquor spills into the patrol car—the man is soused. Why would a robbed man reek of liquor?

The cops receive a radio call to disperse a "disorderly crowd" across from Port Authority. A sorry bunch of street flotsam have bedded down for the night in the driveway of some trucking firm. Skeeter and Parillo step out of the car before a ragged group of discharged mental patients, harmless as jellyfish, with a few homeless teens among them. Whenever these types of critters are arrested, the cops wrap them entirely in a blanket so they don't stink up the car. One of the kids says he's waiting for reentrance into Father Ritter's Covenant House in two weeks. You break the rules there, you're out for a month. He's got two weeks left to scrounge like a rat. The dustbowl group obeys without hesitation, undoing the boxes and newspapers they've assembled for a night's sleep, carrying them across the street and stacking them in neat refuse piles.

"And you'll have to take your friend," instructs Skeeter, referring to one who is unconscious in a pool of vomit. Four of them lift their comrade out of his vomit, a strand of it stretching from his mouth to the street, like pizza cheese. Parillo lets loose with an Ed Norton hoot, turning back to the patrol car to contain himself. The owner of the trucking firm and his wife thank the officers as the mental patients go limping down 40th Street toward the river, like a wounded Civil War battalion.

"Rockin' Robin" comes over WCBS, the home of the hits. Parillo remembers it from high school.

"Yeah, but it wasn't no Michael Jackson version," says Skeeter.

"The rain'll quiet 'em down," he says of his street constituency as a drizzle begins to fall on the windshield. The squeegee bandits at 42nd and Ninth take a moment's break from their particular contribution toward a cleaner New York when the patrol passes. Teenage blacks carrying squeegees make their kung-fu movie cash here by running a soap rag over windshields at the red light, then demanding a tip to wipe it. An old winos' ploy from the Bowery, which amounts to a twenty-five-cent mugging by intimidation. "That's what people's windshield wipers are for," says Skeeter. "Except for this dirtbag white bitch who comes up to the squad car, a real head case, tries to wipe the windshield with her snot handkerchief for a tip." There's not much the cops are allowed to do but chase off the squeegee bandits, some of whom raise their threat to a dollar.

"They wanna stand there at the light and defy all we stand for," Skeeter says through clenched jaw, looking out his patrol car window at an army of black Riker's Island transients on 42nd, whose beat-drug mantra of "Reefer, acid, black beauties" hisses along at people's heels. Older skells at abandoned doorways yap about the proverbial room upstairs with willing girls. There's always some bumpkin with a fat wallet sticking out of his ass who serves himself up like a suckling pig. Younger packs sometimes roam the side streets with pipes and blades. Sure, the cops could launch a paramilitary campaign against this inhuman contamination, and fill up Madison Square Garden with arrests. It poses an interesting argument for one little night of fascism.

"Cops are pawns," says Skeeter, "they change the rules on us constantly. When I was a kid, if you cursed a cop, you'd get clubbed, and you couldn't tell your old man or you'd get belted again. Today, we can't use the billy club except in defense under attack. The skells can even curse us and we have to take it, look the other way. Everything is against the cop, the system protects these guys on the street. We could make an arrest every five minutes, there's enough shit going on out there this moment—but you learn it doesn't do any good, the system lets 'em right out, so why bother?"

"First thing they should do is get rid of that Civilian Review Board," Parillo believes. "These skells might look stupid, but if a cop bops one, they know to go right to Civilian Review, with lawyers ready to represent them and make a few grand off the city."

A short man in a blue uniform waves to the passing police car. "Eddie, he's a head case," says Parillo, waving back. "He's a security guy at one of the welfare hotels. Always calls us whenever there's trouble, then hides in a corner." An emergency call comes over the radio, something about a hotel stabbing. The siren goes on and the driver guns the engine. A backup car meets them at the Hotel Paramount and four officers walk briskly into another of Times Square's once-glamorous hotels, now worn to shit. A black hotel security man, whose white shirt and tie are covered with shiny badges and tie clips, leads them into the elevator, pressing the fifteenth floor. He's familiar with the cops, he's taken them up in this elevator many times before, and they joke about each other's pot bellies, how good their wives cook spaghetti. The security man thinks there's an ongoing dispute between two violent women who live on the same floor. He stays in the elevator as the four cops take strategic positions in the musky hallway, with faded walls and carpet of Broadway's past.

"Open up, police!" bangs Parillo on the door, holding a clipboard in his other hand. And then a second bang. The door creaks open, and peering around the edge comes the ghastly, overly madeup face of an ancient hag, with a blushing smile. This is the second time this week she's called in a false report. She looks mighty pleased that all these virile policemen have come to her door.

"Call back on my night off, will ya, lady," whines Skeeter, while another cop says she should be arrested this time.

Outside the Paramount, the sergeant's car has pulled up for a report. Skeeter jots the incident down on his clipboard, already thick with bureaucratic forms and paperwork. The sarge, a gray-haired gentleman in a hyper mood, removes a large searchlight from his car, clicks it on, and glides a circle of light across building tops of 46th Street, greatly amused. The four-to-midnight shift is nearly through, and these salt-of-the-earth working men will return to their precinct, get out of uniform, and go for cocktails.

It's the anniversary of a fallen officer, and flower wreaths are being placed in front of his plaque at the Midtown South entrance on 35th Street. Parillo points out an older plaque of a policeman "stabbed in the back by a pimp" twenty years ago. He knew this cop from his own neighborhood when he was a kid. The pimp has just been released, after doing twenty years in prison.

The desk sergeant has had a rougher night than the returning troops, his face the perfect choice for an Alka-Seltzer ad. A street-worn black fellow comes up to the desk with a maze of complaints bothering him. "You look like a perfectly decent gentleman," says the desk sergeant, with great understanding. "Why would anyone want to threaten you?" The complainant goes on in an erratic mumble while the sarge makes a final attempt to decipher it. Then, the sarge bolts upright from his seat: "*Take a fuckin' walk!*" He races from behind the desk as the complainant scurries out the door. "Psycho," grumbles the sarge, while two black civil service ladies giggle behind the desk, thankful he didn't refer the fellow to them.

All in all, it was a quiet night in Midtown South.

The Big Cleanup

The first rumblings for a cleanup of Times Square occurred over a century ago. The lore of the region was just as dastardly then as it became during the explosion of porn and pross. Hell's Kitchen, named as such in the 1880s by police, contained miserable tenements, "the lowest and filthiest in the City" according to an article in the *New York Times* of September 22, 1881. Several blocks west of what would be christened Times Square in 1904 was "a locality where law and order is openly defied, where might makes right and depravity revels riotously in squalor and reeking filth. The whole neighborhood is an eyesore to the respectable people who live or are compelled to do business in the vicinity, a source of terror to the honest poor, and an unmitigated nuisance to the police of the 20th Precinct."

Hell's Kitchen—the area west of Eighth Avenue, and ten blocks on either side of 42nd—became known to the public for the exploits of its gangs and hard drinkers. An anonymous photo from the turn of the century shows a dead horse rotting in the cobblestone gutter with oblivious slum kids at play. A mass attack by five hundred gang members called the Gophers was staged against the coppers. In 1910, the railroad corps joined police to defeat the Gophers. A reminiscent report from the *Times* in 1934 recalled how the railroad corps "slugged harder than the gang and shot quicker." The Gophers dwindled, while Father Duffy, the legendary Times Square priest, helped quiet them and the other gangs. Hell's Kitchen was an impoverished melting pot of all New York's nationalities, and in 1934 it was decided that ninety-one of their slum buildings would be razed for the Lincoln Tunnel; even more were razed to make way for the bus terminal, which opened in 1950.

Forty-Second Street was designated a main crossroad in 1811, when Manhattan's future gridiron pattern was carved out by the city commission. John Randall, Jr., who first mapped these streets and avenues, ignored the unruly X made by Broadway and Seventh Avenue when they passed 42nd Street. New York's population was about 100,000 in 1811, and the city fathers couldn't foresee its climbing to a half million by 1850 and nearly a million by the Civil War. Expansion uptown averaged a mile every twenty years.

The Broadway thoroughfare before 1900 was a desolate route of bumps, ruts, and potholes, where a horse-drawn bus could overturn on a winter night and fatally crush the unwary driver. Beyond 42nd Street, squatters in hovels scrounged out a living, harnessing bony dogs to drag carts from which they scavenged. The Broadway and Seventh Avenue intersection was known as "Thieves' Lair." A few blocks west was Eleventh Avenue—its jumble of horses, pedestrians, and railroad cars giving it the nickname "Death Avenue"—where tracks had been laid down in the 1850s. West 42nd Street itself, before 1900, was a respectable enough stretch of stores and businesses, but its outskirts became off-limits by dark.

After nearly seventy years as New York's most magnetic attraction, by the close of the 1960s, Times Square gained its rep for stickups, saw a bold onslaught of streetwalkers, and scared away tourism. This threatened the heart of the city with a fleeing corporate tax base, and some feared for the Big Apple's survival. Broadway, though a lesser concern of corporate interests, saw only eleven of its thirty-eight theaters occupied at one point. The city's course of action took the form of two police "super precincts" in 1972. Midtown South, expanded from the 14th Precinct, handled 42nd Street down to 30th. The 18th became Midtown North, with a 140 percent manpower increase, policing 43rd to 59th streets. North started with a bang, closing eighteen massage parlors, papering windows of porn bookstores, impounding pimpmobiles, and making more than four hundred pross-loitering arrests—all in May, its first month. But by June, twenty-four massage parlors were back in biz. The Westerly, a high rise that headquartered a hundred black pimps, faced Midtown North right in the kisser, from its perch on 54th. Three neighborhood bars—Angel's West, Tommy Small, and Woody's—spilled over with black pimps who mocked, baited and taunted white cops. Every night saw 1,200 prostitutes along Eighth Avenue. The commanding officer of Midtown North, acting out of frustration over uncontrollable street conditions, set police barricades along the Eighth Avenue sidewalk between 45th and 49th streets, creating a path exclusively for pimps. "I told them to make it two pimps wide," he was quoted as saying. A goon squad of ten huge cops kept them strutting within this perimeter.

A criminal element kicked off the Dirty Business in Times Square. It rode the coattails of the "sexual revolution," cashing in on the easing of obscenity laws by the Supreme Court in 1967. Low-rank mobsters, seemingly banished by their superiors to the unprestigious smut trade, spawned a multiplying swamp of pornography, which had grown to 150 joints by the early 1970s. Some paved out a proud industry. "Big Mickey" Zaffarano, who built the Pussycat Cinema's neon façade across Broadway and 49th, owned porn shops around the world. As Joe Bonanno's bodyguard, he took on the toughest of hoods, and later the Shubert Organization, his rivals in the Square. In February 1980, at fifty-seven, he dropped dead of a heart attack one hour before the FBI showed up with a warrant for his arrest in an anti-porn sting. The tabloids fondly observed that not one of Big Mickey's neon displays on Broadway darkened for a moment in his honor.

Massage parlors—a euphemistic tag for street-level brothels—opened in a boom and branched out under guises of model studios, rap studios, even topless shines. They were a sidewalk manifestation of the sexual revolution, a popular talk-show joke. The first were run like counterculture communes, with psychedelic decor and hippie masseuses, in Los Angeles and Manhattan's East Side. The typical parlor in 1969 had a white-walled, therapeutic look, with towels and a choice of body oils or talcum for your "massage," which rarely strayed past a hand- or blowjob. But in Times Square, the fad downgraded into sleazier joints aimed at snaring an even faster buck. Hit-and-run shantytown parlors lined Eighth Avenue, opening and closing at the rate of two per week—some thirty parlors had names like Sugar Shack, Honey Haven, Sensitivity Meeting Room, Beginner's Photo, Danish Parlor, Love Machine. Customers were chased if they requested an actual massage. The short stretch between Ninth and Dyer Avenue, replaced by Theater Row in 1976, contained wondrous cesspools: French Palace, Body Rub Institute, The Studio $10 ("Complete satisfaction featuring the most beautiful conversationalists"), 42nd Street Playhouse Burlesk ("Home of the finest exotics in the business"), and the Mermaid bar.

Martin Hodas, Poppa of the Peeps, turned three stagnant bookstores into parlors, making his entry into massage in 1971. Hodas drilled holes in the walls of The Harem to keep tabs on money exchanges between girls and customers. Five grand per week was a typical gross at these dives. The cops estimated 90 percent of the storefronts and parlors were now mob-financed, as opposed to 1967, when Hodas financed everything. But the mobsters never bothered to deal directly with street prostitution, considering the pimps too stupid. When several black pimps opened parlors in 1971 without paying the mob, their locations were firebombed out of existence.

The "Minnesota Strip"—Eighth Avenue between 34th and 55th streets—picked up its nickname in 1972. Many hookers gave Minneapolis as their home city whenever asked, to the point of its becoming a cynical retort, though some undoubtedly told the truth. Every night through the mid-Seventies, more than a thousand hookers took up their designated posts on Eighth Avenue (this number would dwindle to a half dozen by 1982). The typical pross was required to make a $200 quota every night for her pimp, in $20 throws. There was no coming home until this minimum was reached, and if she spent overnight in the police bullpen, out she rolled without sleep till that $200 was pocketed.

Writer Gail Sheehy, who interviewed dozens of hookers in 1972, found the cycle often starting in midwestern states, and leading to the Square. Many were sweet-looking, smart young white mamas, with kids, some from respectable homes. The white girls, according to Sheehy and cops who ran the pross vans, were raised in predominately black neighborhoods, or from poor black-and-white suburbs outside capital cities—such as "Coon Rapids" near Minneapolis. Their introduction to sex was through black boys, and any teenage pregnancies that resulted in interracial offspring cast them out of their schools and towns as pariahs.

Finding work impossible to get, while carting her baby through hotel rooms, a girl might turn her first trick close to hometown. But a pross arrest there meant a year in prison and a $1,000 fine. Then, an old girlfriend in the same bind would return from New York, in fashionable threads, platform shoes, no kid. She glorifies the oh-so-wonderful family life she's attained in New York, run by her "man." Respectable high-rise apartment living, rent and clothes, affection doled out to each girl (on her night of the week, with all competing to be his "wife"—whoever happened to bring in the most money at the moment). Mr. Times Square Pimp, naturally, had sent this prospector home to *recruit*. Providing a baby-sitter and surrogate father image for her little pride and joy, the pimp as superstar, whom she stocks her fantasy future in, *frees* her to work, explains how she'll be "working for *us*," part of a *com-mun-it-tee*. He boffs her without a trace of emotion, cokes her up, breaks her in among his distinguished colleagues at the Westerly, and no matter how stuck-up and star-struck she is over her *man*, he drops her on a dime for the next young moneymaker. Thus, a role model that the street pross reverses ten times a night with her johns.

To weak-kneed legions of frightened, unlaid men, she was a predator. As they stood naked she took command of their wallets, never disrobing, and issuing orders to come within five minutes into a rubber, or you're out of luck, honey. But each Times Square summer brought out a new killer who practiced his psycho surgery upon prostitutes. And the pimps commonly beat and maimed their girls, some killing them.

Times Square landlords, some of them major real estate conglomerates, silently absorbed profits from prostitution with more stability than the mob, the pimps, and certainly the thousands of moneyless girls. Gail Sheehy decoded the buried puzzle of Times Square pross and porn landowners in 1972. The actual *landlord* for Hodas' Harem massage parlor was Sol Goldman, of Goldman—DiLorenzo, one of the 1984 *Forbes* 400's half-billionaires of real estate. Goldman's holdings included the buildings of more than a dozen peeps, massage parlors, and pimp-hooker apartment houses. Ian Woodner, Madison Avenue builder of high social swim, feigned ignorance over owning the Raymona Hotel on Eighth, where a thousand tricks a day were turned. Dr. Alvin Bakst, renowned heart surgeon from Great Neck, secretly owned the Eros I fag theater on Eighth (Goldman owned the Eros II), along with six fleabag pross hotels and parlors. The Riese Brothers—insatiable land cannibals who would later carpet Manhattan in a locust invasion of fast-food outlets—owned the Lark Hotel lease, a massive pross operation. Edward R. Finch II was principal officer and attorney of the corporation owning 105-109 West 42nd—Peepalive, Roman Massage Parlor, Rector Books, and Bob's Bargain Books, considered the most depraved porn stores in Times Square. Finch was the son of a New York State Appellate Court judge, and the uncle of Edward Finch Cox—then-President Nixon's son-in-law.

On Sheehy's list of porn landowners in 1972 were members of The Association for a Better New York, Park Avenue banks, and members of the mayor's own Times Square Development Council. When Mayor Lindsay announced his coordinated attacks on everything dirty in Times Square, it's no wonder nothing budged.

The Office of Midtown Enforcement is a tactical, twenty-member legal SWAT team whose investigators fan out into every layer of vice in Times Square. They were created in 1976, the pivotal year for Times Square redevelopment, to deal with the unique problems of midtown: specifically sex, although drug dens, numbers, gambling, and after-hours joints would also tumble. (Of all the establishments mentioned previously from 1972, only the Eros I remains today.) They were given more powers than all previous cleanup forces combined. Where pross hotel operators had previously been able to tie up prosecutions in court or ignore their cease-and-desist orders, the OME achieved permanent closures, and heavy fines. Midtown Enforcement's orange sticker slapped across a door, accompanied by police padlocks, meant that location had spurted its last orgasm. They reduced the number of midtown sex joints from 121 in 1978 to 65 in 1983. They closed some forty massage parlors, then enacted a zoning amendment permanently banning new ones.

Here was a bureaucratic cooperation of city agents, an uncolorful group, but with mayoral authority. These white men dealt in graphs, charts, and statistics, using photo surveillance and "conditions investigators" to keep tabs on every morally suspect address in midtown. All data was computerized, every last health violation issued against some peep for semen on the walls. A typical OME task force visit included a buildings inspector, a fire marshal, a Health Department sanitarian, and a cop, all poised over their violations pads. Pinball arcades and peeps buckled under, as zoning regulations were enforced to the letter. The heat even hit newsstands that had leased space to glove or cosmetics peddlers.

Topless bars were the most crooked "dry hustle" dives in Times Square. More insidious than massage parlors, they advertised in the *Daily News* and *Post* sports pages, dangling the false promise of sex, liquor, and chorus lines of beautiful starlets. Even the great novelist and street wizard Nelson Algren, in his twilight, was snagged by the oldest Eighth Avenue topless scam: He was hit with a $30 tab the moment after okaying a drink for a leotarded B-girl on the adjacent barstool. Refusing to pay, Algren called their bluff amid threats. The 250-pound bouncer finally admonished, "Pops, you come around here again, I'm going to get another old man to whip your ass."

The slickest string of topless tourist traps—Guys & Dolls, Adam & Eve, Wild West, and the Living Room—were owned by Sol Sitzer. Suckers were herded into booths and encircled by B-girls chanting "Buy-me-a-drink." Credit cards were billed for fake champagne and $175 trips to an "Erotica Lounge" or "Garden of Eden" room "where anything could happen." Nothing ever did—short of shelling out $500. The B-girls' object was to get the chump so hot to trot, while buying her $10 cocktails (water) every five minutes, that he was ready to sign anything, and handed over his American Express.

A former manager of one "store," who "looked the other way" as he sacrificed his ethics for a $550-a-week job, said Sitzer "would scream and curse at me while his stooges stood by and gloated." Sitzer masterminded an atmosphere of suspicion; employees' jobs rested on how well they could rat each other out. Though treachery was the B-girls' trade, this manager tried to "separate the sharks from the guppies," earning the rep of a "lover boy." He was fired, as was anyone without a thieving nature.

The Manhattan DA and Midtown Enforcement gutted the Sitzer bars in 1982, and Sitzer was sentenced eighteen months to four and a half years for police bribery attempts and credit card fraud.

But Midtown Enforcement had also produced thousands of aimless pross arrests, and shuttered a dozen honestly run, corporate-account East Side spas—like Tahitia and Caesar's Retreat—before going after the topless-bar scourge. Having now knocked the sex industry to the ropes, they branched out to battle other social ills. What with fleeing tourism and corporate abandonment, the Office of Midtown Enforcement's goal was to return Times Square's real estate to "good commercial uses." This white-bread vision was realized to chilling effect in 1984, when the city approved four corporate skyscrapers for construction smack dab at the intersection of 42nd Street and Times Square.

Principal among groups formed around Times Square's "improvement" was the 42nd Street Development Corporation, created in 1976 "to rescue West 42nd Street from four decades of misuse and neglect... to reverse 42nd Street's fall from grace... creating in time a river-to-river Grand Boulevard that would become a magnet for private investment, visitors, jobs and tax revenues, and have a major impact on the economy of New York City and the Tri-State region."

In the Times Square of 1976, this was a tall order. But these were dreams of a board of directors that included Father Rappleyea, pastor of Holy Cross, Gerald Schoenfeld, Shubert Organization chairman, and Jacqueline Kennedy Onassis, herself granting $25,000 toward financing. All of them had a cultural and nostalgic sense of history. Their original fund-raising proposal listed the wonders of 42nd Street starting at the United Nations, the Chrysler Building, the library... then stopping dead at the "physical decay... feeding and providing cover for human decay—vagrants, pimps, pushers, prostitutes—and it is spreading. West 42nd Street is a cancer; it threatens the life of everything around it." They preferred the "nice naughtiness" of Times Square's past, evoking lost shrines, "many behind peeled paint and tinned windows, waiting to be rediscovered." The four decades of neglect 42nd Street suffered presumably began during the Depression. All the legit Broadway theaters on 42nd went into foreclosure. Most were acquired by the Brandts, who converted them to movie houses, instituting a policy of double features for ten cents in the morning, fifteen cents at night.

The Development Corp. immediately took possession of the Crossroads Building at Broadway and 42nd. A sawdust peep scumatorium, where kiddie porn had been available, was evicted and replaced by a police substation. They commissioned a trompe l'oeil painting ten stories high over the Crossroads exterior, mirroring the old Times Tower across the street, as it appeared in 1904; it had been paneled over in 1964 by Allied Chemical. The cops and the painting, both temporary, were "symbolic," they said, of things to come.

The not-for-profit corporation then restored the blue-green Art Deco McGraw-Hill landmark, West 42nd's tallest building. Totally evacuated during the pross boom, the 1930s-style offices were now fully rerented. They created a new headquarters for the Mounted Unit, housing twenty-eight horses in a West 42nd Street police stable. Dozens of developments by others followed in domino fashion. The old Knickerbocker Hotel was reconditioned with quaint office space, its pictorial history laid out in the lobby, as in McGraw-Hill's. The 1978 opening of Manhattan Plaza, 1,700-

unit subsidized housing for actors, anchored the street for cabarets and restaurants nearby—the "New Hell's Kitchen."

But the Development Corp.'s ground-breaking project was Theater Row. Robert Moss, director of Playwrights Horizon, was kicked out of a YMCA in 1974, about to lose state aid if a new location was not found. In utter desperation he rented a crumbling tenement within that unholy massage parlor stretch at Ninth Avenue, from which theater people stayed away in droves. One day during his first "season," he saw men in suits pointing at surrounding tenements, an unusual sight. One of them was Fred Papert, who would next year become chairman of 42nd Street Development; at this location and time, Moss knew urban renewal was an inconceivable fantasy. But the Nat Home Theatre and the Lion Theatre moved in next door to his Playwrights Horizons. The Development Corp. took this cue to condemn five "derelict tenements" (containing the aforementioned wondrous cesspools), and solicit public grants and tax incentives. The entire block was quickly renovated into quaint off-off Broadway theaters.

The 42nd Street Development Corporation's brochure coverline now asks, "What's a Nice Girl Like Estelle Parsons Doing in a Massage Parlor on 42nd Street?" The actress toasts a wineglass in front of a nude oil painting at La Rousse, "a nice French restaurant that was the not-so-nice French Palace, a massage parlor, seven years ago."

Times Square or Bust

Port Authority cops are recognizable by a deeper blue uniform than that of the NYPD. Empowered as state police, with jurisdiction over *two* states—New York and New Jersey—they can chase crooks across state lines, which city cops can't do. Their force, currently reduced to 1,200, polices the three major airports, the shipping ports, tunnels, bridges, World Trade Center, and Port Authority Bus Terminal at 42nd Street.

The bus terminal is a block and a half square, with a quarter million people passing through daily. About 110 uniformed cops are assigned there, not including detectives and plainclothes. Their police station, near the Ninth Avenue sector of the depot, seems untouched since it opened as the Union Bus Terminal in 1950. The same institutional tile and light fixtures, the dreary decor of law enforcement, enveloped within a $150-million expansion and modernization of the Eighth Avenue building. Also untouched is the crusty Mid-City Lanes, with yellowed bowling pins and greasy hamburger-smoked walls, an anachronistic treasure buried behind the exposed steel girders of the rebuilt Port Authority.

But the police deal with bus emergencies that smack of modern times. Officers casually compare their visits to a colleague recovering well from a nearly fatal attack months before: a psychotic Cuban boat-refugee had knifed the cop in the side and twisted the blade up his torso, then stabbed another officer in the leg a dozen times, before being apprehended. "Luckily he kept hitting the bone," says one cop who assisted in the capture, without even firing a shot. On another bus, a rabid bag lady sank her teeth into the arm of a female cop and wouldn't let go for quite some time, while other cops tried to pry her head loose.

Outside the station, a blubbering, sickly, snot-nosed teenage girl reaches her hand out to two cops. The uniforms jump back a yard and order her not to touch them physically; they don't know what the hell she might have.

This is the turf of Sergeant Bernard Poggioli, director of the Port Authority Police Youth Service Unit, who reminisces about his rookie season at the bus terminal in 1971: "Back then, Port Authority had an isolationist attitude. Something goes on across 42nd Street, even property damage—unless it was life and death—we stayed away. Now we've taken the attitude we're part of the community, we've joined the 42nd Street Coalition. I'm amazed how clean it's gotten. When I first came, you couldn't even *walk* on Eighth Avenue. Nothin' but pross and he-shes, animals, derelicts, it was a disaster, and nobody cared.

"In 1971, I was doin' traffic duty, I arrested a pross and she was—he, as a matter of fact—was hailin' cars. I locked the gentleman up, and the sergeant at the time said, 'What are you doin'? That's not our problem, that's a New York City problem.'

"Not only that, Midtown South was the 14th Precinct then, you had maybe seventy, eighty cops, it wasn't a super precinct yet. The pross were all junkies too, and there'd be two hundred gentlemen pretending to be ladies out there morning, noon, and night. You'd be talking to a girl who's six-eight. You couldn't believe there were that many fags out there."

Run like a private corporation, Port Authority is actually a government-sponsored, bi-state agency that turns a profit. A change of leadership involved Port Authority in Times Square redevelopment by 1976, the pivotal year, when forces of good teamed up to battle the bad. They developed a social conscience.

"We used to go across the street, there was a place called Pleasure Studios; somebody'd get ripped off, somebody'd get shot, somebody'd get stabbed, people would fly out the windows. Everybody was makin' money, except the poor schmuck who used to go in there and lose it.

"We shut down topless bars and massage parlors on 42nd Street between Ninth and Tenth. They sent over the manager of the bus terminal to one joint. It was funny, 'cause he walked over with a summons like a businessman, said, 'I'm with the Port Authority, we're closing this down.' The man answers, 'Either get outta here, or we'll kill ya.' These people, ya gave 'em a summons, they didn't know anything. The manager got a little panicky, came back to the terminal. That became the first time we ever went over in force and did something. Once they saw the uniforms, they realized they hadda leave. 'Okay, you're closed, get out.' Manager brought in the maintenance guys, they boarded it right up."

The Youth Services Unit began in 1976 as an alternative to the criminal justice system. Three teams, each consisting of one plainclothes cop and one female social worker, escort kids unable to explain their presence in the terminal to the office, separate from police detention. Runaways are "status offenders"—the same actions by adults would not be illegal. Police return anyone under sixteen home, but they also confer with seven other children's agencies. The unit handles runaways at all Port Authority facilities. Kennedy Airport, for instance, gets about fifteen runaways a year—international ones, at that. The bus terminal is legendary, however, as the gateway into Times Square for everyone who's been run out of town by the sheriff, every discharged mental patient for whom funds have run out, and particularly for the proverbial runaway teens from across the U.S.A. who come here to be prostitutes. In 1983, Port Authority only caught fourteen runaways from midwestern states.

"The Minnesota Strip is a myth," says Poggioli. "We dealt with twenty-five hundred kids last year. Out of that, nine hundred and thirty were runaways. Out of that nine hundred thirty, sixty-nine percent were from New York. You're talking about a majority of kids being from the five boroughs, most from Brooklyn. It's not that we never get kids from Minnesota, but it's more fictionalized. Like all the kids that allegedly come here to be stars, to go onto Broadway. I think I've met two kids that actually came here thinking they were gonna do something. We met one yesterday who we took to the airport today. She walked outside and said, 'Nooo, this is not what I expected, I'm goin' home.'"

The sergeant points to an "upcoming social phenomenon." Kids who've been tossed out by their families to fend for themselves in limbo are known as "throwaways." He estimates some 20,000 desolate teenagers living out of abandoned tenements or rooftops in New York. Runaways at least have a potential place to return; throwaways don't. Enter pimps and chicken hawks.

"They're out there. That's why our major concern is to get these kids before they leave the bus terminal for the street, where they'll become hungry, confused. The pimps don't have to go lookin' for them. Other girls tell 'em. The kid might find another girl who tells her how to work the street, then they move in together. Pimps don't come in the bus terminal too often. Under 21 down the block houses two hundred fifty kids, walking in and out. Why should a pimp come in here and risk getting captured? One thing cops hate are pimps. Especially pimps that prey on kids. You're always lookin' at kids as if they were your own, and out of all the cops here, maybe four don't have children. You see a guy approach a kid, you're gonna hassle him. Right, wrong, or indifferent, that dude is gonna get hassled. He's gonna get bounced. You have their car towed, you create such aggravation that they don't wanna be here. We have a loitering statute. Legalized harassment. If we don't do that, they'll move in.

"The classic pimp, with the big yellow Cadillac and the white-wall tires, they're few and far between. What you do have is a lot of boyfriend-type pimps. When these girls don't do what the pimp tells 'em, the pimp beats 'em, there's no ifs, ands, or buts. This is their philosophy. There's an entire subculture out there. You don't go out cold as a sweet little kid to this big bad pimp. Everybody drills into their kids you don't talk to strangers, watch out for pimps in flashy cars. But you start talking to other kids who've been on the street and they'll tell you, 'What's the difference? So you do this guy, so what? You never did it before?' Some of these kids are embarrassed to say they never did it before, now they gotta show they're street-smart. Everybody's doin' it, so what's the difference? This one's doin' John, Frank, Jim, and Jack, so why not do Freddy too, for a ten-spot?

"A boy doesn't stick out as much as a girl, he's dressed normal. You ask him how he's making money, he'll say 'I rip somebody off, I shine shoes,' most boys aren't gonna tell you they sell their ass. The girls'll say, 'Well, I got a boyfriend who takes care of me.' Now, if a girl decides she wants to press against a pimp, we'll definitely arrest the guy, no ifs, ands, or buts. But chances are it's not goin' anywhere. This court system is so screwed up now, they'll say the kid probably did it on her own, unless she's a first-time runaway that just came out of Catholic school and planned on being a nun until she left."

Times Square's Good Shepherd

In Covenant House's modest chapel—where Father Bruce Ritter, the organization's founder and president, once conducted Sunday services—there are eight huge paintings by a Franciscan priest, a colleague of Father Bruce's. They represent the Covenant House/Under 21 experience. First in the series is a crucified Hispanic male who also bleeds from the crotch, with the face of Jesus superimposed. This, says a Covenant volunteer standing before the painting, symbolizes "Christ still being crucified today in Times Square." The image of this muscular, goateed Roberto Duran look-alike is that of a man, not a boy *under twenty-one.* The second canvas portrays Father Bruce hovering over two ragamuffins, his arms spread in a lordly gesture of acceptance.

A few paintings down the road, we come to the phase of religious counseling, a later step within the strict curriculum for kids who stick it out at Covenant House. It shows a black boy sitting under a rainbow, inwardly reflective. The last painting brings back the crucified Roberto Duran, back on his feet, his soul repaired and rejuvenated, but with crucifixion scars, symbolic of leaving Covenant House successfully.

These days, Father Bruce rarely makes it to the chapel where he is portrayed in an almost biblical confrontation between good and evil. He can now conduct a dozen Masses on a weekend, busily soliciting funds around the country for his internationally expanding homeless-youth crisis centers. The budget for six cities was $24 million in 1983. Father Bruce has described his flagship Times Square operation as "an intensive care unit for dying children."

Covenant's satellite crisis center, Under 21, is out on Eighth Avenue, housing nineteen- and twenty-year-old males. Some of the ravaged faces who appear at its doors could almost pass for forty. The kids deposit their knives at the front desk before being buzzed through for a night's sleep. But Covenant House itself is a large, concrete compound at 41st and Tenth Avenue—formerly a state-prison drug rehab center—which now serves as Times Square's cultish sanctuary for runaways, throwaways, and homeless teens. No questions asked, no background check, immediate grub, roof, threads, medical care, or protection. Closed to all but those "Under 21," with home-made security guards to keep out riffraff and pimps who have threatened to come in shooting if their girls weren't released, according to staff.

In the reception area are several Puerto Rican girls with black eyes, waiting for appointments with their social workers. Nuns in blue summer habits pass by. The furniture, in brightly colored modern shapes, is part of an expenditure to soften up the institutional layout for children's eyes. An endless procession of donated clothes and records comes to the front desk.

A tall, stunning Amazonian lady is escorted in, carrying boxes. She emanates wealth, much out of place here, her hair coiffed, dressed for evening, as if a limo awaits outside from which she keeps producing gifts. None of the nuns or staff inside blink an eye; charity is routine at the desk. Covenant personnel assist her in carrying a rowing machine, donated to Father Bruce's "kids." Someone else has donated a radar detector, sitting on the floor. Staffers will weed through these clothes and records, rejecting unwholesome influences. A woman once came to Covenant House's reception desk with two Blackglama fur coats. The receptionist wrapped himself in one, but Father Bruce took them away. Another anonymous female citizen dropped off an envelope containing five grand in cash. The basement contains stockpiles of extra stuff for kids who've "graduated," deserving silverware, towels, and the like when setting up house.

They're all "good kids," Father Bruce has always said, "my kids," generically, and more than 230 are provided with meals, room, and board each day. Others trample through just for meals, or give it a brief try after living out of subways, gutters, and Playland video arcades where the boys behind the pinballs sell their tails to fags. Incorporated in 1972, the Covenant now mostly houses dispossessed black boys from the boroughs.

"There aren't that many runaways now that go there, just mostly castaways from the city. They're a tough group, and if you're a runaway from the Midwest, you're not gonna last there," says Father Rappleyea about the Covenant youth mission two blocks from his church. He, too, finds kids on the steps of Holy Cross: "If they were a New York City kid, I would send them to Under 21 [the street name for Covenant House]; if they were a runaway, I would send them to the Port Authority Youth Squad, which would attempt to get them home, whereas Under 21 eventually would attempt it, but their policy is not to ask any questions, which has created problems. Father Ritter felt if you became too inquisitive, the youngster wouldn't come."

"A lot of the kids that we pick up," says Sergeant Poggioli of Port Authority Youth Service, "tell you they live at Under 21, rather than tell you they're on the street. A lot of police don't care for it. They feel it's a haven for runaways, which it is. We have our problems with them, but constantly have meetings with them to work it out. We come from two ways of thinking. They take a complete advocacy role for the children."

For example, continues the sergeant, "Under 21 had one kid who said he was getting beat up by his father with an extension cord. They filed an abuse petition, strictly from the kid's point of view. Then we picked up the same kid. He says, 'You can't do anything to me, Under 21 filed a petition against my parents.' 'Okay, baby, but it's my obligation as a police officer to find if you have any alarms.' He had a missing-persons alarm. We call his local police in Jersey and they said, 'Oh, you got him?' I said, 'This kid's claimin' abuse.' They said, 'Abuse, that crumb?' He had shot out his neighbor's windows with a .22. His father spanked him and took away his radio. As he pulled out the radio, the kid got hit in the arm with the cord."

After they walk in, new kids are assessed by volunteers during a process called "intake"—their name, age, health, whether they're selling their ass. Father Bruce's reconditioning program tries to crack the "lying-cheating-stealing" cycle from the street by aiming "our kids" toward the bottom rung of civilized society. A menial job might be held up as a long-term goal. While a licensed public school on the compound handles younger kids, job seminars and vocational counseling are given to older boys. They're taught that the despairing cry—"Yo, man, I need a *job!*"—is not the proper way to interview for a position. When the kid is assessed on his first day, he's asked what kind of work interests him. "I wanna be a rock singer!" is the common plaint. This is neutralized by the counselor's callous answer that it "isn't realistic." Aspiring to a counter job at McDonald's, after proving yourself for six months at the participating Dove Messenger Service, is, however. But only for their most motivated kids.

Eighty percent of the kids admitted suffer from severe emotional disturbance or suicidal depression. The first floor contains medical and legal services. Volunteer doctors treat VD, drug abuse, and rape or send kids with wounds off to hospitals. Above this is a floor for girls, and then a floor for boys aged fifteen through eighteen. The next floor is for pregnant girls and mothers. "'What's your baby's name?'" Father Bruce once asked, reflecting in an Under 21 brochure: "'Aurora,' she said. Lots of our girls give their babies exotic, wistful, wishful, dreamy names.... Somehow that seems to give their children a stake in beauty and faraway things that are not part of their mothers' lives."

Father Bruce cloaks himself in secrecy these days, and his secretaries dismiss interview requests from everyone but puritanical media. Reagan's 1984 State of the Union address singled out the priest as "Times Square's Good Shepherd." His fund-raisers and Young & Rubicam radio and TV commercials help perpetuate the "Minnesota Strip," years after its demise. This titillating fantasy of an Eighth Avenue consumed by kidnapped blond teen hookers prompted a team of Minneapolis detectives to search Times Square in 1983. They could not turn up one girl from their home state. Though no traces of kiddie porn, on paper or film, are available in Times Square, Father Ritter won't differentiate between child abuse and porn, or the fact they are two separate animals. Though young flesh, particularly chicken hawking, appears on the streets, Ritter claims it is "under the protection of organized crime," where "the multi-billion dollar sex industry continues to flourish, feeding off the bodies of these victimized youths—who are raped, beaten, and sometimes murdered."

Two thirds of the kids fall through the cracks, return to the street. They can't cut rules—no drugs, booze, or violence on premises, a 9 P.M. curfew. They are banned from Covenant House up to a month. If or when they return, they might be so dizzy, they won't even recognize their former social worker. ("The street is a brutal parent," says Father Bruce.) About a third, Covenant House says, are "set on the path to a better life."

Pross and Pimps

After Eighth Avenue's streetwalker monopoly was terminated by 1980, girls gravitated to a dozen crosstown thoroughfares, as if dispersed by some antitrust action. The whole city combined would never contain the volume of streetwalkers that Times Square once did. When hookers were still wearing hot pants, blond dime-store wigs, and go-go boots, missionary Arlene Carmen took to the sidewalks of Times Square: "What we call the 'immersion process' in the church—immersing myself in *the life* to find out what it was, whether there was a place the church could be of service."

Carmen believes hookers today "have been affected by the women's movement, there's a greater sense of independence than eight years ago. More are renegades who live without men. The women stand out less visibly than they used to in dress, there's less decoration of the body."

Judson Memorial Church, Carmen's headquarters on Washington Square, acquired a National Car Rental bus once used for airport shuttles and made it their mobile unit for hookers: "The bus is to give the women access to the square world, to help them with social services, baptize their babies, marry them, bury them. It's a church."

The mobile church snakes its way up Eighth Avenue in winter, offering hot coffee to cold-legged wildlife. No males whatsoever are allowed in, except the priest who drives. A sign on the door reads IF YOU'RE RUNNING, RUN RIGHT BY, IF YOU'RE WALKING, WALK RIGHT IN. Speaking in a whisper at her church administration desk, Arlene Carmen says she won't open the bus door for girls evading cops. Middle-aged, with frizzy black hair, she is solemn, humorless, possibly a bit shell-shocked after being engaged in "the ministry of prostitutes" since 1976. Judson Church's denomination is American Baptist/United Church of Christ. Judson's goal is to decriminalize prostitution.

Carmen deals only with streetwalkers, bottom feeders in the hierarchy of hookers: "They prefer working outdoors because they have a choice about who to go with. When you work inside, management doesn't permit you to say no. That's the only freedom in that life—to move around and choose who she goes with. Some have tried and just couldn't hack the boredom indoors.

"Most of these women are mothers," Carmen continues. "In this city there are baby-sitters who care for the children of prostitutes twenty-four hours a day in their own apartments. The mothers pay up to $150 a week for that care, a very informal network. The women don't know if they're going to jail, so they can't keep their kids with them. Children are very important in that life."

All of Carmen's hookers bring pictures of their babies to paste up in the van: "It was their idea to put up the board. That was the only thing they ever asked us to do. Because they can't carry anything—any minute they could go to jail. They can't open bank accounts for the same reason they can't get apartments, you need references. You move to a hotel, but you can't stay in a hotel with a child for any length of time. So they move around a lot. Then they get arrested and they lose their hotel room, all their clothes and belongings, and are always rebuying. These things come together to make for a terribly unstable life. You can't save, you don't have an apartment, you can't have your kid, you're a criminal, you're labeled and you go to jail. So life is filled with instant gratification, on impulse rather than planning. You spend all your money, there's no place to save it."

Carmen claims prostitutes could break out of this cycle if they ceased being chased by cops, having to pay fines, and spending three-to-ten-day stretches at Riker's. On the other hand, she won't acknowledge residential neighborhoods that are plagued by whores turning tricks and littering rubbers in their lobbies and courtyards.

"You think of it as a short-term profession, maybe eight years. She's thinking about getting out by her late twenties or early thirties. An athlete has a short life span, and a woman is pretty much in the same business—she's using her body, and her body gets tired. She's tired of going to jail, she's ready for something quieter. But we've criminalized her. Her opportunity to move into the square world is restricted. She's got a record, so she sees her choices as being narrow; either go into another illicit activity that carries a harsher penalty, like car thefts or drugs, or go on welfare."

In the early 1970s, Times Square police felony warrants were rife with pimps who beat or killed their troops like so many expendable pawns. King George, for instance, poured boiling water into a bathtub that he made his whores sit in. Fast Black, one-time possessor of a twenty-bitch stable, staged shoot-outs when acquiring other pimps' girls. A decade later, there's a less flamboyant *man*, steering a budget pimpmobile, perhaps a white-walled Skylark instead of the customized Eldorado of Superfly's day.

Though Carmen has recently conducted four memorial services, she believes, oddly enough, "There are some really nice pimps who are good to their women, just as nice as anyone might be. It's her choice to be with a pimp, because not everybody is."

Carmen takes a softer line on pimps, stating that "Tricks are very dangerous people. Here is a population of women who are criminalized by society. Therefore they're easy targets. 'Cause nobody gives a damn what happens to them. When a woman gets murdered who's a prostitute, no one's going to waste much time trying to solve it, it's a low priority. I've known more women than I could possibly count who've been murdered out there, died anonymously. For me, if a dozen people I know die, that's a lot."

"The pimp squad was dissolved five months ago," says Officer DeMerle of Public Morals, the division from which the squad operated. "There just weren't enough complaints against pimps anymore."

"Pimps are *slime*," counters DeMerle's partner, Officer Lenz. Heavily pockmarked and indignant, Lenz assumes the bad-guy role. The Public Morals division (formerly the vice squad) is on the fourth floor of the Traffic Precinct on West 30th. In the mildew-green office, a dozen plainclothes protectors of our morals plot out routine busts and roundups at Times Square's sex shows, sometimes in concert with Midtown Enforcement.

Plainclothes make "righteous arrests" of the pross, playing the johns, catching them with their skirts down. Uniforms just round them up when loitering-for-the-purpose-of. The Morals boys go to swing clubs, peeps, burlesque shows—all of which they soberly return from, leading a handcuffed chain of girls and managers. Conversely, DeMerle says he gives full protection to hookers as citizens, should they need police. But the lawmen here consider all porn joints illegal, despite their ability to operate freely in Times Square. "The police are not an entity unto themselves," explains Lenz, who would personally banish the blatant stuff: "I can't bring my wife and kids to Times Square, even though I'm an officer with a gun. Who my gonna look after first—my wife, my daughter?"

Morals cops only stay in this division for two years, then are transferred before becoming too comfortable with the Square and its bribe system. Every nationality is represented here—only their regulation .38's in their shoulder holsters are the same. They spend most of their time out in the field, working toward the gradual elimination of the porn machine, which they're confident will crumble. Cupid's Retreat, the last massage parlor in Times Square, was shuttered in May 1984. Roundups of Show World booth girls and Harmony Theatre strippers, though seemingly futile, continue. Mention the Harmony to one seasoned dick at the front desk, and he sneers: "Don't worry, we'll get 'em."

Castrate the Bastards!

October 20, 1979: It is a cool, bright Saturday in late fall, and between five and seven thousand women assemble at Columbus Circle to march on Times Square. This spectacular turnout will deliver the crowning war cry, thus far, of Women Against Pornography. Thousands arrange their placards and banners and move into parade formation at 1 P.M., bristling with revolution. They will stampede down Broadway to 42nd Street, the pornography capital of America. Midtown traffic has been rerouted for the day; hundreds of police barricades are in place. Forty-second Street is sealed off, and it will be theirs. These girls *know* how to apply for a right-to-demonstration permit.

TALES OF TIMES SQUARE

TAKE THE HARDCORE OUT OF THE BIG APPLE

WOMEN SAY NO TO MEN WHO READ PORN

Women Against Porn was given a storefront at cost by the 42nd Street Development Corp., at Ninth and 42nd, a former hooker soul-food restaurant. Martin Paints sold discounted whitewash to cover the slimy walls. Tony's Bar provided hot water and a sink. "It's about time!" said the neighbors, and the exclamation became the slogan of WAP buttons. A former *Newsday* reporter, and a California activist who'd spent four years with the United Farm Workers, were full-time directors of the office. Carl Weisbrod, Midtown Enforcement director, gave the feminists their first Times Square porn tour. Susan Brownmiller, who spawned the porn-equals-rape belief—a fantasy fueled by wishful propaganda, contrary to what every scientific study had thus far concluded—led twice-weekly smut tours. Giddy groups of women, each donating five dollars, had a high old time touring the peeps, though always emerging nose-up and indignant. Show World was most cooperative in admitting the broads—maybe they could help clean up the area, close the sleazier joints, make it safer for three-piece-suits, the favored customers.

And now, more thousands have shown for the march than was dreamed, after months of handbilling the city and countryside.

TWO-FOUR-SIX-EIGHT, PORNOGRAPHY IS WHAT WE HATE! Banners proclaim the Sarah Lawrence Feminist Alliance, and another cute contingent from Vassar. A group of stubby, mustachioed dykes in green janitorial uniforms chant, "No more profits! Off our bodies!" Gloria Steinem is at the front line of the parade, smiling, waving her fist like a football cheerleader. Bella Abzug marches at the helm, making sure no one will exploit her bod. A couple of old cunt-licking professors march in step, plenty anxious to gain favor with the girls.

PORN IS RAPE ON PAPER

CUT SMUT

PORN IS THE THEORY, RAPE IS THE PRACTICE

The tension mounts with each block as the thousands approach 49th Street. Here is the first target of their aggression: the Pussycat Cinema and Showcase. They halt before the neon monolith.

"We say no! We say no!" They chant and wave fists. Thousands more converge. "No more bucks! Off our butts!"

OUR FEAR HAS TURNED TO ANGER—WATCH OUT!

The feminist march resumes toward 42nd Street. Here, emotions reach fever pitch. They stop before *House of Psychotic Women*, an R-rater at a Brandt theater. ("Their flesh is bloody, their lust will suck you in.")

PORN IS THE MALE DEATH CULTURE!
DEATH TO PATRIARCHY!

Peepland locks one of its front doors. Cashiers watch from windows, laughing out of nervousness. The huge procession clogs the street, sidewalk to sidewalk, as if they could momentarily purge the smut by exorcism.

"We say no! We say no!"

A row of peep show girls emerges from the New Bryant live-sex theater facing the protestors squarely: "We say yes! We say yes!" A quarter cashier stands in the doorway next to the peep dancers holding aloft a copy of *Screw* and a fistful of dollars, chanting, "Money says yes!"

An old black hound dog on 42nd stands outside a peep parlor and admonishes the crowd: "Know how many quarters I put in there every night to get my joint hard? They got all those fine young girls inside. How else my gonna get my joint hard, you just tell me that!" He points to the marchers. "These is some asshole women. Get outta here!"

PORN MOLESTS MINDS! PORN PROMOTES RACISM! PORNO HURTS KIDS!
CASTRATE THE BASTARDS!

The thousands march back and forth between Sixth and Eighth avenues, an area that harbors the thickest concentration of pornography in the world. Then they retreat into Bryant Park, behind the Public Library, for a rally. An old bag lady with an anti-abortion poster has it grabbed and ripped up by man-hating dykes. The rage of a dozen feminist speakers vents itself from the podium. The wackiest of these is Robin Morgan, whose voice screams to a tearful crescendo on the podium, attacking the very fabric of American manhood: "Ted Kennedy has left one of us dead, and a battered wife. Am I the only woman here who still mourns for Mary Jo Kopechne?"

PORN POISONS! PORN IS PAINFUL!
CHILD PORN IS SCARY! MAKE LOVE, NOT PORN!

Signs are leaned up against trash containers so the message can continue to ring out until the garbage men arrive.

A LONER'S PARADISE

Save Our 42nd Street

Item from the *Forty-second St. Bugle*—if such a paper could indeed ever exist:

Forty Deuce, Jan. 1978... *"They gone fuck up everything," said Williamson BoJeffries, a man in command of fifteen prostitutes whose strategic base is the corner of Eighth Ave. and 42nd St. Gazing out from his customized Eldorado, he could see the bulldozers and cranes transforming his beloved block. "Another year from now, this neighborhood be ruined." A cop car crawled up alongside his Cadillac and Williamson sped off. He had been complaining, of course, about the 42nd Street Development Corporation, which has begun construction on the Theater Row project, west of Eighth Ave. Five perfectly suitable condemned buildings are undergoing a loathsome renovation intended to provide "off-off Broadway theater." Will the plague spread eastward and eventually do in all of 42nd St.?*

It started with the new Port Authority structure. Then came Manhattan Plaza, an eyesore that now houses hundreds of "performing arts" people. Theater Row is the latest architectural plan to undermine the fabric of the Times Square area. Although the directors of the Development Corp. insist their mission is a nonprofit one, they are backed by the likes of the Ford Foundation, every major greed-inspired bank and the infamous Port Author-

ity itself. Imminent peril looms over this once thriving community.

"I've seen the directors of this committee," said one massage parlor proprietor. "They don't leer at our prostitutes, they refuse to purchase dildos or rubber cunts, and they won't even come into our peep-show viewing booths and jerk off into the window."

Who are these people and why are they invading the area?

"They call themselves theatergoers. They say they're trying to make our street suitable for more of their kind. I tell you it's sick."

The Kinney parking lot chain, once a fast-fellatio service for late-night thrill seekers, has recently been ordered to restrict its clientele to car owners. Additional parking facilities are being cleared for the sole purpose of harboring automobiles—while the owners frequent Theater Row.

"I can't understand it," said an elderly parking lot attendant. "Used to make an extra fifty bucks a night lettin' them gals suck off customers in the back. For a dollar, you could rent the back seat of any parked car in the lot. And they was fine young ladies, too. Left a trail of used condoms and douches all over the place. It was a pleasure coming to work."

And who is responsible for turning this paradise into a grim cars-only desert?

"Thank yer former mayor for that. Gave out some hefty fines to my boss. If the new mayor would only come down and get sucked off in our parking lot, it might persuade him to bring back a great New York pastime."

The unfortunate situation plaguing greater Times Square goes beyond building-renovation and prostitute crackdowns. It has even affected the children. Not long ago, a dozen bookstores in the area were raided in an attempt to rid them of all photographic material dealing with minors.

"Not the kids," cried one bookstore owner during a recent raid. "When marshals came in and started emptying the shelves of our kiddie porn, I just broke down and cried. 'You can't do this to those kids,' I said, blocking the aisle. 'They're just innocent young tots trying to earn a living.' It was no use. Those bastards cleaned out some of our best-selling stock items. They grabbed every copy of Infant Ward Enema,

Kindergarten Lezbos *Nos. 1–6. They even took our last edition of* Sally's First Menstruation, *which was culled from serious medical journals."*

If they go after children, then there is no telling what they'll go after next. Apparently nothing is held sacred in Times Square. This is of particular concern to Skids Grant, an urban ecologist and self-appointed chairman of the 42nd St. Wildlife Association. Lying half conscious in a puddle of urine, Skids was reached for comment at the IRT subway platform, his home and office.

"Dear God, I loves rats. Rats is the only natural wildlife we got around here. And they been trying to drive 'em out for years."

Just what, if any, new measures are being taken to exterminate them?

"It's those fuckin' train conductors. They likes to run over the rats. Many's a rat I've scraped from the bottom of a subway wheel. Slow and bow-legged rats is, just like old Skids. But rats'll be here longer than the IRT. They comes from deep down under the subways, up from hell. It's just a cryin' pity that rats gets such a raw deal. They're cleanin' up subway garbage now, and rats needs garbage to eat. They's tryin' to get rid of old Skids, too. Old Skids is the only friend rats has."

Although the neon still shines brighter than the sun, some of that old sleazola that once glamorized Times Square has gone. Residents and tourists alike feel a sinking loss of spirit and pride as they stroll through the gutters of 42nd. The inflow of fresh young prostitutes has been interrupted by a "runaway squad" stationed in Port Authority. An NYPD "information center" stands where the statuesque World Porno Palace once stood, now just a memory of old New York. A 'Lite Bite' sandwich shop inhabits the building where "7 Live Nude Girls" once operated in sainted squalor. A Hardee's burger chain store took over the site where a trio of Danish porn parlors once flourished. Ghosts of dead sperm cells haunt the crevices that ammonia rags can't reach, but Hardee's patrons seem untroubled as they chew their hamburgers in a location that once inspired a thousand gallons of jizz.

Though most of the three-card monte sharks, unemployed Harlemites and fleabag-hotel transients who dwell in the district seem apathetic, several are willing to stand up and fight for their neighborhood. One such patriot is filmmaker "Loupy Sales," whose ten-minute spools are featured in many 42nd

St. peeps. Harnessing his talents for another medium, he plans a TV campaign to engage the support of smut sympathizers everywhere. Breaking from a hectic schedule of anal-penetration close-ups, Loupy was anxious to talk.

"We all got to do what we can to stop those morons from ruining the whole area. You got fuckin' priests and detectives out there stealing the best new blondes. I mean, it's getting so that a man can't publicly masturbate anymore. The least I could do was shoot these commercials to let people know what's happening around here."

Just what will the commercials show?

"Well, the first one goes like this: A six-foot-tall black hooker in a blond wig comes strutting down Eighth Ave. 'Wanna go out?' she asks to businessmen walking by. No response. 'Looking for a date?' No one acknowledges her presence. She stands more aggressively in the middle of the sidewalk, grabbing pedestrians. 'Wanna date, honey? Lookin' for some sex? Wanna good time? How 'bout a suck and a fuck?' Everyone just brushes her aside. She feels desperate and screams, 'Don't no one wanna pay for mah pussy?'

"Two big men in blue come over and clasp her hands in cuffs. There's a loud snap, lots of echo. The cops walk her to the squad car, they pause, and we see a profile of the hooker's face peering down the street. Then a slow pan of the avenue, showing the new Port Authority site, a Disney film on a marquee, mothers walking children to school. Not a peep show or urban blight in sight. A full head shot of the hooker turning toward the camera. There's a tear running down her cheek. The frame freezes on this as a voice-over says: Bring Times Square back into the gutter. Stop the renovation now."

Twenty-Four Hours On the Square

Night was its natural hour. By day, many of the lights were turned on impatiently as if the proprietors could not wait for the sun to get out of the way. Nature was in large part eliminated.... Even on clear nights, the stars were outdazzled, as if a supernatural furnace door had been opened. If you hunted long enough over the building tops, sometimes you could see a pale moon moving through its lonely orbit in the sky. Like a discarded mistress, it kept its distance. It looked reproachful and humiliated.

—*Times* drama critic Brooks Atkinson, describing Broadway in the 1920s

Poor Brooks. Oh, how the elders of *The New York Times*, namesake of the Square, must have choked in the filth and smut and sleaze that steadily grew around the Paper of Record. The venerable old drama critic, for whom a Broadway theater was named, was appointed to the *Times* in 1925. He passed on in 1984. Ol' Brooks perceived the gradual corrosion of 42nd Street from the Depression on, but saw his whole nabe shoot to hell during the late Sixties: "Go-go girls in striptease attire," he wrote of the 1969 season, "danced as sensually as they could in the windows.... Crowds of dazed civilians in Duffy Square gawked at them all winter in a mood of sophomoric incredulity."

The establishments sharing the back road of 43rd Street with the *Times*, at 229 West, make up a motley block association. The once-quaint Strand Hotel resembles a flophouse, but only its $35-a-single-room charge prevents this. Happy Place was the name of a bustling $12 fuck parlor, across the street from the *Times* during the Seventies. The Van Dyck, at 268 West 43rd, is a time-warped cafeteria whose menu still carries a Longacre telephone exchange. Blue's, across from the Paper of Record, is the block's exclusive black gay bar, the butt of *Times* reporters' jokes and target of police billy clubs.

"Sorry, but we only admit orientals," says the fellow barring entrance to the Rose Saigon, a small Asian nightclub. The Hotel Carter cashes in on city welfare contracts, while winos and junkies linger outside the Times Square Motor Hotel. Such is 43rd between Seventh and Eighth avenues.

Union and management reps of the *Times* met with police chiefs in 1969 to call for, as the paper stated, "a crackdown on drunks, homosexuals, loiterers and other undesirables" who'd been harassing them. Drunken panhandlers who slept in the area "preferred sidewalks with high-intensity lamps and a flow of relatively trustworthy pedestrians." Like Brooks Atkinson.

Any midnight, a pedestrian might grab a free paper fallen from the loading docks of the *Times* delivery trucks. But most midnight people on this block don't read the *Times*. Round the corner—past the Playland, Joe Franklin's Memory Lane studio at 1481 Broadway, the Rialto I, the Funny Store gag shop, and finally La Primadora Quality Cigars—you've reached the Crossroads of the World. Stand on the corner of Broadway and 42nd, the old legend goes, and you'll eventually meet everyone you've ever known.

Forty-second Street, at midnight. Denizens of the old Times Square might not appreciate the romance of this sublime ugliness. Slum snot, hatefully hawked out of flaring nostrils, strands of phlegm coughed out onto the sidewalks, each offering an opinion of the world. Characters up to no good from every slum within subway fare come to bathe in the neon. Let an entrance stay blocked too long—any store owner's Little League bat will chase most of 'em a mile. The actual corner is Seventh and 42nd, but establishments on both avenues use Broadway for their address.

Victory's Defeat

If we stroll around the corner, the first joint of note is the Victory Theater, 209 West 42nd, where sidewalk evangelists are handing out tracts warning "There Is No Water in Hell" to porngoers. This is the Brandt Organization's only porno house. The box office woman seems disgruntled: "Nobody stays too long. Even men who come here with their women don't stay that long—just long enough to get hot. Then they leave."

On the first balcony, however, is an enfilade of slobs, the same wasted, drowsy bums who've been farting up there since this was Minskys' Republic burlesque in the Depression thirties. None of them, who shelled out three bucks for the triple bill, are watching the triple bill, though several absentmindedly yank their schmucks. Only difference between now and fifty years ago is that most are Negroes. Ask any theater manager his take on the customers and he'll shrug: "This is 42nd Street."

The Victory is the oldest theater on the strip, built in 1899 by Oscar Hammerstein I ("The Father of Times Square"). *Gypsy* and *The Night They Raided Minsky's* took place here. The interior has a splendid old European quaintness, now raw and worn. The third balcony and four opera booths are sealed. Even the quaint bidet-style urinals in the men's room date back to pre-burlesque days, when *Abie's Irish Rose* played here. A beefy security guard is on the prowl. Brandt theaters are the most professional on 42nd—they know their popcorn. Each bucket movie seat has probably felt the weight of a hundred thousand asses each. With a little spit 'n' polish, you'd think you were back in the balcony of Minsky's, farting along to Gypsy, Ann Corio, and Pisha Pasha from Persia.

Back out on the strip, rookie police come to attention as mounted cop Barney Devine rides by. A trim, tan, and gruff sixty-three years old, Devine is a cop skells won't mess with or taunt. Every night, in his leather jacket, boots, helmet, and custom-fit striped knickers, he patrols the shadows of fifteen marquees on the block. His faithful partner, Jim, is an immaculately groomed horse, Devine's third mount in thirty-seven years on the force. Devine makes the law look stylish, even pretty. He dismounts at the curb with more authority than any cop on the beat, ready to clear the sidewalk, smack a skell's beer bottle out of his hand, or kick some ass. He is fighting in court to stay on the job since passing the NYPD's mandatory retirement age.

So drab is the interior of Cupid's Retreat, across from the Victory, that when the hookers change sheets between sessions, it is a moving experience. Inside are six fully pitched camping tents, where quickies are available to the Times Square outdoorsman. The next entrance, sandwiched between Blackjack and the New Amsterdam, was the short-lived Keystone Books. The racks of this tiny outlet were divided into she-male, transsexual, and hermaphrodite sections, and no hermaphrodite should have passed up a visit when in the nabe.

Skell's Nutrition

An endless stream of scar-faced skells appear at the window of Alsaidi's candy stop, at 678 Eighth Avenue, off 42nd. Abdul Steve, from Casablanca, Morocco, runs the Friday night late shift, when the store gleans its profit for the week. This is one of a handful of support systems where the world-renowned lowlifes of 42nd Street come for their nutrition. The grubby kiosk is stocked with potato chips, beer, soda, candy, cigs, and headshop gear. Abdul Steve can grab a forty-ounce Bud or a pack of Newports, bag it, make change and toss in a straw without turning his head or taking a step. It's real cozy inside—there's always a moonlighting friend or two among this small society of Arabs who interchange work shifts at a dozen tiny all-night headshops in Times Square. Rent is about three grand a month, but the owner can make himself a thousand-dollars-a-week profit.

A couple of burnt-out white kids from Jersey appear at the waist-level open window. "Two packs of Marlboro, box of whippers," says one. "Whippers" come in ten-packs for eight bucks, and are ostensibly used as charges for whipping cream. The little metal torpedoes have a warning on the package: "Pure N_2O under pressure. Do not inhale." Popular items with girls mostly, Abdul says. A black swish appears at the window, contemplating whether to buy a tiny bottle of Rush, Quicksilver, or Hardware, inhaled as an orgasm enhancer, or for a fifteen-minute kick. Abdul tells him each brand is identical, they just put a different label on the bottles.

But Rush is preferred among junkies. Next in line, a fat welfare woman, dressed to party, says, "I'll have me a Pink Champale—the big bottle!" Abdul Steve is like your friendly downtown flying-carpet salesman. He calls the ugliest, most haggardly drunken faces "sir," thanks each one, listens to their orders, and smiles in such an unthreatening manner that virtually no one gives him a hard time. Most of his 2 A.M. customers on an August Friday night are up to no good—predators and gutter alcoholics.

"Quart a Colt 45!" demands a skell, fist hitting the narrow wooden counter.

"I cain't drink no Colt 45," whines his crony, "my stomach won't take it."

"I seen this muthafucka drink gasoline," says the skell, swiping the bottle in the bag. "A buck fifty, shit!"

An old, ravaged white face appears next at the window, bags hanging miserably under his eyes. "Camel filters," he wheezes. He's a quarter cashier at Show World finishing up a sixteen-hour double shift; each shift pays $39. Show World employees are among the best customers, they buy a lot of orange juice, and security guards, forbidden from drinking, sneak their beer in paper bags.

A massive rhino, who looks like a pro wrestler in a suit, thinks a white Jersey boy has cut ahead. "There's a line here!" he snarls, half laughing that anyone has the audacity to step in front of him. It seems the whole store might collapse if he expands his rib cage in anger. "You are not part of this conversation!" he belches to some skell mumbling behind to *hurry up*. Abdul cools him out with a flying-carpet smile.

"That was my best customer," he says of the rhino. "He work nearby, and every day at six o'clock, he go next door to the Blarney Stone and sits drinking till four in the morning. Every day." The guy who was not part of the conversation is now hanging in a seasick manner over the counter. Two tall Ballantines, he manages to sputter, his hands a mass of scar tissue and scabs. "Whazza matter, you don't like the way Spanish look?" he says to the ghetto-blaster boy behind in line. Abdul says this bozo works as a janitor in one of the bogus burlesque dives around the corner, he drinks too much Ballantine every day, and he doesn't sleep. Ever.

Little kids drop by for potato chips after 2 A.M. "Their mothers are drunk in the hotel," says Abdul, of the welfare families who now stay at the Carter, around the block. "I have little daughter, I'd *never* bring her here." A fellow in an athletic jacket wants a tube of Sta-Hard stud cream. The proprietor sells only five Sta-Hards a week, which, like the Gold Star-brand rubbers, are bought mostly by black and Puerto Rican girls. Abdul can't recall seeing a white woman come up to his window after 11 P.M.

A serious request for the evening's biggest order—six-pack of Bud, Kools, rubbers, glass pipe, ammonia—this dude's got a lot of party left in him tonight. Abdul refrains from all vices sold in the headshop. Some of his beer drinkers, he says, claim they get higher if they drink through a straw. Every customer gets a straw with their beer, and even the most gruesome of faces become pacified when he tosses the straw in their bag.

Abdul Steve likes to sweep up, pull down the heavy metal gate, and close shop after 3 A.M. "This is when the type of people out there get really bad," he grins.

Morning on 42nd Street. Thornton Wilder imagined archaeologists pausing with their pickaxes over the Square someday, saying, "There appears to have been some kind of public center here." Times Square is the only part of the city whose very architecture seems to sleep with a hangover from the night before. The hulking neon voltage takes a hard-earned snooze to fuel up for another shift. Commuters from the tri-state area flood into Port Authority, Grand Central, and the stations of five converging subway lines, which disgorge here. These were the daytime invaders who poured in at sunrise when actors and gamblers in the Times Square of yore donned their eyeshades and earplugs for bedtime. Thousands of phrases were coined here, one of them being "out-of-towner." Rosy-cheeked, corn-fed, star-gazing, hand-holding couples who say, "Excuse me, please." They used to be called the "white-shoe trade" each summer at the hotels; "hicksters" by bus drivers; "farmers" by lunchroom managers; "popeyes" to the theater.

If Marquees Could Talk

A limo stops at 229 West 42nd this morning to let off Martin Levine, head man of Brandt 42nd St. Theaters, with the organization through six decades. He leaves every afternoon before the ghetto brigades arrive. Levine's office is on the top floor of the six-story Brandt Building, above the Grand Luncheonette hot dog counter and Selwyn Theater. An old patch-cord switchboard operates up front, taking calls for all seven Brandt-owned movie houses on Forty Deuce—the Victory, Lyric, Apollo, Selwyn, Times Square, Liberty, and Empire. All were among the thirteen legit theaters built on 42nd Street between 1899 and 1920. Wire spools of ticket stubs represent the daily take—each Brandt movie house on 42nd grosses between $25,000 and $75,000 a week.

"We had a good diversification down here," says the white-haired Levine, in his seventies, the son-in-law of founder William Brandt. "We developed this into the biggest movie center in the world." The hall leading to his dark, professorial office contains publicity stills from Levine's heyday. Here he sits at a dinner with Jack Kennedy and Eleanor Roosevelt; a bland-looking businessman posing with Cary Grant, Gina Lollobrigida, or Nelson Rockefeller.

Levine defends the epochal Brandt takeover of 42nd Street's legit theaters, resulting from the Depression in 1933: "The banks had foreclosed and taken them over. The dominant party back then in legit theater, as today, was Shubert Theaters. They were very happy to see these theaters convert to motion pictures 'cause it removed potential competition. They might have been demolished if we didn't take over."

Levine was particularly proud of the Apollo, 223 West, his "art house." Honorary plaques from the French, German and Russian governments decorate his wall: "For thirty-five years, the Apollo Theater was the most successful art house in the country. It played nothing but foreign films and art films, films dealing with opera and ballet. One of the first pictures we played there was *The Life of Beethoven*."

The Apollo was also the first to exhibit foreign nudity, making it, perhaps, the archetypal American theater imagined to be attended by truck drivers, murderers, and raincoat wankers. Levine supervises today's bookings on 42nd Street, even approves the custom-made showcards depicting mutilations, for which Forty Deuce is infamous. "What we call 'Fronts,'" says Levine. "As long as I've been in this business we've used Fronts."

"Action-oriented," he describes the movies he books, some of them first-run, which he couldn't get in the old days. "*Broadway* was first-run in those days, big gala openings, lotta hoopla. We never had that 'cause we were second- and third-run." (Hollywood studios booked movies into their own theaters, until a federal antitrust suit opened up the business.)

"A lot of people have their own impressions," shrugs Levine, defensive about 42nd Street's fare. "Look at today's bookings: At the Lyric we're playing a picture called *Conan*, which is playing all over the city." Levine fumbles with schedules on his desk. "The Apollo is playing *Beat Street*. The Selwyn is playing *Cannonball Run II*, a major-company release. The Empire is playing *Escape from Women's Prison*, also at the Criterion on Broadway, for example."

Levine neglects to mention *Trap Them, Kill Them*, playing at the Liberty. He says he'd like to see porn eliminated from 42nd Street but doesn't acknowledge the weekly bill of Seka reruns at the Victory. He won't mention *Splatter University*. Or next week at the Times Square: *Doctor Butcher, Medical Deviate*. ("He is a depraved, sadistic rapist, a bloodthirsty homicidal killer … and he makes house calls.") *Make Them Die Slowly*, a regular return engagement at the Liberty, is chock full of graphic castrations and disembowelments, highlighted every day on the TV monitor outside.

These flicks would be forever relegated to Southern drive-ins and sleaze-film fests, if the $1.6 billion redevelopment project succeeds in condemning all fourteen theaters between Seventh and Eighth Avenues on 42nd Street. Half would be demolished, while the others would allegedly be consigned to the Nederlanders for legit theater conversion. Although if they remain dark without bookings, developers would likely soon convert the remaining old palaces to office space. The Brandt Organization filed three antitrust suits in 1984 against the government to save their business chain. The Great Black Way versus The Great White Way. The Brandts cling to this volatile issue, the "low-income, minority group" defense, championing a last stand to save the last wildlife preserve of cheap-ticket, ghetto entertainment for "the masses."

"These theaters would be dark unless showing motion pictures," forewarns the old motion-picture booker.

Remembering Hubie's

The peeps click on their neon by 11 A.M., to grab the lunch crowd. Peepland, at number 228 West 42nd Street, sports the blinking neon eye in front, peering through a keyhole of lights. *In God We Trust*, says the 1978 Washington quarter, a replica the size of a tractor tire. This is the most unabashed shrine to legal Peeping Tomism on the block. (Live Nude Girls are only available in parlors along the downtown side of 42nd.) Gaze up the building front and you'll notice the old vertical neon HUBERT'S sign rusting in the shadows.

Hubert's Museum and Flea Circus was the forerunner of bad taste, signaling to some the downfall of Times Square. At the turn of the century, the approximate location had been Murray's Roman Gardens, an elegant restaurant that featured an "Egyptian Room" with mummies and ancient artifacts on display. Hubert's opened in the 1920s (it moved a few doors over in 1940). Its preeminence in the pantheon of Times Square sleaze was noted by Brooks Atkinson himself:

When the culture quotient of 42nd Street began to decline during the thirties the Flea Circus was blamed. It was rated as one step lower than the burlesque houses, which, in turn, were the poor farm of the theater. ... By the time 42nd Street had become the most depraved corner of the Broadway district, patrolled day and night by male and female prostitutes, Hubert's

Museum was the ranking cultural institution. The trained fleas turned out to be the finest performers on the block.

Hubert's was an ill-famed rumpus parlor for kids playing hooky. It had Skee-Ball, pinball, Wild West badman duels, kill-the-Japs submarine torpedoes, a shooting gallery using war-surplus .22's on chains to knock down cornball ducks. Karoy, "the man with the i-run tongue," lured people into sideshow exhibits. Gawking sailors could discover the "Hidden Secrets" of sex, solely consigned to Hubert's by the "French Academy of Medicine, Paris, France." A fat lady wedged into a tiny booth at the back of the arcade was startled out of her dreaming each time a customer approached for a fifteen-cent ticket.

Soured careers that ended up on display at Hubert's included pitching great Grover Cleveland Alexander, old and fat; Jack Johnson, thirty years after his heavyweight championship, having sacrificed God knows how much pride. Tiny Tim played Hubert's in 1959 as the Human Canary, up on a platform in a tux with his uke, making $50 a week.

Down the steep flight of stairs were the likes of Sealo, the boy with flippers instead of arms. Estelline, a 200-pound female who tilted her head back, opened wide her mouth and slipped four swords down her gullet (a "doubledecker sword sandwich" she called it). There was Andy Potato Chips, the Midget; Congo, the Jungle Witch Doctor; Presto, the Magician; Princess Wago and her Pet Pythons; Sailor White, the Strong Man; Lydia, the Contortionist. During each of eight daily shows, the curtains would open over individual linoleum platforms where the freaks posed, telling their stories, then gracefully turning clockwise to wave the spectators on to the next attraction.

Professor Roy Heckler, with a bald kidney-bean head and horn-rimmed glasses, recited the same spiel every day for thirty years, taking his trained fleas through their turns. When Albert Goldman wrote of Lenny Bruce's fascination with Hubert's, he recalled the Professor during a typical visit by Lenny in 1960:

> *The man seems so spaced, so indifferent to whether anyone is listening, you instinctively look to see if he has a mal-*

> *functioning hearing aid. "And now here's Napol-ee-on Bon-ee-part dragging his cannon. And here is Bru-tus pulling a chariot. Brutus and Napol-ee-on Bon-ee-part are going to do a race. Brutus is ahead. No, the winner is Napol-ee-on Bon-ee-part."*
>
> *With his chin right on the table only a foot away from the fleas, Lenny watches barely visible little mites dressed in ballerina costumes, kicking soccer balls, turning carrousels, lying in their cotton wool "flea hotel" and feeding greedily off the Professor's arm. ... He even breaks up when the Professor cracks his one joke: "If a dog were to walk by, I'd lose my act."*

Hubert's discontinued live attractions in 1965. The arcade closed altogether a decade later. Peepland blinked open in January 1978, its bottom level rife with freak loops of donkeys and eel sex, continuing the odd lineage of exhibitions that began here with mummies at the turn of the century.

In 1984, the Longacre Building at Broadway and 42nd still lists Hubert's Museum, Inc., Room 725. Firms' names are lettered over clouded glass doors, private-eye style, as the Longacre remains unchanged through time, even its directory. But a peek through the mail slot reveals Hubert's executive offices now to be a custodial closet, with mops, pails, and cleaning supplies.

The New Amsterdam, at 214 West 42nd, was the first land-marked theater on the block. A turbaned dude sells incense under its marquee this afternoon. The Astaires danced here; Ziegfeld *Follies* ran from 1913 to 1927. A kung-fu house in recent years, it was boarded shut in the 1980s, and is the most likely theater in Times Square to be haunted. A handyman claimed to see Olive Thomas, a statuesque Ziegfeld showgirl, float down a staircase onstage waiting for the curtain to rise. Buried inside are the original marble fireplaces, allegorical Shakespearean paintings, and Art Nouveau pillars that made it the most opulent theater ever built in New York. Ol' Brooks draws us back to the Depression, when the theater "began to look seedy and the florid uniforms of the ushers, tarnished and worn." Its last legit production was Walter Huston's dispirited *Othello*, in 1937, after which it became a grind house. "The elegant façade was disfigured with a bulbous-shaped excrescence; the expensive wood paneling inside was neglected, and the New Amsterdam became a slum," remembers Brooks.

The Harem, 249 West, is actually the only porno grinder on 42nd that operates twenty-four hours. A double bill of second-run porn is currently showing: *Never Enough* and *Titillation*. Two long, narrow rows of seats are occupied by black transvestites, pre-op transsexuals, subway toilet queens, and confused Japanese tourists. Night or day, they *live* here for five bucks. Not one empty seat. Ghastly, open-mouthed faces lie unconscious, others are smoking, wheezing, spitting, festering in the warmth of each other's disease. Thank God Brooks never saw it. The sleaziest theater in America.

(If you run low on cash during your quest for sexual fulfillment, you might recoup your quarters at the storefront between Dating Room and G&A Books. This is a winos' blood bank at 251 West 42nd. The counterman, a dead ringer for Igor, pays six dollars a pint [sans orange juice].)

Twenty-Four Hours On the Square (Part Two)

CHOP SUEY signs were once prevalent in Times Square, the neon catchphrase for Cantonese cuisine. ("Chop suey" literally translates as "leftovers," making the meal an age-old inside joke among Chinese waiters.) The last CHOP SUEY sign to go was at 259 West 42nd, second floor, replaced by the Soul City restaurant and topless bar in 1983.

"We got some *Soul City* women upstairs," says the barker on 42nd Street, with ethnic pride. It's now 5 P.M. Two pool tables are filled, their players quietly engaged, while one topless dancer on a makeshift stage wriggles to a loud juke.

"You shoulda been here yesterday," says the bartender, leaning toward the barstool. "This *beautiful* woman walks in, say she lookin' for a job. I sent her in the back to get in her costume. Best-lookin' woman you ever seen comes out. Gets up onstage, has a *cock* this big." The barkeep holds his hands a foot apart. "I say, 'What you got under them panties—you havin' your period?' She say, 'What's the difference, it's only topless here,' then she hike up her skirt to show me. I say, 'You can't work here with that, get out!'"

Hell's Shoeshine Stands

Twenty-four-hour shines are available across from Port Authority on Eighth and 42nd. Each shoeshine man has himself a *job*—a small seat of business, which in turn spawns a cottage infestation of several winos, junkies, or lowlife con men at each stand who leech off the shoeshine action. Sometimes they all interchange shifts at the stand. A white customer who sits upon the lopsided cushion and props each shoe onto a podium will indulge in the most nervefraying dollar-fifty shine this side of hell. Even during the evening rush hour.

As the shoeshine uncle goes to work, first attacking the shoes with an alcohol rag, a scar-faced boogeyman comes alive from the edge of the stand. "Hey, how much dem shoes cos'?" A second skell joins in, admiring the black Zodiac sneakers.

"About fifty bucks," says the customer.

"Yeah, fifty?" say both lowlifes, incredulously. Both want to know where they can purchase such a pair, they've been looking all over. Neither can pronounce words, however, doing gross injustice to black English. Many of the skells here, who intermingle like roaches in a garbage spill, talk in such broken, junked-out voices—often jabbering simultaneously in each other's faces—that there is a total lack of communication.

"Where you live at?" the first boogeyman asks the customer, who names a Manhattan vicinity. "Lotta rich people up there," says the skell, continuing to size up the prey. The shoeshine man smears on a dab of Kiwi polish from the tin. The skell leans up toward the customer's face. "You smoke?"

"Naw," goes the customer, "people are watching me, they'd find it in my piss."

"*Urinalysis*," the skell says, with sudden Shakespearean clarity. He leans up against the customer, quieter: "My man got seven 19-inch TV's, five 12-inch TV's, a carton of Sony cassette-radios and stereos, in that truck behind you in the parking lot."

"What kind of TV's?"

"Zenith. He's with the company."

The customer is amused. How enterprising of those rascals at Zenith and Sony to establish authorized dealerships at this 42nd Street shoeshine stand. "How much?" he wonders. The skell says wait, he'll be right back. Standing at the parking entrance, sure enough, is a short, serious fellow in a raincoat with a toothpick in the side of his mouth, whom he consults with.

"Seventy-five for the 19-inch, fifty for the 12-inch. They brand new from the warehouse."

"Lemme get a cab and pick one up in the parking lot," offers the shoeshine customer.

"Naw, man," says the skell. "We *deliver* to your home."

"Oh," says the customer, laughing now at this punch line. "You'll *deliver*, just like the *Seven Santini Brothers.* I don't have the money now, I gotta come back."

"Well, what you got?" asks the con man. "You can gimme a *down* payment to show you mean it." And then the raincoat guy with hands in his pockets struts over, on this sunny afternoon. The shoeshine is through, and lousy to boot; the shine jockey makes room for his entourage to work. "Buy me a beer to show you'll be back," says the first skell.

"Oh, I'll be back in an hour," says the customer.

"No guarantee we have any TV's lef'," warns the TV salesman in a raincoat. "But if you a *man*, you'll be back like you say!"

"Save me one of them TV's—I'll be back," says the recipient of a second-rate shine, never to return.

Theater tourists who spill onto the Eighth Avenue sidewalk are safe, so long as they keep a steady pace. Stagger from a few intermission drinks and you're fodder for lowlife scramblers keenly interested in reaping the Broadway audience's wallets, watches, and earrings. The more professional takeoff artists were no strangers to McGirrs, the last poolroom to close in the Square. Its unassuming doorway on Eighth Avenue led downstairs to a cavernous, smoky den, clubhouse to the old pool hustlers of Broadway.

The next shrine we come to on Eighth is Show World, at 42nd. One of its wackier incidents occurred when some old duke became over-aroused by a loop and dropped dead of a heart attack. Personnel and customers stood around and laughed. The emporium racked up 279 arrest convictions for disorderly conduct and obscenity in its first six years, before the courts eased up on obscenity raps. The Show World towers—originally the Corn Exchange Bank Trust—is structurally sound, foiling attempts by the city to close it for building violations.

Fewer than a dozen sex parlors remain along Eighth Avenue, and they draw mostly gays. Though only one of four little theaters dotting 44th Street shows fag movies, all are cruising grounds for hustlers, old queens, business suits, pickpockets, drug addicts. Re-creating the ambience of subway toilets is what Times Square's dozen gay joints are after. Eighth Avenue's first-run Adonis theater and Show Palace burlesque are the slight exceptions.

Liz Dumps Dick for Mort Fineshriber

Your Name in Headlines, at 200 West 48th, is Times Square in its purest state. "By and large," says the owner, "the American public likes a gag." For four bucks, he'll set your name or nearly anything you desire into a hot-press headline on the cover of *The Daily Tribune*—a realistic-looking make-believe newspaper. The cover stories underneath have remained the same for twenty-five years. "The beauty of this is to watch it being done in front of you," says the owner, as his counterman works the flatbed press.

"And I make damn good copy," says the counter guy, "much cleaner than the crap you'll get from souvenir sellers around the block. This is all we do here." The counter guy has a political science degree from Fordham, and is now working his way through law school. On the wall is a Supreme Court ruling about freedom of the press, with a footnote scrawled in by the owner about reserving the right to refuse anything "obscene."

"This is a family operation, we don't use dirty words," the boss explains. "The worst offenders wanting off-color headlines are women. Two Spanish women once had me write something in Spanish about a guy, calling him a fag. They sent it anonymously. He came here with a dick. The cop grilled me to identify these women, while the guy went wild. Now, I make everyone translate."

"We won't print 'fuck' or 'shit,'" adds the counter guy, "but we will print stuff about farts." The counter provides twenty outdated suggestions: __________DINES WITH ROCK HUDSON; __________MOBBED BY SCREAMING GIRLS; __________TO STAR ON ED SULLIVAN T.V. SHOW

"Most people have an intuitive feeling not to ask for dirty words, thankfully," says the counter guy. "I want to give 'em what they want, make 'em happy. My most memorable headline was for a guy whose girlfriend was afraid of water: L. NORRIS GOES DOWN & SETS NEW DEPTH RECORD OF 6000 FEET … WITHOUT SWALLOWING. The boss wouldn't let me hang it up, wasn't general enough."

"How much dis booshit cos'?" demands a young Negro, barging into the tiny shop.

"It's four dollars.… And it's not bullshit," says the political science major.

The Ol' In And Out

The Doll Theater, at Seventh and 48th, revolves around an emotionless palooka ramming his three-quarters hard-on into some broad's snatch atop a pink-spotlighted mattress tilted toward the audience. That is the whole of its theatrical endeavor. But, says the projectionist, an old junker who thinks he runs the show, "Video is killing our whole business. I give this only two more years."

Featured tonight at eight o'clock are Passion Young and Shark. "My favorite place was the old Follies Burlesque," says Passion, where she debuted in Times Square. "They watched me dance and said, 'You're fat, but you're damn sexy,' and they booked me steady a year."

Shark, a newcomer to dicking onstage, comes from Cuba, perhaps a gift from Castro's boat-people exchange. He doesn't speak English. Though Passion claims to have a whole burlesque wardrobe ("from my own designer"), she won't break out the costumes here. They're not paying enough. Couples who fuck onstage get $10 per show. A few years back it was $15.

"It's not worth it to get better-lookin' stars," says the projectionist, in his decrepit booth. "You lose money paying their expenses and salaries; the theater don't even seat a hundred. The best way to make a profit is with what we got now, 'cause it's a losing business anyway.

"I gotta worry 'bout the guy outside clippin' me," he continues, stuck back here running the huge reel of rickety stag porn and announcing the "love team" every ninety minutes. "These guys should be grateful for a job. But the kind of man you get is one who can't keep a job," he says of the box office barker. "Same problem with stage couples. We'd rather have them married or living together. I don't like that boy-meets-girl crap—two hustlers who meet on the street, usually on some stuff, they come in here to do a few shows and get some money in their pockets. Then they're out after two days. That's why we always have a standby."

The Doll keeps a live-sex girl working at the New Paris, a sucker's burlesque dive two blocks down where they offer "private shows." They call her in when some fly-by-night live team deserts their engagement. The barker comes in and *schtups* her onstage.

"Wednesday I call 'China Night.' That's when all the waiters come up from Chinatown, but don't ask me why. I try and get good couples for that night," he says, dismissing most performers as "crap."

Passion does perform with enthusiasm, eliciting a groan or two among the thirty patrons as she slurps up Shark's tool. The projectionist works the pink spotlight, perfectly framing Shark's schlong as it slips into Passion's squack. And that's what the whole fuss is about.

Twenty-Four Hours On the Square (Part Three)

Greatest Of Grease

There's no better way to fuel up for our evening tour of the Square than with a charcoal-scorched, four-dollar side of Times Square beef. Tad's Steaks, at 50th and Seventh, provides the greatest of grease, from which you can emerge with full belly and slimy hands to descend upon the cheap thrills of the Square. There are five Tad's Steaks in Times Square. Many a derelict would be surprised to learn that Tad's operates coast to coast. While their arch competition, Flame Steaks, around the corner from every Tad's, chars the meat, it is a pale performance compared to Tad's, where you observe the world's cheapest steak devoured by an infernal grill. Tad's is the Lutèce of Skid Row. But part of the charm and ambience of Tad's—

for anyone who leaves a few bites—is watching a derelict descend upon your leftovers the moment you leave the table.

Varsity Dancing, Satin Ballroom, and Tango Palace, all at the top of the Square, are sordid anachronisms, persisting a few decades after they died a natural death. They are rotting, musty ballrooms. At Tango Palace, Brazilian transsexuals eke out a living as $20 dance partners, dry-humping the occasional geek who braves the ominous staircase. The trannies are lined up in shadow behind the wood railing. Same as Joan Crawford and Barbara Stanwyck, who were once dime-a-dance girls here at 1587 Broadway, founded 1910. Sinatra once played here. Tango Palace had a six-piece band and seventy hostesses, struggling actresses in sequined gowns who stared off into the distance when some GI accidentally pawed her fanny. Occasionally, some old mook comes in today and actually wants to tango. So they still keep a few tango records in the juke.

After nightfall, the billboard of Popeye's Chicken on 48th and Seventh amazingly transforms to a Negro Popeye, through lighting effects. Fifty Japanese businessmen from the Sheraton Centre line up outside the World 49th Street Theater for *All American Girls.* Many open their tall wallets, chock full of freshly minted, unfolded fifties, long before their turns buying a six-dollar ticket. They are the favored customers of the sex industry, from peeps to bordellos, the biggest tippers, the least troublesome.

The former location of the World, across the street, was converted to a family theater. Under the stewardship of Sweetheart Theatres, a porno chain ("Bring Your Sweetheart"), the World had debuted *Deep Throat* 1972. Exactly a decade later, Sweetheart sold the theater to new owners who promptly switched the bill to Walt Disney's animated *Robin Hood.*

Less trivial in movie history was the 1914 opening of the Strand, a million-dollar cathedral at Broadway and 47th. With three thousand seats and a thirty-piece orchestra, it was the first theater in New York designed exclusively for silent movies. Not a trace of the heavenly Strand exists at the RKO Warner Twin now on the block. Even more dastardly was the fate of the Criterion. Its locale was originally part of Oscar Hammerstein's Olympia, built in 1895, the pioneer theater on land that was soon to become Times Square. The Olympia consumed the entire 44th Street to 45th Street block on the east side of Broadway; it contained three massive and ornate theaters, which quickly led to bankruptcy. Vitagraph purchased one of the three in 1914—the Criterion—and it remained a Broadway movie mainstay for generations. Today's "Criterion Center," however, has been butchered into six claustrophobic multiplex screens. Several RKO Twins on Broadway take this a step further—some of their reconverted "theaters" economize space by stacking the rows on a steep incline, directly before the screen. Patrons of this scam must hold their armrests—one slip on a Milk Dud could send them tumbling down to their death.

Leighton's, at 1571 Broadway, sells bland, middle-of-the-road men's apparel. You'd never figure that in the 1950s it contained high-priced Broadway flash for blues singers, gamblers, and pimps. The quality spot for a Billy Eckstein roll-collar shirt, or alligator shoes. A jaywalk across from Leighton's is the "tkts" booth in Duffy Square, selling half-price leftovers for that night's shows. This triangle originally contained the statue of "Virtue." This was a forty-foot miniature of Liberty, erected by The Association of New York in 1909 "to challenge indiscriminate abuse and criticism of New York City." Her shield read *Our City*, and had dark blotches symbolizing the mudslinging it warded off, with her plaque inscribed *Defeat Slander.*

The old neon façades of Broadway's numerous Playland arcades remain untouched, but video has obsoleted pinball. Here are schlock art galleries; flash T-shirt-poster shops; dozens of bargain-bidding Sephardic camera-electronics gyp stores—the same ghetto blaster here might be half-price next door. Fat guys with cigars are slowly being replaced by Third Worlders.

In advertising, Japanese electronics dominate today's galactic center of Times Square. The voltage is peaking now at ten o'clock. American beverages and designer jeans are outjazzed by superior billboards for Panasonic, Fuji, JVC, Toshiba, Nikon. But none have the cherished vulgarity of the three-dimensional, pre-pop art engineering wonders of Times Square legend. Only in recent times was the Camel Smoker scrapped. He blew several perfect smoke rings each minute (through Con Ed steam pipes) for decades—"And never coughed once," said his builder. Maxwell House coffee dripped an eternity past its last drop; Little Lulu hopped eight stories high to pull out a Kleenex; the 10,000-gallon Pepsi-Cola waterfall, above Bond clothing and the Criterion, was an entire block long. Immigrants of the World War I era stared for hours at such spectaculars, entranced by American know-how. (All were creations of either Artkraft-Straus, or Leigh.)

A guy wearing a sticker that said "I need a better job" recently handed out flyers for one of the topless clip joints on the side street of 45th, between Sixth and Seventh. Lucky Lady advertised "$13 Complete," while a baggy-pants bouncer frisked customers at the entrance. The girls in the waiting lounge were the best on the block, but the session wasn't "Complete" until the customer's choice was greased with another $25. Lucky Lady was busted every year. It always reopened under a new incarnation, such as Her Place, Harlow's, the Silver Slipper, the Blue Garter. Across the street were scuzzier parlors, like Heaven's Paradise and International Rooms, charging a flat total of $10. Illegal aliens from South America turned nonstop tricks on stained mattresses in cardboard-walled cubicles. Grunts, groans, and cursing filled the air as the poor man found his paradise. Smiling black messenger boys, in between deliveries, counted out loose change to make the $10 entrance; they exited five minutes later, euphoric over a taste of syphilitic pussy. Next door, at the Luxor Baths, in a condemned hotel, hookers themselves ran the manual elevators up to the ninth floor.

But the Grapevine took the cake, as the block's crowning wonder. Here was the smoky hangout of Times Square's several hundred pre-op transsexuals. He-she-its. Some were astounding sex changes, the more gifted of whom appeared on the Grapevine's cabaret stage. Bringing down the house one night was a remarkable early 1960s look-alike who pouted through the song "I Wanna Be Jackie Onassis." Cheesecake patriotism.

Like a huge can of Raid, Midtown Enforcement wiped out the entire side street of 45th.

Riese's Leases

Lindy's restaurants are a perfect example of the phony commercialism filling the vacuum caused by porn closures. The original Lindy's from 1921 to 1969 had been the most revered hangout on Broadway—where even a starving comedian could order the seventy-five-cent Fruit Compote, pass the front-center tables manned by the heavy funny men, and be "seen." Sadly, rights to the name were acquired by the Riese Brothers, ten years after its demise. They opened a spate of mundane, overpriced tourist traps bearing no resemblance to the original Lindy's, which each purports to be. Sorry tourists at the 44th and Broadway branch stare at posters of comic legends who once hurled one-liners and insults at each other at the old restaurant. Their quotes appear on wallpaper—public relations remarks made forty years ago about an entirely different restaurant. At a time before a sandwich, salad, and drink totaled $27, a cheeseburger $8.

Each of eighteen sandwiches employs the good name of a Buster Keaton, Milton Berle, even Richard Pryor, along with "Laurel & Hardy Combos," "Will Rogers Steakburgers," "Jack Benny Eggs," or "Groucho & Harpo Juices & Fruits." Storefront billboards recall the rapport between famous comics and legendary Lindy's waiters, noted for their wit. (Bing Crosby: "Do you serve crabs here?" Lindy's waiter: "We serve anyone. Sit down.")

"I have no jokes," states the poor waitress at today's pathetic "Lindy's." "But you should go next door for dessert, the prices here are ridiculous."

In the esoteric world of Times Square junk food, a division might be made between good and bad. Nathan's, Barking Fish, Tad's, Popeye's—these contain some element of style or soul. But like a locust invasion of Times Square comes an unscrupulous influx of hit-or-miss chains, overseen by one family. The Riese Organization, which operates as landlord and franchisee over many hundreds of locations, are the ghouls of Times Square junk food. Their cannibalistic real estate conquests are aimed at building a four-thousand-restaurant conglomerate. At Penn Station, for instance, they own a dozen restaurants, yet all are surreptitiously served from one central kitchen. On the block of 44th and Broadway, they run Häagen-Dazs, Roy Rogers, Godfather's, and Lindy's, side by side, with similar clusters ad nauseam through the city.

The Rieses disguise their holdings under a hundred shell companies. Their Times Square storefronts are standardized franchises, with bored ghetto workers who hate their jobs answering to suit-and-tie managers. In 1983, the Rieses began another onslaught with twenty-five Godfather's Pizzas ("A Pizza You Can't Refuse") in midtown, fifty in the suburbs. Thirty new Roy Rogerses were slated for Manhattan, while they took over seventeen Chock Full O' Nuts for $62 million. The fallen Schrafft's and Lindy's, Ma Bell's, Boss, Childs, Brew Burger, the Bagel Factory, Pete Smith's Hall of Fame—people don't eat at these joints for pleasure. Rather, to the hungry lunch crowds, the Rieses are fast-food Big Brother, peering out from every corner in another disguise. Junk food at its worst.

And as the Rieses monopolize the lunch counters, the public use of Times Square has come under the private-developer's ax. Historic real estate is overtaken and emasculated by modern-day robber barons eager to extract as many dollars per square foot as they can lobby for themselves. "People are still hung up on the goddamn corny image of what's there on Times Square, and yet Times Square is horrible," said Atlanta developer John Portman in 1973. "There's not one thing great about it." And indeed, eleven years later, Portman's Marriott Hotel, like the adjacent Astor Plaza, looms up over 45th Street like an extraordinary vision of concrete and corporate ugliness. Ironically, not one peep, scumatorium, or topless bar was razed for the Marriott—just the Morosco and Helen Hayes theaters.

The most inherently corrupt and immoral power group since Tammany Hall—real estate speculators—circle like buzzards above the dying Forty Deuce. These are not visionary architects, but cold snakes who exist only to amass fortunes through land. They don't need art, or fun, or spontaneity. With each demolished theater, they destroy more of New York's history. Cheaply constructed, inflation-era skyscrapers of glass, cement, and plasterboard replace finely tuned, homey theatrical inns, one tower obstructing the view of the next. The reigning architecture of New York has become corporate.

The $1.6 billion Redevelopment could make the whole sense and place of Times Square disappear into the all-connecting Mall of America—a chic, commercialized, phony shopping center, with an insincere wink toward its past, like the South Street Seaport. Super rents for 30,000-square-foot floors could drive out dance studios, agents, costume and tailor shops, all the little guys who spice up Broadway.

"Architects and planners, as much as they try, cannot design urban spontaneity," states one architect, opposing the plan.

Even the *Times* wonders, "Is there a legitimate and irreplaceable street life on 42nd St. that would be wiped out?"

Real estate values make three-story theater buildings obsolete, but the legacy continues across 44th Street, where Broadway reigns. God bless Sardi's Restaurant, unchanged in its splendor for fifty years, the symbol of old Broadway glory.

The armed forces recruiting station for all four services is an anachronism of the military's recognition of Times Square. It sits on the island before the Times Tower, where three-story-high cash registers became war chests for bond rallies during two world wars. People once signed up to defend America here. George M. Cohan made this pavement synonymous with patriotism, having written and performed "It's a Grand Old Flag" and "Yankee Doodle Dandy" in the nabe. Now, there are more who sign up for the Sweep-Up Project here, where recovering alcoholics take to the Broadway gutters with Hefty bags.

The 375-foot *Times* Building, No. 1 Times Square, was constructed in 1904 as the new home of the paper. Adolph Ochs embedded his presses fifty-five feet below street level, under August Belmont's IRT subway, built to coincide with the *Times* at this intersection. This subterrain has long been a silent cavern, last used by Hotaling's News Agency on 42nd Street to store international papers. Take it away, Brooks:

A Loner's Paradise

In 1964, the Allied Chemical Corporation bought the Times Building that had presided over the neighborhood for 60 years. Modeled after a Renaissance Florentine tower, the Times Building had a grace and elegance and seemed to take pleasure in being part of an affable community. The Allied Chemical Corporation stripped off the original stonework and junked the decor and covered the steel frame with blank marble slabs. It is a cold, self-possessed building that represents a cold, self-possessed industry and it is totally detached from the crowds that stream through Times Square.

Feelings

11 A.M. Back out on 42nd Street, between Sixth and Seventh Avenues. The New Bryant Theater is managed by Mac, a cigar-chomping huckster from the old school. "I got a great act in from Chicago," he says, leading his guest down the aisle proudly. "Sit down, relax and enjoy."

Some fifty heads remain insanely silent as the stag film blacks out and live sex is about to occur. The "act" begins when red spots go up over a mattress in front of the screen. A chubby slut muddles through her striptease, then calls to a shill in the audience to come up and have sex. He is unable to even feign surprise over his odd good fortune, but merely obliges, zips off his clothes onstage, and runs through some standard foreplay (to the soundtrack of "Feelings"). He inserts his semi-erection and they perform the ol' cock-in-cunt routine, same as the first day it began here, nothing's changed, not even the sheets. The stud has trouble keeping it hard and goes limp by the end of the twenty-minute set, as if on cue. There is no applause. The stag projector abruptly flickers back on. "You gotta give 'em an X-movie too, they love it," says Mac.

Then Mac strolls into the dressing rooms to check his acts. Crowded into a narrow space are three couples who travel the live-sex circuit around the country. One of the couples feels they are "sexual pioneers," risking arrest and performing in a medium that they insist has artistic merit.

Outside the theater, a tape loop barks incessantly about hot sex inside. "My boss swears the speaker makes 'em stop and look," says the box office cashier, who looks suicidally depressed. "We got fined $250 once for noise pollution.

"I know the troublemakers on the street, not to let 'em in. Usually the three-card guys. They'll offer to pay, then stay inside for hours, looking for marks, or let in a partner through the exit."

The Bryant's lease will be up any time now, but the landlord won't renew. Same goes for the three sex theaters across the street. Up on Broadway they charge $5, while the live-sexers down here are $4 or less. "Forty-second Street," says the box office. "Gotta keep with the crowd."

Next door, an occasional customer braves the winding mugger's staircase that leads up to Delicate Touch, at 140 West 42nd. A sign advertises "Topless Shines." Sure enough, a corridor of makeshift shoeshine stands, polish tins and all the trimmings. An old black fellow addresses customers from behind the counter: "It cost $5 for a girl and a room for fifteen minutes. Anything extra is negotiable.... But if you fool enough to wanna stay out here and have her shine yo' shoes, that be fine with me."

Out on the strip, in front of the Bryant, a squealing dog man walks by, barking and whimpering without a trace of healthy brain tissue in his head. Two scantily clad white teenyboppers have the audacity to walk down this route, a subliminal search for niggerman trouble. "They your daughters," jokes one disgusto to another. Then an aspiring Superfly jumps out blocking their path and poses Mr. Universe style, but the chicks walk around it. Another couple from the Bryant stage, slammin' it to each other only minutes before, exit the theater after their eleven o'clock show, walking arm in arm down 42nd like Mr. and Mrs. Front Porch, out on a summer stroll—which they are.

Across the street is the Times Square Boxing Club, where Boom Boom Mancini works out every morn. An old barker hands out cards that say "you Are the King." Holiday Hostesses looms above, at 113 West Forty

Deuce. The elevator bank is Art Deco, reminiscent of a finer day, long before dishonest whores took over. Only one tiny room exists for suckers who believe they are indeed "the King." Angry ghetto chicks, after extracting a $10 entrance fee, will roll out a filthy rug for the King, tell him to "make himself comfortable," then *dare* him to try something, muthafucka. Sex rarely occurs.

A young white guy runs the elevator. His entire job is to press the second-floor button whenever gentleman callers arrive. Every five minutes he sprays the elevator cab with Evergreen air freshener. "I'm a forest ranger out on the range," he sighs, inhaling deep. "If I smoke enough pot and spray out a can, I'm a forest ranger."

Nedick's, on Seventh and 42nd—the southwest corner of the Crossroads of the World—has maintained its mediocrity on this spot since the early Twenties. The old Grant's Bar, a few doors over, didn't survive the ages with Nedick's. Described by the city as "a center for intense criminal activity," Grant's became a Kentucky Fried Chicken in 1974. The skells then took over Topp's Bar, a block east on 42nd, which in turn choked in its own filth by 1982. Forty-second Street's renowned street scum currently toast glasses at the Golden Dollar Topless Bar, within spitting distance of Nedick's.

Which brings us to the peak of a hot Saturday night for ten thousand honest slum kids. Where else can an eighteen-year-old A&P stockboy from The Bronx escape with his girl on a Saturday night date for twenty bucks? They hop a D train down to 42nd, all snazzy and dressed to kill. This is a heavy date, and the boy wants to impress. Charcoal greasy sirloins *upstairs* at Tad's, at $4.39 a side, including rubbery garlic bread, watery onions, and baked spud with melted lard! They set a candle on the table and block out the world. They stroll arm in arm down 42nd, their pick of fourteen movies before them, at $3.50 per ticket; the rest of the city charges $5. It might be *cinema du* kung-fu (*Kill or Be Killed*), slice-em-up (*I Spit on Your Grave*), black exploitation reruns (*The Mack*), violent sexploitation (*Barbed Wire Dolls*) or first-run Hollywood (*Breakin' II: Electric Boogaloo*).

Movied-out afterward, at eleven-thirty they might pick from a dozen

Playlands, where a photo-booth souvenir costs a buck for four poses. Finally, they take a neon suntan under the Godzilla-size Japanese display ads, and with his johnson rising, he embraces her closely for a $3 color Polaroid, on the advice of a cultured street photographer. Ah, ghetto romance.

"Everybody knows it's gonna go, it's just when," says an old, irritable stagehand, sipping a midnight coffee at Grand Luncheonette, 229 West 42nd. "Those theaters coulda stood another hundred years, if it wasn't for the real estate. I've worked in each one."

The old stagehand claims an elevator contraption built by Houdini for his Disappearing Elephant lies dormant and forgotten under the Victory Theater stage. "That whole side'll come down first," he says, pointing at the south side of 42nd Street, "everything but the Candler Building." Though the plan calls for saving at least seven theaters, he doesn't believe it for a second. Even the New Amsterdam, once the neighborhood's Sistine Chapel, will go. "They found out the steel's bad, it has to come down. They just won't say.

"On this side," the old hand continues, pointing north, "we'll be lucky to save just the Lyric, the Selwyn, and the Apollo. Apollo's just like it was sixty-five years ago, I remember."

The old stagehand saw them paint over Abbott and Costello's graffiti when they restored the Apollo a few years ago. Although showing movies now, "It's ready to convert to legit on twenty-four hours notice."

In the years following a gruesome Chicago fire in 1902, all theaters were prohibited from having any construction above—thus, the theatrical homes along 42nd Street, with no skyscrapers squatting over them. Three-story buildings rotting on the hottest commercial real estate in the world. Those theaters have gotten away with murder, sitting there with all those "air rights" over them for eighty years. And allowed to become a slum carnival, no less. They've had their laugh.

So long, sucker.

TIMES SQUARE PAST

The following pictures are an aside to this book—not a photo record of the chapters. Several shots, taken in 1986, may vary slightly from descriptions in **Tales**, *which deals primarily with the years 1978–1984.*

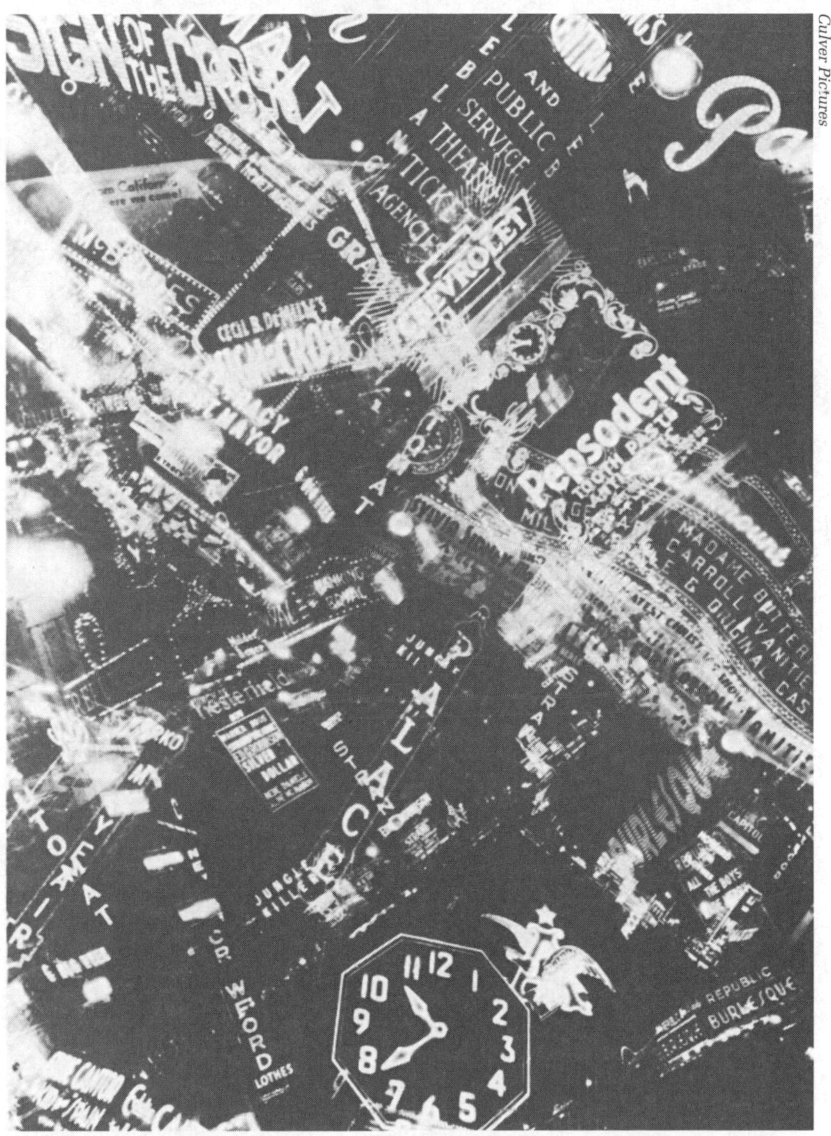

Culver Pictures

Pity the sky with nothing but stars. Montage of electric signs on Broadway in 1932 (when theater had already passed its pinnacle).

Broadway traffic in 1938, facing the Times Tower. Archaeologists with pickaxes may one day say, "There appears to have been some kind of public center here."

Wide World Photos

Wide World Photos

Even the subway had its own marquee, a few yards west of the Crossroads of the World—Broadway & 42nd Street. Burlesque, such as Minsky's Republic, would be outlawed by Mayor La Guardia the year this was taken, 1940.

Forty-second Street, closed for a stickball exhibition in 1943.

Culver Pictures

Culver Pictures

Hubert's Museum and Flea Circus, late '40s. Forty-second Street's legendary bowels of show business. On exhibit here in the basement, the Great Waldo, wolfing down live mice, and a Filipino jungle creep. *Lower right:* Night in the Square, late '40s, before 25¢ became the community exchange rate.

Wide World Photos

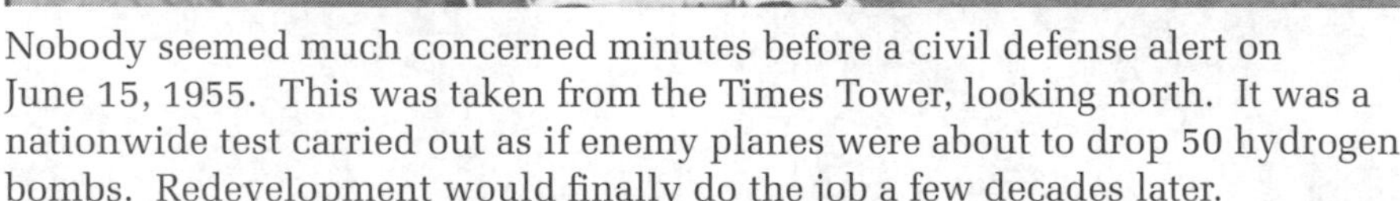

Nobody seemed much concerned minutes before a civil defense alert on June 15, 1955. This was taken from the Times Tower, looking north. It was a nationwide test carried out as if enemy planes were about to drop 50 hydrogen bombs. Redevelopment would finally do the job a few decades later.

Wide World Photos

The streets were cleaner and the faces whiter along the all-night theaters of 42nd Street in August 1958. Truck drivers and murderers in raincoats could catch the latest Bardot flick at the Apollo.

TIMES SQUARE PRESENT

The Final Days

Twilight on Forty Deuce, 1979. Worn down to splendid disrepair.

© Jeff Goodman, 1986

Peepland, at the former locale of Hubert's Flea Circus.

© Jeff Goodman, 1986

Quintessential gag shop, stationed near the corner of Broadway & 42nd since 1953. *Right:* On Broadway.

© Jeff Goodman, 1986

On Seventh Avenue. *Right:* Forty-fifth Street at night.

Raven De La Croix in 1982 during her Melody Burlesk days. At right, an Uncle Lou scrapbook pose with his number-one niece, Raven.

Courtesy Harmony Theatre.

© Jeff Goodman, 1986

Amazon peep-queen turned stripper, Candy Staton. *Right:* "These crazy nuts off the streets walk in and I straighten 'em out," says Pee Wee, pacing like a hen at Hawaii Kai's entrance since 1960.

Porn takes no holiday. The six major peeps grind 24 hours, each day of the year.

The Lord & the devil side by side: Holy Cross Church, built on 42nd in 1870; Show World, a half block away, established in 1974.

Eighth & 42nd subway entrance, above penny arcade, on an innocent Saturday afternoon. Wait until dark.

Following photos from the collection of the author, except where otherwise noted.

CHINA VAGINA: The Stud on a roll at the China Club, 1986.

FEMALE DANCERS WANTED
GIRLS
HOTTEST STARS IN TOWN
First Rate!
GIRLS

IDENTITY VICES: Playland, Broadway near 42nd, where countless bobbysoxers came of age.

OBSCENE ACRES: Fresh air! Times Square! Josh on Forty Doo-Wop.

DOWN IN THE ALLEY: Josh, right, on dumpster detail for *Screw*, with Annie Sprinkle and Marc Stevens.

BUILDING
ENJOY A
MOVIE
TODAY
42nd ST
APOLLO
FIRST NEW YORK
LOUIS GOSSETT JR
FIRST

LIVE
NUDE
GIRLS

PRIDE OF THE YANKERS: The Great One, Al Goldstein, marshals instructions during twilight years of *Screw* and *Midnight Blue.*

SQUARE GUY: I always got the sense that Don Normal, right, considered *me* the oddball.

A WORKING ACT: Former Hubert's attraction Harold Smith dispensing quarters at Playland, 1986.

BOSOM BUDDIES: "Mr. Burlesque," Bob Anthony, left, and B'way boxer Manny Rosen at the Melody B. in the late '70s.

WHEN SEX WAS DIRTY

GOD'S GIFT TO WOMEN

I had just suffered a month hanging out with New York's reigning "strikeout king"—an otherwise cunning men's magazine editor named Sammy Grubman. Poor Grubman spent his summer dreaming up endless ruses to score women—bogus rock video auditions, swimsuit contests, photo "test shoots" for his mag. Dumbstruck, I joined him in his nightly rounds at the Palladium and Studio 54 as he hit upon ballrooms of females. In his rumpled suit, skinny black tie, thick glasses, with nasal whine and Sen-Sen breath, I watched him viciously strike out under the rotating disco ball. I even got into the rhythm of failure with him, tossing out some dumb pickup lines myself. Losing wind after a hundred No's, he repositioned to the girls' powder room. The most common retort from spandexed chicks exiting, as Grubman propositioned each for a drink, was simply, "Fuck you." By 4 A.M., reeling from the dread of such monumental rejection, Grubman would bomb himself to sleep with codeine pills.

I too began wondering whether all women in New York were paranoid men-haters, terrified to smile at a stranger. Or was it just Grubman, rubbing off on me?

During this time, a fringe show-biz agent pal of ours named Shark began relating tales of the greatest barroom pickup artist alive. Shark reflected upon his own glory years in the 1960s. His organs malfunctioning from middle-aged alcoholism, Shark grew moist in reminiscence over the only activity that really mattered—sliding his pecker into trainloads of girls. He called this perpetual state of scoring a "roll."

"It's a beautiful thing, being on a *roll*," Shark recalled, his voice hoarse from substance abuse. "Catching the rhythm and keeping it up night after night. While you're fucking one broad, you're planning tomorrow's menu. You establish your turf, your nightclubs, your clique of celebs, then the broads flock to *you* each night. But once you're out of the rhythm, Jack, it's *very* hard to get back in."

Shark definitely seemed to have lost his chops as a pickup artist, along with his best clients and his dough. He ran a skid-row agency, Tops Models, for mostly unemployable bush-leaguers—A&P checkout girls and bar hostesses with big dreams and bigger tits. Real lookers some were, but cursed by being an inch too short for Ford, a pound too heavy for Elite. They were unschooled and gawky in their runway gait. Some had white-trash bruises that healed slowly.

But Shark had become spiritually rejuvenated by the discovery of this protégé. He referred to him as the Stud. Through the Stud, he could vicariously live out the longest roll of his career.

"The kid's incredible, like DiMaggio on a hitting streak," claimed the agent. "There's no one can touch him. He's got fifteen broads a day callin', beggin' to go out, Ten more from last week beggin' for seconds. Walks out of clubs with three, four at a time, the best-lookin' ones. He's not interested in amenities, he don't send flowers. He don't wanna know their names, their jobs, where they're from… I hung out with Namath. I hung out with Elvis. I hung out with Engelbert. None of these guys could hold the Stud's jockstrap."

I was suddenly struck by the antithesis of Grubman. The Stud seemed heroic, swimming upstream like an erect salmon against the tide of '80s abstinence in the face of AIDS. The Stud's reputation drove Grubman crazy. I decided to do two articles: One on New York's premier pickup artist, and then one on New York's foremost strikeout king (a title no man would relish). I would take a journey like Gulliver; I had been to the land of the Lilliputians. Now I would visit the land of giants.

God's Gift

Mike Florio is the Stud's name, a special effects man in Local 52 of the movie business. At thirty-one, he's been on a twelve-year roll, according to Shark, who passed the Stud my number. On the phone Florio is a far cry from Cary Grant. The timbre and accent of his voice could be that of any Brooklyn garage mechanic. Florio makes it clear, at first, that he hates men. "I always go out alone," he explains. "I don't need dead weight dragging along."

A nephew of rib restaurateur Tony Roma, Florio began his career as a stunt man on *Kramer Vs. Kramer*. The production chief wanted him fired, Florio recalls, for "bangin' dozens of chicks on the set." So this very morning, a decade later, he reports for work on the Michael Douglas film, *Fatal Attraction*. He's setting up special rain effects, which he feels will garner him an Oscar nomination. The same production chief is on the movie, says he's impressed with how Mike's "matured," become professional, not chasing skirts on the job. "Then SAG calls the set this morning," huffs Mike, "claims there are four sex harassment complaints about me, looking up girls' dresses and stuff."

The Stud claims to be immune from disease, refuses to wear protection: "The last time I wore a rubber it ended up in forty pieces." As we talk by phone, the Stud's call-waiting device is constantly clicking. These are the frustrated attempts of girls phoning around the clock. Mike clicks in some of his call-waiting gals, then phones a list of this week's conquests, with me listening on the party line. His voice is a haunting reminder of a night in which they slept with a stranger. In a dozen calls, the Stud arranges dates with roommates of girls who aren't home; a secretary will risk being fired and see him that instant; a girl in bed with a fever will come out that night; three girls are each assigned to visit a different club—Arena, Limelight and the Milk Bar—pick up another girl, then come to his apartment, at two-hour intervals. Each girl whispered her willingness to sleep with him again. Mike has fucked many of them up the ass, he says, within an hour of meeting each one.

Perhaps these were self-destructive wackos, from amongst the exploding buyer's market of girls out there. Nightclubs are bursting with available females. There must be a dozen Studs in every city, I told Shark. Why glamorize the bastard in print?

"You've heard him with one type of girl over the phone," Shark insisted. "But he's a high roller. Take him out. There're a lot of supermodels at the clubs around Christmas. The Stud's as good at scoring broads as Picasso was at painting."

That Saturday, I made the rounds with one of New York's premier pickup artists. Strikeout kings, read on.

Café Pacifico, 10 p.m.

We decide to rendezvous at Pacifico, a Columbus Avenue café which looks like a rejected stage set from *A Clockwork Orange*. "You'll *know* who I am," he predicted over the phone. Sure enough, several girls are milling about the front barstool. The hottest blonde in the joint is stroking some bloke's generous brown curls. He's wearing black suede boots, pleated slacks, a T-shirt under a fluffy cockpit jacket that momentarily makes him resemble a Saint Bernard pup. It's the Stud. He looks like some indeterminable pretty-boy corporate rock star. Somebody girls can't quite pinpoint.

"I love this chick. She's so sweet." Mike narrates the situation as if she's not in the room. Having just arrived himself, he removes his coat, professing to love all his jackets. He has dozens. Each jacket carries "a unique vibe," whether it cost twenty bucks or $500. As a matter of fact, some chick wouldn't leave his apartment last night. He finally tossed her clothes in the hall to get her out. But the heap included one of his beloved jackets, a Willywear, which she kept. It was like losing a friend. The Stud had no way to contact her to retrieve the jacket. Why get bogged down with names when you're banging several chicks a night?

The blonde stroking his hair has just signed with some new modeling agency. She's dripping with homemade jewelry. Her painfully long legs are twisting around the barstool, and she's terribly bored with everything in the world except this foxy guy who just took the adjacent stool. The Stud whispers in her ear, to her utter delight. Then her girlfriend enters the restaurant.

It's the girlfriend's twenty-fourth birthday, they're out to celebrate. Round of champagne, says Mike, an $18 pouring for the three of them.

"Yeah, I like this chick," he says aloud of the blonde, "but I like her girlfriend better." And *voilà*, the brunette birthday girl, an expensively decked-out lady with profound cleavage, is slayed by one insincere Mike Florio smile. The Stud reaches around the wall where the bartender unquestioningly allows him to rearrange the mood lighting for the entire bar. In this darkened atmosphere, he takes the birthday girl's hands, introduces himself as her birthday present, and begins soul kissing. The blonde model is miffed, a spurned pout on her haughty face. I feel invisible to both girls. The Stud's girl-mechanic hands travel over the outside of Birthday Girl's body like sonar, taking a reading on what's underneath those Bergdorf threads.

"Let's leave this dump and go to Columbus," demands the Stud, to both dames.

"I don't wanna go," whines the rejected blonde, swaying her jewelry to Huey Lewis on the jukebox. "I wanna dance at the Palladium."

"*I don't wanna*," sing-songs the Stud, in mock imitation. "The Palladium's a dump."

In actuality, the Palladium, Stringfellow's and Nell's have banned Mike from their premises—as pool sharks are banned from pool halls.

"You're giving me trouble," spits the blonde.

"The world is full of trouble," counters Mike. "Trouble makes the world go round. But imagine how much fun we can have when the trouble stops...."

The blonde giggles at this lame philosophy. Florio's style is to *parody* pickup clichés, with a wink—women love to laugh along, part of a spontaneous joke. Birthday Girl has her hands all over him, and pleads with her stubborn friend to follow us guys to Columbus. But the Stud feels he's given them both too much of his time, and stands to leave. Birthday Girl is deflated. But they exchange phone numbers. She enters his right into her address book in pen. He takes hers on a napkin, which he'll blow his nose with later.

Columbus, 10:45 p.m.

The way most guys work a bar, Mike explains, reminds him of a moronic stop-action silent film. They flicker around in a circle. Mike centers himself at the middle barstool, where he can track all girls coming through. He sucks them over in two's and three's. "I've got eyes in the back of my head for chicks," he says, surveying the room like a speed reader. "That table's all married; forget the blonde in the corner, she's with a Colombian coke dealer; I already fucked the shit outta that table..."

Columbus Restaurant is this year's celebrity hangout on Columbus Avenue. Its vacuous soul is that of a mall—there's no hearth, just unadorned windows for celeb gazing. The Stud comes through like a barroom Frankenstein. Ice-breaking one-liners spew out rapid-fire.

"Hey, I like you, what can I do about it?" *Bam*, one chick at his side. "A woman is a noun. I am a verb." *Zap*, a second girl takes up position. "I got brand new bed sheets, never been slept in." *Kapow*. "Take off your hat, what're you trying to cover up, chemotherapy?" he cracks, grabbing the hat off a passing girl's head.

Before you know it, he's got an admiration society. All are TKO's, any of them ready to leave with Mike should he so desire. I am virtually invisible at his side. Even the two at Pacifico were scored as TKO's. "They'll call," Mike shrugs, matter-of-factly, "I'll bang both of 'em."

Every line he speaks with blushing boyish charm, a sarcastic, Ultrabrite smile, creating instant camaraderie. "I'm married," one girl retorts to his come-on.

"That's your problem," says the Stud, quickly disinterested, his Saint Bernard puppy expression fraught with disgust, making her feel it really *is* her problem.

When Florio sees a chick he likes, all he merely has to do is "Give her one of these." He demonstrates waving his finger with effortless superiority, like Buddy Love in *The Nutty Professor*. This draws the attention of two curious girls. He introduces himself as the "lead singer of Cinderella."

"Yeah, I'm headlining The Garden next week, wanna go?" One of the chicks nervously jots his phone number down, thinking she's scored some heavy metal clod. "Yeah, gimme a call, I'll be waitin' by the phone *like a dog*."

After several Heinekens, the Stud hiccups obnoxiously into every girl's face at the Columbus meat rack. He intermittently apologizes, or snaps at them to "Shut up!"

"Wha'd he say?!" demands some guy, joining his girlfriend after a respite in the restroom. "Should I belt him?"

"... I hate men," replies the Stud, with a cosmic sigh to the complainant. He leans over in confidence toward two mouseburger girls, out of the side his mouth: "I'm so horny. Just gotta get laid. But there's no *good* pussy here tonight, you dig?" He hiccups in their faces.

"Please don't do that in our ears," say the homely girls, unflattered. The Stud gets more obnoxious with each downed beer.

"Would you prefer I do it up your ass? *Brrappp*. You know, you two remind me of Mutt & Jeff. I won't say who's Mutt."

The Stud approaches a group of hardened, out-of-work actresses in their early thirties. They're indignant over his demeanor, having overheard the last ten minutes. They're onto his game and they don't approve.

"I'll tell you something, all you women," he announces, with histrionic presence. "If you didn't own a pussy, you wouldn't have a friend in the world." After a half-dozen beers, the Stud seems to have slipped. This group doesn't want him. So, he blows his cover and confides to them he's a barroom pickup artist: "I'm God's gift to women. I really am. That's why he put me here—for you, and you and you. I live for women. I was born for you. I have a great job, in the movies, I work two, three hard days a week. Make lots of money, then come out at night for pussy. If I don't get it here, I go across the street. If I don't get it from you, I'll get it from her. But I'll *get* it," he shrugs.

The group listens with amused disdain. "I have a great penthouse apartment, full of *life*. It's filled with plants and Pacific Ocean fish tanks." Indeed, the Stud keeps two sharks on the premises in his living room aquarium. The first is a one-and-a-half-foot leopard shark, the other a three-foot nurse shark. Both are capable of taking a serious bite out of a man, but they have a hypnotizing effect on women.

Still holding their attention, Mike quiets down to a soulful confession. "Don't analyze me in ten minutes, baby, I got hours." Florio never had sex as a teenager, he says, was rejected throughout high school. Then when he was nineteen, he fell deeply in love with a girl. They planned to marry. Shortly after, one day, a doctor told him his father had ten months to live. This hit him like a sledgehammer, since his dad was closest to him in the world. Thank heavens his girlfriend's father was chief radiologist at New York Hospital, who could provide the saving care Mike's father needed. But on the same day he planned to ask his fiancée for her family's help, she showed up arm in arm with another guy. Mike was dumped on the spot, at New York Hospital. "From then on," the Stud recalled, "I decided that *I'm* the one who'll do the fucking over, not girls."

The actresses are moved. They're talking softly with Mike now. Three more TKO's for the Stud. "I'm God's gift to women!" he bellows, a jungle cry to the bar at large.

"God's gift to women is a dildo!" screams back some drunk.

"Hear, hear," toast some hearty male voices at the bar.

Florio needs some grub before he can reach a second wind. The hostess seems hot for him and gives us a reserved table. This is an exclusive area at night, beyond the meat rack. The table next to us contains four young, high-toned models, strategically placed at Columbus' front window like an advertisement. Some heavy metal millionaire sits with them. At the table in front of them, however, is a big-time beauty with several male escorts. "Point me to whoever you want, I'll get her," he says, like a hunting dog. I tell him to turn around for the first true 10 of the evening. This knockout will be his target for tonight, he decides, deciphering her body as if wearing X-ray specs.

The moment the heavy metal idiot goes to the john, the Stud reaches over and taps a model on the shoulder. She's a black-haired heartbreaker with a cute, upturned nose job and pyramid tits.

"What's your name?"

"Courtney."

"Hi, Courtney. Joe Perry," says the Stud, extending a sturdy handshake. For the rest of the evening, he'll pose as a member of Aerosmith. "Say, Courtney," he goes, waving her closer in confidence. "Who's *that*?"

"Why, that's Carol Alt," says Courtney. Carol has a natural, outdoorsy look, without much makeup. She's wearing something like riding pants, as if she just stepped in from an afternoon of British polo. An elaborate fur is draped around her chair, and she's seated with three male chaperones. She's one of the world's five top models, yet she doesn't look so self-consciously *modelly* as the girls behind her.

The Stud has heard of her. "Look how *bored* she is," he ascertains, as if she were in dire need of rescue. He can tell she goes to bed by one o'clock from her clear skin. "Got to work fast."

Carol starts table-hopping. She stops by Mike Tyson's table, and he rises to kiss her cheek, looking pretty as a *GQ* cover after his three-round KO over Trevor Berbick. She schmoozes with the owners of Columbus, then Danny Aiello. Then she stops at Courtney's table. Warren Beatty takes a table, sits there innocently, not bothering anybody. "Look at him, he can't even get laid anymore," says the Stud. Neither can a member of Kiss, striking out left and right (anonymous without makeup and costume).

The Stud fidgets over the time the young models are spending with Alt. "These chicks are gonna fuck it up for me. They're all like monkeys together." Alt returns to her table, slips on the fur. All the minor models at Courtney's table put on *their* fur coats. "Like monkeys," he repeats, making his move.

Florio sits right down at Carol Alt's table, introducing himself as the lead guitarist of Aerosmith, about to leave to play with Gino Vanelli, and headline the Garden next month. He blurts out a few lines from "Walk This Way," with a high cackle. Tells her he took lessons from the guitar player in the Tonight Show Orchestra as a kid. She says she was about to call it an evening at midnight. The Stud brings her back to our table, offering his last forkful of chicken pot pie.

"No, really, I'm just having one Scotch tonight," she giggles.

"A Scotch in Carol Alt's perfect bod?" he gasps, incredulously. She's sweet, innocent and gullible. One of her chaperones is a bulky ex-Hell's Angel and Vietnam vet, keeping an eye on her. The Stud says how much he would enjoy dancing with her at the China Club. Alt agrees to go. She's very polite toward me, whom the Stud has introduced as his manager (an incarnation I shudder from).

While she goes through the saying-goodbye ceremonies to friends, the Stud's table is approached by several pairs of women who seem to know him. Some are former one-night affairs. Being invisible next to this caballero, I must suppress my ego. "Just remember," Shark the agent had cautioned, "don't even try to compete. Most guys' egos couldn't handle a night with him." The Stud lays out tonight's situation to the girls, who shrug and wish him luck. They are *rooting* for him to fuck the model.

The Stud engages two hot-looking chicks as he's about to exit. "C'mon, let's go dancing at the China Club," he orders, as though they were anything but strangers. Both accept. They're from Oklahoma, and have a BMW outside, offering us a lift there. But the Stud peers first into a double-parked Lincoln Town Car, pretending his chauffeur has disappeared.

Jackie Mason, at a nearby table, was confounded as to why so many broads came and went from our table. His lawyer, Jesse Vogel, one of Mason's entourage of alter cocker flunkies, is propositioning blondes, and asks the Oklahoma girls if they'd like to sit for a drink with a famous Jewish comedian, headlining sixteen weeks on Broadway.

"I can play a romantic lead," declares Mason to his table. "Why shouldn't I? That ugly dumb bastard, Dangerfield, was the romantic lead in that last picture, what was it?"

"*Back To School*," comes the table.

"Yeah, he gets the goil, that Sally-what's-her-name, he was a romantic lead. And you mean to tell me, this skinny putz, wid the big nose and glasses, this bent-over sickeningly ugly weasel, Woody Allen, can play romantic leads, and I can't? He can sleep with Diane Keaton or Mia Farrow?"

Both girls decline Mason's lawyer's invitation, waiting patiently for the Stud.

"You think I have a chance?" Florio wonders, his first glimmer of insecurity about scoring the supermodel. Quick deliberation—should he *walk* Carol Alt's party to China, or get into these chicks' BMW? Best Carol see him exit with other girls, he decides. We hop into the Okies' car. Alt shrugs—oh, well, there goes Mr. Aerosmith.

The Stud makes the Okies park before a fire hydrant at the side of China Club. They're afraid of getting a ticket or towed. Florio guarantees he'll pay any ticket, and offers them full usage of his "limo" if they get towed, until he can bail out their car. They believe him. The Okies park.

China Club, Half-Past Midnight

The Okie girls expect to be whooshed in for free on the Stud's comet. Instead, he ditches them at the door. Florio claims to have "lost his pass" to the China Club box office marm. He flashes his Ultrabrite smile, and bullshits past the door charge.

It is a matter of honor that the Stud *never* pays the stiff entrance to clubs. Stringfellow's, for example, is the type of joint that considers it utterly uncool to admit human beings from New Jersey. The last straw occurred when Mike showed up with Miss America of 1980, her sister and an Elite model. "Just because you're with three gorgeous girls, you think you can come in for free?" sneered manager John Hawkins, with a British laugh. "That'll be a hundred bucks." The Stud started a fracas, threatened to hit the guy. The cops hustled Florio into a squad car, telling him he was going to the Pig Bar, a nearby establishment.

"But I don't want to go to the Pig Bar," Florio protested.

"You either come with us to the Pig Bar or get arrested." Florio accepted a police escort to the Pig Bar.

Now at the crowded China Club, Florio has bigger fish to fry. Alt's entourage won't arrive for fifteen minutes. He has time to exercise his pickup muscles, do some warm-ups. The Stud grabs a reserved table in a cordoned-off side area. Already, girls are flocking around, something I take for granted, the world is always like this.

A tall blonde hugs him, saying, "Hey, how're ya?" Mike leans to me, whispering, "Never saw her in my life." Girls often approach, acting like they know him. This one's an ex-Playboy Club bunny from the recently defunct New York branch. He plays it as if he remembers her, says she's even gained weight. Her girlfriend eagerly takes a seat on the Stud's right. A third female sits at the table, vying for Mike's attention. She also claims to know him. Reminds him that he fucked her six months ago, a memorable night. "Sorry," he shrugs, "I guess it wasn't so memorable to me."

The Stud's act is so well oiled, he can slip and slide women through these seats like a Detroit assembly line. As the big blonde is vacating her chair, the Stud simultaneously reaches over to an adjacent table, clutching the hand of a brunette stranger conversing with some fellow. She takes his hand, continuing her talk. Neither have even made eye contact. But then she sort of slithers into the vacant seat within seconds of the blonde's departure. An average-looking girl, overwhelmed by this groovy guy grabbing her hand. But she didn't even see the sucker, she must have responded to some primal musk.

"What's your name?" she asks.

"Does it matter?" The Stud isn't interested in names, occupations, he could care less about sentimental dolls girls keep by their pillows, or cooking tips. I remember Shark's initial testimony—"He don't send flowers, he don't care where they're from. He just lives to fuck."

"What do you do?" asks the enchanted girl.

"Does it matter? I thought you recognized me… Do you wanna fuck me?"

The girl's face closes in until they lock tongues, mouth to mouth. She's a goner, you can see stars around her head.

"Your place or mine?" he whispers. She practically comes in her seat, needing a spatula to be removed. She then gathers her composure and explains she visits the China Club often. If she's seen walking out with him, it will be assumed she's going to sleep with him. If the door bouncers see this more than once, they'll think she's a "slut." Therefore, they should exit separately and meet by the corner payphone. As she runs her hands through his hair, the Stud's head spins to some foxy chick in the aisle, and he excuses himself for a minute.

"You seem to have landed my friend," I suggest.

"I know," she smiles, primping in her pocketbook mirror. "But *who* is he?"

"All I can tell you is a lot of girls have been after him tonight. But I haven't seen him take to any like you."

"I know," she glows, confident of her big score.

I ask if she'll go to his place or hers, and she says definitely his. I ask her what she sees in him, having known him a total of five minutes.

"I love long hair," she says. "I want to run my hands through his hair all night. You know, I didn't really feel sexy tonight. But he brought it out in me. He's very oral, and so am I," she squeals, eyes widening in anticipation, as though I'm not even there.

"Are you ready?" she asks the Stud, upon his return.

The Stud is intently staring off in the distance, whale-watching for Carol Alt. She repeats herself. He gazes beyond, giving her the silent treatment. She looks at her watch, lights a cig, a bit confused, not yet hip to the game. The Stud turns to me and blurts, "I ain't gonna fuck *that*," hitching his thumb toward her. She tugs his sleeve. He swats her hand like a fly.

"Hey, what's going on?" she demands, horrified.

"I don't wanna fuck *you* any more," he says, sour-faced, like he's dealing with total shit. She doesn't believe her ears. "I don't wanna fuck you any more," he repeats. "Get lost."

"What!?" After it sinks in, she puts her hands on her hips. "Kind of brutal, huh?"

But Mike's not even paying attention, spotting his big-time prey at the entrance. The reject is mumbling incoherently, can't quite bring herself to accept the humiliation.

"Look—" says the Stud, with sympathetic compromise. "You still wanna fuck me, you have to go pick up another girl to come along. One better-looking than yourself."

She's shell-shocked, but starts to consider. "Jailhouse Rock" comes over the house speakers, and the Stud lets out a battle cry of "Everybody wants to suck my cock!" in sync with the chorus. He's off in the crowd, lots of familiar faces from Columbus, like part of a duck-breeding migration. "Ya gonna sit in on drums with my band at the Garden?" he asks Mason Reese, passing the orange dwarf whilst following Alt to a prime table.

He's pure gentleman now, won't use any low blows in acquiring the supermodel. The Stud is past his feeding time—by now, he could have been home and back for seconds. Alt is clearly in charge of her entourage, it's her table. The Stud and I are invited to take seats.

"Are we mixing in London or L.A.?" The Stud asks me.

"Whichever city will let you in," I say, cringing at the thought of it. Sometimes Mike forgets which rock star he's already impersonated, and blows his cover with the prey. But this more likely happens at home, by which time he can convince the girl she should be flattered he went through the trouble.

The Stud guides the supermodel onto the China Club dance floor, where they appear like royalty. They get along famously, doubled up with laughter after four dances. She even requests "Walk This Way" from the DJ. But then the million-dollar model reveals she is happily married to hockey star

Ron Greschner of the New York Rangers. The Stud trudges back to our table. "Something's wrong with the way she feels," he confides. "She doesn't have as great a body as I thought. If she was available, I would have had her already... There's not a woman on this earth I can't pick up when I'm hot as a pistol."

The Stud professes a code of honor that respects newlyweds or women in love with other men (unless they so much as wink first). And so, the Stud disappears into the horizon to divide and conquer new female territory. He leaves me with the supermodel.

She's out celebrating her father's birthday tonight, though she vowed to be home by one o'clock. He was a decorated fireman who passed away several years ago. I ask her a stupid question, like how many endangered species went into her fur. "It keeps me warm," she sighs, curling an eyebrow with interest. "So, you believe in things?"

God's Gift To Women reappears ten minutes later to take his last shot. He tugs on Alt's elbow like a child trying to get a grownup's attention. But she doesn't respond. Nevertheless, he's lined up a pair of sisters, two barroom Doublemint twins in their early twenties. Both are running their hands over his leather cockpit jacket, caressing his neck, purring and anxious to get back to his big brass bed. They look like two dumb little lambs being led off to slaughter. He'll give them the thrill of a year, then show them to the door after he comes. Maybe he'll hit the Milk Bar before 4 A.M. for another score. Valuable minutes are ticking away, and he has to make his quota. Carol, meanwhile, has rejected him. But she engages me in an awfully friendly conversation, and it's the first time tonight I don't feel invisible.

Postscript

Several months after my rounds with the Stud, I spotted a most unusual patron slumped down in his seat in the dank third-floor Triple Treat Theatre at Show World. It was the Stud! He slumped further in his seat, leather cockpit jacket unfurled around his neck, hoping I didn't see him. Like a dejected puppy dog, he finally owned up that it was indeed himself and shook my hand. In the company of dreaded men—legions of unlaid masturbators, to boot—he looked around, sizing up the place. Some porn starlet was onstage. "You come here?" he asked. I was making my weekly rounds for *Screw*'s Naked City listings, my weekly column.

"Hey, this is my first time here," he swore. "My first time ever." And then he let out a trademark sarcastic chuckle and choked a bit, like the cat who ate the canary.

THE STRIKEOUT KING

The I.D. Girls

As any network news program told you with relish, drinking by teenage girls was on the rise. Lushes by eighteen. So many a teen alcoholic got caught in a bind when New York State raised its legal drinking age to twenty-one in 1985. Nymphs who'd been swigging it down legally suddenly had to come into the city for fake I.D.'s. Enter the Playlands of Times Square.

A pal of mine, Sammy Grubman, took immediate notice of this political situation. A men's magazine editor in his thirties, Sammy spent many a lunch hour enraptured by the teenagers lining up at Playland headquarters—Broadway between 42nd & 43rd Streets. Mobs of boppers would subway into Times Square at school break to purchase fake I.D.'s. The I.D. girls became a New York phenomenon.

Sammy had a self-admitted weakness for young bloods, and he gazed for hours at girls in braces. His office was just around the corner, and since the liquor age rose, he often returned late from lunch, drooling like a dingo.

They subwayed in from Jersey, Queens, Brooklyn, the Bronx and Staten Isle. Sammy imagined them later in the evening: "Carloads of liquored-up dirty girls going 100 mph, talking about blowjobs until they get into a wreck."

The Playland off 42nd & Broadway became the most booming fake I.D. franchise in the city. (This was the same location where I got my *Screw* press pass laminated every year.) Gals filled out a form at the counter, in English or Spanish, which was then promptly punched out along with a tiny Polaroid onto an official-looking $8 card. *Voilà*, they instantly came of age. A bartender's signal to pour. The girls left squealing, their freshly laminated Times Square I.D.'s at the ready, so they could go out club-hopping with their underage boyfriends and become drunk-driving fatalities.

"Let's go to a bar and get fucked up!" said a Puerto Rican tamale to her accomplice as they nervously scattered out of Playland one Friday. A new wave entered, affecting phony tough-girl façades. "Remember, you gotta be anonymous," said the ringleader to her girlfriends. Some lost their nerve at the entrance. Strangers to this funky Times Square locale—the Crossroads of the Third World—they were afraid they'd be stopped, questioned or arrested.

"You've got bumper crops of 'em coming in to Penn Station from Long Island," said Sammy, leering near the arcade entrance. "They have braver girlfriends who've done it first, told 'em how ya walk eight blocks up from Penn Station. This is the first time they've been to the city, they don't know anything about it, they're terrified of getting lost. They're doing something naughty, they think they're going out drinking in the city. After they buy the I.D., they look around a few blocks on the way back to Penn, but they won't find anything. Maybe they'll stop in McDonald's, the only thing they recognize. Then they run back to the train before dark. That's the whole I.D. Girl itinerary... Here's a new I.D. train from Great Neck," Sammy sputtered. "Look at King Bozo, the protector," he fizzled, over their young male chaperone.

"You can't overestimate their intelligence," explained Sammy, who rarely ever actually talked to one. "They'd be terrified if some older guy came on. There's no way to pick them up. They don't know the Palladium or Studio 54, you can't show them tickets, they've never heard of anything. You'd have to tell them something they can relate to in TV terms, like you're an actor trying to make it in New York, something they've seen on soaps. You're a photographer, you shoot rock bands like Kiss.

"Look, there's a group that just went shopping, they're dressed just like a commercial for The Gap." The girls giddily made themselves up in a photo booth mirror before their Polaroids were snapped. They wore leg-warmers and pre-faded jeans. "You also get your real *goyisha* Dirty Girls," he added, panting after a new group entered, dressed up to get messed up. "You might as well just pass out," sighed Sammy at his pervert's perch.

Just what makes them so appealing?

"Young sluts are adventurous," Sammy explained. "They don't smell, everything that comes out of them is sweet. Another few years, they start to stink."

Trains indeed pulled into Penn Station with new waves of I.D. Girls, images Sammy would toss and turn over. But he never had the gumption to approach them. He knew well the dangers of procuring jailbait, what with cops and plainclothes all over this corner.

"There goes Mr. Racial Ambiguity," he said of another chaperone, wishing it could be him.

The Palladium

I accompanied Sammy on his nightly rounds pursuing females by the thousand. He always returned home alone. An industrious fellow, Sammy's workaday world was permeated with endless ruses: "All my desires, the magazines, my movie company dealings, the exercise tapes, all stem from wanting to meet girls," said Sammy. "Every idea I have, every motivation, comes from my obsession with girls. I hate the Palladium, you'd never get me there unless I had a good friend giving a party or some business deal. It's repulsive, the music is sickening, the people are pathetic. It's only good for taking some dumb slut, using my invites to proposition some bimbo who has to wait on line and can't get in, but thinks it's hot shit to go. If I had a girlfriend, I'd never go there. My idea of a great evening is to go to Chinatown, order off-the-menu, run home, fuck her, then watch TV in bed while she tells me how great I am, how happy she is to be with me."

In his unkempt midtown apartment, littered with watches and hot Panasonic racing bike parts (not his), Sammy splashed on a handful of Paco Rabanne cologne, arranged his skinny black tie and donnned the rumpled black Brooks Brothers suit bought wholesale at Syms. He'd worn it all week. His black glasses were thick, as was the scent of Sen-Sen upon his breath. He popped two Valium. He carried a pocket full of special passes to upcoming oh-so-exclusive Palladium events, which he would flash to females. These were easily obtained by New York media mockeys like Sammy—whose primary vocation was nine-to-five editor of *Oui* magazine. We cabbed it to the Palladium.

Sammy also fronted a semi-legitimate office for exercise and swimsuit models seeking "print work." He called such prospective amateurs "Cargo Models."

"Fly 'em up for a look, if I'm not satisfied, send 'em back down in five minutes, it's only a few hours to Miami. Are you kidding, a modeling interview in New York, fashion capital of the world? They gab to all their friends, ba-bah-bah-bah, I'm flying to New York. This is the dream they see in every stupid TV show and magazine. But ya gotta ask to see *all* their pictures, not just skin photos. You wanna see their contact sheets, any stupid Polaroids. You can never tell from model pictures, they always look different, you tell 'em to Fed Ex all of 'em up quick. That way you can almost insure it won't be a total bust. Some models look terrible in person, they're great picture girls, not fuck girls. You need a front, an office with the bullshit, a secretary, sit there in a suit with phones ringing, a switchboard. A front is essential. Have 'em sign some stupid paper, makes it look important."

Two of his recent prospects were the Bai Sisters (pronounced *bah-hi*). Sometimes, he hired girls for an actual project, and in this case, he flew the Bai Sisters up for a video box cover. He arranged the shoot to take place at the Palladium. "It was terrible, a disaster session," Sammy moans. "The Bai Sisters have huge tits, like half watermelons. But I noticed they sagged a bit. They wore these huge wire bras that threw me off. Wouldn't let me touch 'em. Then the cameraman, the Palladium guy, the lighting guy, all went crazy as soon as the tits came out, started using every come-on they could think of. I demanded that they behave professionally, but they didn't and I couldn't control 'em. The sisters freaked out."

Sammy cut their visit short and sent the sisters back to Miami. He waved them off at the airport with a fond "Bah-hi!"

Outside the Palladium—AKA "the torture club"—were what Sammy called the "Line-Up Girls." Fifty of them, a bit older than the afternoon I.D. Girls, anxiously awaited selection for the honor of paying tonight's $10 entrance. Exclusion was the currency here. *Let's all get excited about parties to which we're uninvited*. Even more rarefied were Friday nights in the Mike Todd Room, where Ladies Only roamed. The backroom bar was known as Shescape. Not even Don Johnson and David Lee Roth were allowed to crash it.

Hundreds of chumps also braved the line each night, raising their hands like schoolboys, dying to get in. A few gutter blacks outside worked a tired scam ("I'm friends with the do' man, gimme twenty, I getcha in.") Sammy scanned the line. One chick, with boyfriend, struck up a friendly chat. When she asked how he acquired the special passes he flaunted, Sammy said, "We're bigshots from Hollywood." Sammy cemented a friendship with the Palladium's mailroom clerk for invitations. Feeling gregarious, he handed an extra pass to her. He conceded to me, "half your power is lost" at this point.

Sammy presented two passes to the goons at the door. Once inside, he set sight on his first prey at the bar. He took a seat next to the lass, but couldn't rev his engine for a few minutes. Finally, he hit with the lamest of come-ons: "What do you do for a living?"

She rolled her eyes and soured her expression without an answer. Three of her girlfriends strolled over, all oblivious to Sammy and myself. They were bubbling over about Boy George, who was in the Mike Todd Room upstairs. The four were trading off their one special pass to get in. Sammy volunteered that he possessed a pass and that "Boy George works" for his company.

"Would you like to meet Boy George?"

The sour-faced cutie became animated, suddenly interested as Sammy pulled out abundant Mike Todd Room passes. "Would you like me to introduce you?"

"Would you?!" she cried.

"No," said Sammy. "You could have said 'No Thanks,' or said you weren't interested politely. But you made a face and didn't answer. You sit there for twenty minutes in the Palladium then get upset when some guy approaches? Fuck you. Now I'm leaving to go up and see Boy George."

Sammy walked off smugly, having scored himself a rare TKO.

"They're just girls, sometimes out of high school," said Sammy, veering off to observe the female powder room exit. "Yet trying to land one requires all the cunning of a corporate takeover."

We walked upstairs where the cocktail party was in progress for Boy George. Boy and 500 of his very closest friends. There was an open bar manned by a butch bartender. "I like seeing barmaids in uniforms, with their hats tilted at a jaunty, subservient angle," said Sammy, from the side of his mouth. The butch bartender happened to be a charter member of Women Against Pornography, I would later learn. She spotted Sammy. As Grubman recovered our drinks to leave, a large bouncer laid a beefy hand on Sammy's shoulder. He ordered him to halt.

"I thought it was Open Bar?" cried Sammy.

"*You* pay," yelled the bartendress from behind the bar, eyeing him with venom.

The Mike Todd room had a more elite clientele, barring most Line-Up Girls. Remember, *exclusion* was what made the Palladium's engine tick. While models flitted about us, Sammy imparted this theory: "Their whole career is trading their body one way or another to get ahead. What's modeling but a life of what they think is glamour, meeting famous people, traveling, show biz? So they're another form of hooker, basically.

"Unfortunately, a beautiful girl is the highest status symbol in the world. I don't care what car you have, what clothes, how much money. When you walk in the room with a beautiful girl, even if you look like a slob in jeans, everyone thinks you must be hot shit, you must know something… 'Look at that old fuck with the models, he must be the owner of a famous design company.'"

A Continental chap named Fritz was Special Events coordinator at the Palladium. Sammy didn't fancy Euro Trash. Every one of the regulars here who seemed to score with models was named Lars, Horst, Otto, Helmut, Hans, Sven, Rudolph or Da-vid. A Venezuelan beauty queen, whose airfare to New York was paid for by one of Sammy's ventures, escaped his clutches. Instead, she made her way through every Tom, Dick and Adolf here at the Mike Todd Room. Fritz, a high-roller with the broads, let out a cosmic sigh of cigarette smoke.

"I'm so sick of zeze hard, stressed-out professional chicks with zere insane schedules," he told Sammy.

"How'd you do with the Venezuelan?" asked Sammy.

"Ze girl takes so much coke—not just enough to get high, enough to kill somebody," complained frazzled Fritz. "She orders sushi at the restaurant—every single piece on ze menu. Zen she doesn't touch any of it. I hear her doing bulimia in my bathroom. She *j'accuse* me of trying to poison her with sediment at the bottom of the wine. She call my penis 'Mr. Droopy.' She hit her female roommate over the head with a bottle during an argument, so she can't go home. She crashes in my bed at 7 A.M. and sleep the sleep of ze dead. She awake at 4:30 in the afternoon and demands tea and caviar on crackers. So I take her to Zabar's. She wants the

$110 tin of caviar. Oh, no, I say, you can have the $20 crab meat. We went back to my apartment. She washes her hair over ze sink in Evian. Zen she takes three hours putting on makeup, blow-drying, doing ze hair. Zen back out to the clubs for same routine. You want her back?"

"No thanks," said Sammy. "What do I need with another night of horror and humiliation."

Fritz said hello to Mike Florio, the Stud, who was also working the Mike Todd Room. "The reason I'm not in a band," he told Fritz, "is I know I'd be goin' through fifteen or twenty girls a night. I like to keep it down to four or five."

"I know what you mean," agreed Fritz.

Sammy observed the Stud casting out his own line and reelin' 'em in. "I've made a study of this for years," Sammy explained. "The most fucked-up jerks are fucking the hottest sluts. You have five seconds to catch their attention before they walk away, so anything you say is going to sound ridiculous. You have to scream, so you use words that trigger their interest, like 'millionaire' or 'MTV producer,' mention a few dumb celebrities. That's why they get all dressed up and slutty and come to the city. They're tired of shlubs from Brooklyn, some plumber asking them out on a date. The media has created this whole fantasy you already have to work from. Mention the trigger word, the fantasy of jets around the world, the Rolling Stones, fur coats, coke. Their biggest dream is to come to New York and meet someone in a limo they think is glamorous, who'll rescue them from selling nail polish behind the Woolworth's counter. *They're interested in the sizzle, not the steak."*

Sammy began handing out his professional business card. He gave out hundreds a week to girls "in the field."

"All my life," he explained, "I've tried to get girls without success. Finally I figured out how."

The card reads:

> *YOU HAVE BEEN SELECTED as a potential model for OUI Magazine. To arrange for a test shooting and an interview, please call Monday to Friday, 10AM to 4PM.*

About one in twenty might call, and maybe one in fifty would actually show for an appointment.

"The Palladium is too chic to tell men not to use the ladies room," said Sammy, staking out the long line. "Sometimes I think of giving my passes to burly Negroes on the street, with the provision they all file in and take a dump. It would be interesting to see the ladies' reactions."

I finally tried tossing out a few pickup lines myself, Sammy Grubman-style. Sure enough, the girls kept walking. "He's a millionaire!" Sammy shouted after one. She hesitated a moment, then her friend grabbed her arm to pull her along. A ringleader emerged from each clique to steer the prettiest or most amenable girl away from Sammy. "Sure, walk away. We're casting a major movie!" Sammy reverberated, as two bolted away from him like frightened does. Then two chicks in a lounge chair accused Sammy of eavesdropping. He asked if he could buy them drinks.

"We have boyfriends upstairs."

"Well, if they're giving you any trouble, let us know."

"They give us love," said one girl cheerily, and both headed for the stairs.

"Your boyfriends are garbage men," posited Sammy. He became more indignant over every fellow he saw accompanying a beauty. "There goes Mr. Bozo. I'd like to pull down that guy's pants and humiliate him in front of his girlfriend," said Sammy, voicing his own worst fear. "Oh, ugggh, there goes one, you might as well pass out."

Thousands of single chumps paid twenty bucks to enter and six bucks per drink. And every one of them sounded like a schmuck, you couldn't *not* sound like a schmuck. Even a Nobel Laureate like Jonas Salk or Isaac Singer or Senator Daniel Patrick Moynahan wouldn't have a chance in hell, they'd be spat upon here. But Sammy was leading the League of Schmucks with the lowest batting average I'd ever seen.

Shark's Office

The next morning Sammy and I visited Shark's agency, Tops Models. The Stud was also there. Catalogs from the real top model agencies were splayed across his desk. Tear sheets of models whom Shark had never met were ripped from fashion magazines, affixed to walls and sticking out of files. The telephone was on the ring "from the coast."

During business hours, Shark wore his coyote fur and cowboy hat with stained bell bottoms circa 1967. There was always the suspicious air of a colostomy bag about. Sammy believed Shark wore one, but never dared ask.

The other night, Shark and the Stud were rejected at Stringfellow's entrance as *persona non grata*. Sammy suggested Shark call the crack hotline on the doorman. Shark turned stone sober: "I don't drop a dime on anyone," said Shark. "That's no joke. I don't even wanna associate with a man who jokes like that."

But Shark did associate with Grubman and his shabby model agency steered dozens of girls Grubman's way for "interviews."

"All I do is sit at home," said Sammy. "You'd never in a hundred years figure such an easy way to meet girls. I've got 'em comin' right to the door, don't have to lift a finger... God takes care of men like me this way."

"It ain't God, buddy," explained Shark. "Anyone good enough to give my girls work is good enough to fuck 'em."

Occasionally the more experienced models who came to Shark's office would stand up and yell, "Fake! Fraud!" then bolt out the door. But most prospects stayed through their interviews. Shark would take on almost anybody. He delivered soulful, eye-to-eye pep talks to secretaries and A&P checkout girls as they left his office with a printout of modeling leads—usually pilfered from that week's *BackStage* magazine.

The Stud, decked out in his cockpit jacket, was headed for a model's convention at the New York Hilton. All the best cunt on the planet would be there, he said, licking his chops. He was aiming for Paulina Porizkova tonight.

"I don't care how beautiful she is," said Shark. "Someday her husband or someone is gonna get tired of fucking her. I think you got a shot, pal."

And then Shark looked me over, as I was initiated into the club. "You wanna gamble with top models," he said, "you get bigger payoffs, or bigger rejections. You gotta remember, as consolation, when these girls reach thirty they start to fall apart, they're going to spend the next forty years looking terrible with nobody paying attention to them. Meanwhile, you'll be on the rise, Jack."

"I take great pleasure in realizing that," said Sammy.

The Stud himself had a hard time last night at the Palladium. He denied botching it with Ford model Meg Calendar.

"You struck out," came Shark, "you hit the mud with her, buddy."

"I talked to her for ten minutes."

"That's right, buddy, all you did was *talk*."

"What?! I'll eat her brains out. I'll fuck the shit outta her! When *I* want to!" yelled the Stud, jabbing his finger.

"She'll spit you out like dirt!" came Shark. Disgusted, the Stud downed his beer and headed out for the convention, slamming the door.

"There goes the consummate professional," said Shark of his protégé, shaking his head, bemused. "Don't ever underestimate him. He's a 15th round knockout artist. Bastard'll probably fuck Paulina, Vendela *and* Helena. Doze chicks'll be all over him like a cheap suit. He's lethal. Michael can get any girl he wants, girls who've turned down hundreds of guys. The later it gets in the night, the more the killer instinct comes out. This is like Leonardo da Vinci designing a ship. This is like Michelangelo painting a chapel."

Then he chuckled knowingly. "Except Meg Calendar… I dunno."

Meg Calendar was the crown jewel in Shark's stable. "Boner City," said Sammy, leafing through her portfolio, wincing in pain. An absolute 10, she made the rest of Shark's stable resemble, in Sammy's estimation, "a pig sty." She was a Ford model who maintained some mysterious allegiance to Shark from her early days. Meg still sought Shark's career advice, perhaps out of pity. Somehow, Shark procured Meg a small part in a *Miami Vice* episode, along with bikini walk-ons in a few Hollywood movies. He kept her Ford Agency portfolio front and center on his desk.

I skimmed through it. Every pose was haughty, superior, sophisticated. Height 5'8", size 8, bust 34D, waist 24, hips 34. She had a blonde mane teased around her forehead like a lion. But apparently Meg Calendar was too cold for anybody to *like*. Too fabulous for her own good. The only thing people viewed her as was a goddess. Shark showed a clipping of her from last week's *Post*, posing with Fabio, her male counterpart, at the Palladium. If a cartoon thinking balloon were to accompany the photo, it would say, "Don't even *think* about it, Fab."

"Diz chick don't need Fabio," said Shark. "All she's gotta do is stand in front of a mirror and masturbate."

"When I first saw her I turned my head away," Grubman confessed, "'cause I knew I'd feel deprived the rest of my life. Why go on living? When I see her pictures, I know I'll feel sick for years for not being able to get her."

"I walked up to Menahem Golan [of Golan-Globus Productions] at a party with her," recalled Shark. "He cleared people away and treated me like royalty. 'Mr. Golan,' I says, 'I'd like to send you her pictures and résumé.' He takes out a pen and writes down my number and everything, says to make sure I send 'em pronto.

"Lemme tell ya about diz chick, okay," continued Shark. "She's the most ruthlessly ambitious model I've ever known. She's a stormtrooper of ambition. She eats up guys and spits them out. Lesbians try for her, just like construction workers. As a matter of fact, there's only one guy who might have a shot at her."

"Who's that?" I asked.

"You, my friend."

"Me?"

"You could have her. Meg Calendar can be in your bed. But only if you follow my instructions. I know diz chick like the back of my hand. She don't need sex with nobody, she just looks in the mirror and comes. She's a narcissist."

Shark did seem to have some sort of odd past with the model, who long since left his humble agency for Ford. She was a glacial tower all right, and wouldn't look twice at another human being unless they were an A-list movie director. Yet she still called him, the lowest modeling agent in New York, even had lunch with him between $10,000 assignments.

"Lemme tell ya 'bout diz chick. She pisses ice water. I know guys with a little money who hang around model agencies, lookin' to take 'em out. They don't even try. Meg is high-stakes poker, pal. You're playin' cards with Amarillo Slim. You'll never be the one to fuck her. She'll fuck you."

"Literally or figuratively?"

"Both… Okay, lemme tell ya how ya gotta deal with diz chick," said Shark. His voice lowered, as if imparting the most classified military instructions. "Ya gotta bullshit a little the first time, it's the only way one of dese models will see ya. Do you have any movie contacts we could start with?"

As a matter of fact I had, sort of. For starters, a couple of old friends up at *Saturday Night Live*. I occasionally attended rehearsals. In a few weeks the guest host was going to be Francis Ford Coppola.

"Francis?" said Shark. "That's perfect! She'd kill to be in one of his movies. I'll call her right away."

Shark called Meg on the spot, told her he's got this good friend he'd like to fix her up with who's tight with *SNL*. He said who the guest host was going to be and that the friend could bring her up to rehearsals in a few weeks, introduce her to Francis, then maybe attend the cast party after the show airs.

"You're rollin', buddy," said Shark, hanging up the phone. "When you meet her, just tell her *Francis*," he instructed. "Don't even say his last name. She'll know Francis. If you say his last name, you'll blow the whole deal. You let her meet Francis, get a few drinks into diz bitch, don't take much to get 'er drunk, and buddy, she'll fuck you so long and hard you'll have to fight your way up for air. I won't even hear back from you for weeks, you'll be so busy. She's got Beatty, Nicholson, Michael Douglas callin' her every day, desperate to get in her pants. None of 'em scored. But they ain't no match for you, Josh, so long as you follow what I say."

Sammy had been speechless but now felt compelled to offer his own expertise. "Ya gotta pretend you do this every day at *Saturday Night Live*," he coached. "Like it's nothing, you're a big shot."

"Remember," said Shark, "all she wants is to become a movie star."

"And if she gets it, then what's she gonna do?"

"That's a philosophical question," replied the wizened model agent.

Sammy's Office

In Sammy's universe, he faced opposition on three fronts: Women Against Pornography; lawsuits from enraged parents of wayward girls who'd come to New York to do porn; and Stephanie Mason, his stiffest competition, who edited a handful of fetish publications. At this moment, they were both working for the same company.

"I hate her," said Sammy of the tall female editor down the hall. They competed for girls. They sent jailbait prospects each other's way. They were both out to sink each other's ships. Stephanie was a master pornographer, also considered a goddess by many admirers. A witch at getting girls *nekkid*. A female Svengali at the seduction game necessary to keep the pipeline of puss happening. (Which paid most gals, incidentally, a measly few hundred bucks per photo shoot.) She had a greater grasp of the male sexual point of view than any man in the business and could hold her own with any misogynist.

"Check out this cover shot," said Stephanie, behind her desk. She displayed one of her ass magazines featuring the derrière of an aging porn starlet. She opened the photo spread. "Look how her asshole remains perfectly clefted, which is amazing considering the multitudes who've fucked her up the butt," observed Stephanie, with scientific detachment. "And she never needed lubricant. I asked how she did this and she said it was just natural excitement. She gets wet there."

Half Amazon, half intellectual, Mason oversaw five titles a month, each a masturbatory bible for a different fetish. Current mags she edited catered to asshole obsessions, fake jailbait and feet.

"I won't run photos like these," she said, scrupling at a box of color slides on the desk. "I showed them to a proctologist friend of mine. He explained the girl, who's a crack addict, had a prolapsed anus. A very bad trend in the industry."

Stephanie Mason's girlie copy resounded with psychodrama. The fantasy personalities she bestowed upon photos of unwitting nude models were sweet, sticky, psychodramatic and charged with girlie frustrations. ("Hi, my name is Linda, and I love going around sucking out used scumbags.") It's speculated that several young lovelies committed suicide as a result of reading their own girlie copy.

Stephanie presented a vibrating plastic tongue. She sent out dozens of them as Christmas favors to older fans, whose own tongues had perhaps lost steam. She loved awkward proletarian porn, amateur Kodak moments from heartland Americans who fell for the porn hack con. She received hundreds of letters. She opened every one, her favorite part of the job.

"Look at this one," she said, unfolding a letter from one of her regular readers—a Queens janitor who signed his correspondence as the Monistat 7 Man. "He worships at the altar of yeast infections."

She unveiled a set of photos from her latest brainstorm, introduced in her newest title, *Untouchable*. "Locker Room Dare," in which college girls are challenged to snap one another naked for publication. The first contacts are hot indeed—two nifty chicks surreptitiously posing at their basketball team lockers. Stephanie receives the film rolls fresh from the girls' cameras for her own smut laboratory to develop.

In the cynical, insincere racket of newsstand sex magazines, run by formula hacks whose contempt for the "readership" echoes with every cliché, Stephanie stood out as genuine. She understood and empathized with male sexual obsessions. Readers were taught to wear their perversions as badges of honor, to shed their debilitating embarrassment. Monthly essays espoused masturbation as the ultimate safe sex. Fetishes were nature's way of diverting DNA from reproduction in an overcrowded world. Did excessive masturbation further separate people from human contact? Wasn't it harder to come back to earth for a relationship? These questions were overlooked, because one thing obsessive masturbation led to was larger magazine sales. There's nothing more stale than last month's pornography.

Mason was forever on the prowl in search of feet. She was recently ejected from the biggest topless bar in New York, trying to recruit talent. She asked male acquaintances at social events whether she could view their wives' feet. Would they consider having them photographed? Apologetically, she was forever checking women's toe spreads, arches, seeking sharply defined angularity as opposed to stubby or corny features. She considered her own feet lacking in angular grace. She used great photographic care in striking the most flattering pose for her own monthly leg snapshots, which accompanied editorials. Like silent screen stars knew how to angle their faces, Stephanie knew which side of her heel was her good side. She loved dressing up and posing her models at photoshoots, like a big girl playing with demented Barbie dolls.

But, like Sammy, she was also known to do subtle, not-so-nice things.

In walked Yvette Venice, a veteran stripper, here for a model interview. She sat before Stephanie's desk draping her fox fur behind the chair. Stephanie glared at the portfolio. "God… you're old," blurted out Stephanie. "I'm thirty-two. You must be at least ten years older than me, right?"

Yvette was only in her mid-thirties, hoping to play younger. She squirmed in discomfort but kept her composure. "A lady never tells," said Yvette.

Though Stephanie would find a place for Yvette's pictures somewhere, she kept playing the cruelty card. "These must be your swan song shots, right? How many kids have you had? Be honest."

Yvette never had any kids, at least none that she can remember. This interview stung.

Stephanie Mason learned the joys of her trade from her mentor, the late Pete Fox, another enemy of Sammy's. Stephanie and Pete were once inseparable, founding several sex magazines together in the 1970s. They invented the gonzo style of editor participation.

Pete would go to work on new recruits that he flew in to New York from Southern trailer parks. He humiliated prospective models from the get-go. Like Sammy, Fox's eagle eye strained to find a stretch mark, a scar, evidence of motherhood, anything to play upon an insecurity. He knew how to zero in on a fault: "So, where'd you get the nosejob? Is your tit tuck starting to sag again?"

"C'mon, Peter, that's not nice to say," came Stephanie, playing good cop. If a girl was willing to put up with this, if her self-esteem was that low—and most girls were masochistic—Pete worked that fault for all it was worth. Of course, girls took negative criticism to heart. No matter how beautiful the girl was, if she stayed, he knew she regarded herself as no better than a sack of shit. When the recruits first laid eyes on this skinny-assed, alkie editor, who looked like Willie Nelson's grandfather, they'd think, "Oh, my god, I'll *never* fuck *him*."

Fox resembled an aging "Hell No, We Won't Go" hippie from 1969—which he was. He wore a gray ponytail, torn blue jeans, a biker bandanna. Once, when he was editor of *Outlaw Biker*, he was confronted by a motorcycle gang at a rally. Fox couldn't name a single part of the Harley. He walked off in humiliation before the laughing bikers, revealing himself as a total dilettante.

Fox's predatory talent lay with the girls. He never came on at first. He waited until breaking down what little confidence the maidens possessed. Here they were, flown all the way into the Big Apple from some Missouri pig farm at the expense of a national magazine, thirsty for a few crumbs of recognition and a compliment or two for the only tangible assets they had—their bodies. At the end of Fox's procurement sessions, he'd invite a few girls back into his office. Then he seized the moment, holding aloft several mockup covers with their photos attached: "I can put either *you*, *you* or *you* on the cover. It's up to all of *you—you* make the decision.

"Now… Who goes home with me?"

That was Fox's legacy to Stephanie, before he dropped dead of a heart attack in his late forties. Now Stephanie ran the whole ship by herself, and was quite gifted.

"I guess we could put you in our new *Over 40* magazine," Stephanie told

Yvette, finally offering a concession. "But don't call us, we'll call you."

The aging stripper trudged on. And soon after retired.

Down the hall, Sammy took pains to avoid contact with Stephanie in their workaday environment. Sometimes they made cold contact when passing the reception desk or water cooler. Stephanie got Sammy in trouble recently by clipping a particularly bad review of *Oui* which she made sure their publisher in Connecticut saw. A "horsey" woman, Sammy dismissed her as an "ugly bitch who blabbers too much."

Sammy dressed like a stock analyst in a suit and tie every morning. Gynecological slides were scattered across his desk.

"We're waiting for this one to turn eighteen," he whined, passing over contact sheets with a loupe. A shoot with a seventeen-year-old brunette sucking dildos. She had that dumb "sloe-eyed" expression that Sammy so covets—eyes rolled up in swallowing abandon, only the whites showing.

Grubman suffered a hard lesson with this exotic beauty. The mother presented fake I.D. when she accompanied her daughter to the office for Sammy's mandatory "test shots." Sammy went bonkers over the girl, got her oiled up and soon she was deep-throating a veiny, black rubber dildo before the camera.

Five months later, when the photo set hit the stands, the mother filed a $1-million lawsuit. If that ain't entrapment. It became one of Sammy's ongoing headaches, but one he planned to avenge. Sammy had a second, even dirtier photo shoot with the girl, which he intended to publish after her eighteenth birthday.

All kinds of trailer-trash mother-daughter scams befall poor schmucks in the girlie business. Although the lawsuit named only Sammy, he was a smokescreen for the real publisher. There were a dozen men's magazine goniffs in New York, each with their own independent second-rate empires. None were proud frontmen like Hefner, Guccione, Flynt or Goldstein—who made up the frontline, the Detroit of sex. Sammy fronted for the shadowy, second-string imitators. Ashamed of their work, these businessmen remained hidden behind layers of paperwork. They hid behind shell corporations with noble-sounding names, like Knight Publications. One secretive smut king stirred up the ire of environmentalists by building a heliport on his pristine Connecticut land, scattering geese and ducks every time he coptered in from the city.

Sammy had worked for most of them. They saw in Sammy a younger version of themselves. They would perhaps like to have done badder things on a grander scale, but like Sammy, they all lacked the balls to be murderous. So they settled on being shrewd, deceptive, eager to cheat—characteristics they also admired in Sammy. They were actually no different than publishers of most mainstream publications, maybe better. If Sammy was sly enough to embezzle a few shekels from the budget, then by God, these men wanted him fronting their operations.

Sammy's Childhood Heroes

Sammy Grubman's personality was shaped by the pawnbroking business. Pawnbrokers were his heroes growing up. His mother didn't love him and his father gave him beatings. "Not on the head, not on the head!" Mrs. Grubman screamed at Sammy's father as he flailed away at little Sammy. Sammy's only solace after school was retreating to Simpson's Hockshop to revel in the company of old Jewish pawnbrokers and their fabulous mockey cons.

Sammy's favorite memory was when a black hustler came rushing into Simpson's demanding a hundred bucks for some jewel. Old Mr. Simpson laughed, said it wasn't worth a tenth of that. The black dude then asked for $50. The pawnbroker said forget it, it was worthless, a fake. Maybe he'd pay five bucks. The black guy left in a huff. But a minute later he walked back through the door, asking $25. The pawnbroker, with great impatience, totally disinterested, said he'd give the guy ten bucks. The black guy took it.

The moment the black guy left, the broker was on the phone. A group of diamond district merchants from 47th Street with loupes arrived ten minutes later. They gasped when they saw the gem, *oohed* and *ahhed*. They offered twenty grand.

What impressed Sammy was how the broker Jewed the black guy down to $10, risking a twenty grand loss. It was all a game, the spirit of it being to see how much you could get for nothing. The broker sensed the black guy's desperation, knew he'd be back in a minute. And he derived his satisfaction by acquiring the gem for a sawbuck, rather than even giving the guy a hundred bucks, still a ridiculous fraction of its worth.

"Why not give the guy a few hundred—it would still be ripping him off?" I asked Sammy.

Sammy recoiled, as if I'd missed the whole point, the beauty of it. "The guy stole the gem anyway, why should he *not* get ripped off?

Sammy's sunken eyes were like loupes, the kind used by jewelers and by sex magazine editors who pored over contact sheets. He sold hot watches to magazine publishers—notorious old *schtarkers* of the newsstand wars, like Myron Fass, Murry Traub, Carl Ruderman, Harvey Shapiro. And that is how he first came to meet them. From selling them watches. They saw their younger selves in Sammy, a shrewd throwback Jew, the kind they didn't make anymore. They hired him to helm their skin divisions, the second-rate tits-and-assers that were last-choice impulse buys on the newsstand, after the masturbator had already gone through that month's *Playboy*, *Penthouse* or *Hustler*. Sammy would siphon off a thousand for himself, scrimping and cheating his way through the cut-rate monthly budgets of each rag. When bosses caught him raiding the cookie jar they only admired him more. Sammy would rip off a writer here, a nude model there. Just like a pawnbroker.

"You have to get on your knees to get paid by Sammy Grubman," moaned one photographer to Shark.

"Lower," said Shark.

Sammy also fenced off bicycles. He'd pay ghetto thieves $20 for freshly stolen bikes at the corner of St. Mark's Place, then resell them to shops.

After several weeks in the bike black market, he learned to take apart a new Panasonic Japanese bike, then put it back together with cheaper cannibalized parts—so he could resell the bike, and then the parts. Grubman made regular visits to city marshal dispossession auctions with his ancient pawnbroker cronies. They acquired stereos, TVs, tape recorders. Sammy had his own clique of old-Jew customers, including the sex publishers, who bought the merchandise from Grubman, all of them satisfied that the merchandise came at the price of someone's loss. Sammy derived great pleasure in knowing the stuff was stolen.

One of the oldest pawnbrokers, Sam Katz, once advertised himself as "The Honestest Man in New York." He taught Sammy the secret "scratch test" for gold. When Sammy was a child, Katz took him into the vaults harboring fine jewelry, sterling silver, athletic trophies pawned by down-on-their-luck sports champs. He was a star pupil of Katz's, who'd taught him how to appraise gems, watches, estimate the worth of stereos and TVs, a jack-of-all-merchandise appraiser. Sammy appraised girls the same way—notating blemishes, pimpled asses, cellulite and future wrinkles on their naked bodies. He was never really able to enjoy any of this merchandise himself—either the stereos or the women—just appraise and resell it. The enjoyment was in the turnover, making money he would sock away and take to the grave.

Sammy was currently editorial chief at *Oui*, and the conceptual editor of endless one-shot specials. An *idea man*. He didn't bother with nuts-and-bolts copy editing. Other editors took care of the mechanics while Sammy played the field. Guys like associate editor Michael Melville. A nerdy sort who never participated in any sexual endeavors of the magazine, Melville did line editing, proofreading, took care of punctuation. But judging by endless typos and grammatical mistakes in any 1980s issue of *Oui*, one might gather the proofreader was a bit distracted.

According to Sammy, he was just dumped by a blind girlfriend after he bought her a stereo which she considered the wrong brand. So he went back to dating a "welfare Negress with three kids," says Sammy, one who stole the furniture out of Melville's apartment before she last left him.

"Somehow," said Sammy, "the Negress got Michael to pose for some weird pictures. Pictures of Michael standing there examining his own penis under a microscope. The Negress convinced Michael that this was so funny they should make prints and send some to his friends. Then she convinces him to send them to his own mother, father and relatives. So, reluctantly, he did. Now the parents want to have him committed to a mental institution."

Meg at SNL

"This is beautiful," said Shark. "'Meet at the NBC security desk,' they love those kind of words. 'Checkpoints' at NBC, that's great, ya have to keep it a professional thing the first date."

I arranged a visit to a *Saturday Night Live* rehearsal the week Francis Ford Coppola hosted. Several friends on staff at the show made this easy. Sammy and Shark coached me over the phone like I was pinch-hitting in the playoffs, coming off the bench to replace the Stud as cleanup batter. Everybody, it seemed, wanted Meg Calendar to get a good stiff banging, maybe for the first time. Then they could vicariously enjoy hearing the details of conquest. Shark called Meg throughout the day, repeating the "Francis, Francis" mantra. As if the fix was in for a part in his next film.

"Diz girlz got Don Johnson callin' her every day, Michael Douglas callin' every night, she's confused, she called me cryin' yesterday morning, wonders if all they want is to get in her pants. But now you got it over them. Ya take diz bitch to *SNL*, get her a few drinks, then a few more drinks, till she's drunk, and you can fuck the shit outta her all night. I'm the closest friend she's got, I know. Just follow my instructions."

"Make her be a mercenary," adds Sammy, pitching his own strategy. "She thinks you're a big shot. But if Francis sits down next to her to discuss movie stuff, she'll walk off with his 300-pound belly. If you forget that and think she likes you for your looks or 'cause you're a nice guy—if you let down your guard and reveal your desire—you've blown it. You're merely her liaison of the moment into the world of movie directors."

Grubman remained awestruck over Meg. "I'd be a nervous wreck in your shoes," he admitted. He once asked Shark what he could cook up to get Meg, but Shark said Fuhgeddaboudit, Jack, you don't have the guns to deal with diz chick, she's outta your league. It was the movie biz, and nothing but, that got her attention.

On the day of the *SNL* rehearsal, mid-week, I received a morning call from Shark. "Remember," he reiterated, "just say Francis to her, that's the key word. Don't say Francis Ford Coppola, that'll fuck it up, just Francis. That's music to her ears. She loves Francis, she's totally mesmerized by diz guy, she almost met him once, she'll do anything to get in one of his movies. But make it sound familiar. Just say, 'Francis'll be there.' Then call me back in a coupla weeks when you come up for air."

Shark caught his breath a moment, showing fatherly concern toward my welfare. "Just remember one thing with diz girl… Don't ever let down your guard. It's easy to fall for her, surrounded by all her beauty and largesse. Then you let down your guard and get hit by a right cross and it's lights out. She's a maneater."

Shark was spent. His work was done. Working diligently for several weeks to secure this event, he could now bow out and let nature take its course. Thereafter, with Meg on my arm at parties, according to Shark and Sammy, every big shot in the room would stop in their tracks; women would act catty and jealous, important people would gravitate toward me, anxious to exchange numbers, to ask me for her pictures and portfolio. This was the type of pimpish power that Sammy and Shark craved more than anything in life.

That afternoon, right on time, my doorbell rang. "Meg Calendar," sang the voice at the intercom.

"Want to come up?"

"No." I went down, exited the elevator and saw her in person for the first time through the lobby window. Her photos did her a disservice. She was a goddess, blindingly beautiful, the effect of which could not be experienced from any photograph. She wore what might be considered a tastefully expensive ensemble. A scarf wove through her flowing blonde mane, impossible curls bouncing with vitality. Eyes of charismatic blue sparkled, creamy flesh radiating health. Her cleavage revealed just enough bosom to inspire wonder, yet not be offensive at a PTA meeting.

For some reason, I wore a turquoise V-neck sweater as a shirt. I'd never worn it this way before and felt like a schmuck from the get-go. I hailed us a cab. Meg allowed me to open the door and stepped in. I introduced myself. Slightly annoyed, she felt obliged to mumble a few words back.

"I've been with the Ford Agency since I was fourteen. Now I'm twenty-three," she confessed, with a sorrowful shrug. "I looked exactly the same when I was fourteen as I do now—built the same."

"Wow, you must really be… used to yourself."

"Well, now I have a few wrinkles."

There were no wrinkles. She began to tell of her background. She was the only white girl at an all-black school in Virginia. A tomboy who learned to fight. It was hard to imagine Meg ever being remotely boyish. However, I jumped on this odd coincidence. I'd once been the only white kid at a black school on Long Island. For an exhilarating moment I imagined we'd bond on this. But she didn't hear me and continued her own story. She met Shark when she was a child. Somehow, her parents trusted Shark to escort her to a football game where they sat at the sidelines of the visiting team. The visiting team was the New York Jets and Shark was part of their entourage. She never knew in what capacity. But it was a special day and they'd been friends ever since.

As she spoke I inhaled complicated layers of her fragrance. She wore only a hint of perfume, but more than that, Meg exuded some hormonal charge that touched nerves I never knew existed. Enclosed in the back of a funky cab, her scent touched off sensations of early childhood when the taste of ice cream or the scent of a Christmas tree was brand new.

"Francis'll be there," I blurted out, as I was coached.

Meg fell silent. The rest of our ride was silent.

Outside 30 Rock and once inside the cavernous RCA Building art deco lobby, the heads of male pedestrians turned. Meg had learned to act oblivious. But I found the attention terribly unnerving. She couldn't walk a city street without hearing catcalls, whistles, hoots. Jayne Mansfield heard the same on walks, but she craved it. I imagined the pressure some poor boyfriend or future husband would have to endure. Meg Calendar was possibly the most beautiful woman on earth which, by definition, made her a sociopath. I was walking with a freak.

Hardened NBC stage crew—Local 1 union palookas used to seeing beautiful women every day—dropped their jaws as we strode past. A group of electricians led us through the labyrinthine corridors toward Studio 8C to make sure we got to the right destination. Every time I looked over at her face I grew weaker, tripping over words. I searched for any sign of imperfection I might focus on to dull her effect. Voluptuousness was out, so perhaps this is what held her back in the industry. She had none of the heroin-faced teenage waif look currently in vogue.

We reached Studio 8C. There was a bustle of activity. Camera men, sound men, electricians, lighting crew, set builders, musicians, writers, directors and cast members. It appeared they were putting together a show. If you so much as touched a mike boom, you risked physical ejection by the National Association of Broadcast Engineers and Technicians. Meg scanned the terrain, taking it all in and she came alive. This was the promised land, the road to stardom. Camera men were notating shots, actors blocked out scenes as grips laid down masking tape for position. Her cold heart warmed even more the moment she stepped on center stage. She began asking questions to a makeup assistant. Meg had now ditched me as her escort.

In the middle of the hurly-burly was Francis Ford Coppola. Or should I say, Francis. He looked like a bearded slob. But Meg homed in, distancing herself from me. Fly, Meg, fly.

An extra on the show, some struggling soap opera actor who'd auditioned with her once, stopped by to chat. He approached with manly confidence.

Meg stood by a popcorn machine looking positively perverse. Hundreds of kernels bubbled over the top in fluffy buds. She helped herself, pumping melted butter over the popcorn with a cockeyed look of satisfaction. The extra left a minute later looking like a woeful bloodhound.

Meg and I finally took chairs near Francis. As he rehearsed some sketch, she kept sliding her chair away from me, a few inches more toward the hirsute director. Each time she laughed insincerely at a cast member's joke, or touched one's arm, a stab of anguish shot through my gut, like I was losing rope.

But the cast of *Saturday Night Live* wouldn't really give her the time of day. They were into some advanced stage of anti-glamour, and turned up their noses at models. So did Francis, apparently, who didn't acknowledge her presence. Only stagehands came close for a sniff.

We rode the elevator to the lobby, where Meg abruptly shook my hand, offered a tight goodbye smile and was off to hail her own taxi. I cursed my turquoise sweater.

The next morning I debriefed Shark, who absorbed the information like a general. "We're picking up our wounded on stretchers, reforming our battle plans," he said. "Remember, you're in the league with Babe Ruth, Jack."

I told Shark how Meg always kept five paces away from me.

"Five feet away?" said Shark. "Ain't that better havin' a super knockout, just five feet away—than showin' up with some everyday dog fawning all over you. You walked into *Saturday Night Live* with Meg Calendar! But this is gonna take a little more of a push than I first thought. What was that other thing you mentioned?"

"The cast party?"

"The cast party!" yelled Shark. "That's perfect! You take her back to that *SNL* cast party on Saturday, sit her next to Francis when he's hot off the air—buddy, you'll have her like a hole in one."

"Won't she wonder why the hell I'm doing this for her?"

"No," said Shark, "that's the thing with narcissists. She's so self-centered and obsessed with herself, she thinks everyone else is too."

"I dunno."

"You've got to get her to that cast party," said Shark.

The Exercise Tape

Sammy had his hands in a few extra-curricular operations, one of them called The Exercise Tape. It purported to be a clearinghouse for models needed in the burgeoning exercise video market. Every out-of-work celeb was a fitness guru all of a sudden, from Marie Osmond to Debbie Reynolds. They were the latest snake oil salesmen. In Sammy's case, as always, there was a small degree of legitimacy to the operation. He did occasionally land girls in minor modeling jobs. Ads for The Exercise Tape appeared in community papers and on bulletin boards and telephone booths.

The ruse took place at a respectable-looking midtown office. Sammy and his partners kept a professional production atmosphere, with editing equipment, video cameras on tripods and a white backdrop. Even a receptionist.

"A lot of these girls are great at camouflaging their flaws from ten feet away," said Sammy. "You get a big boner, but on close examination they look terrible." If a girl came in wearing a floppy dress, Sammy instantly knew something's amiss. "If they're not showing it, they're hiding something."

A typical appointment at The Exercise Tape went as such: A toothy, disheveled girl entered who had no chance of getting a modeling gig whatsoever. She was accompanied by a short Italian boyfriend with a pompadour and a black eye. Their car exploded on the Jersey turnpike, drenching her clothes. Sammy was mortified. The poor girl was too nervous to answer questions during a videotaped Q&A. She had a bad smile, bad body, terrible speaking voice.

"Do you exercise?" asked Sammy, off camera.

"I give my boyfriend a workout every night." She was given the obligatory five minutes for showing up, then thanked. In such instances, Sammy didn't even waste tape, he secretly unloaded the camera.

"I hate it when they come with a boyfriend," explained Sammy. "It's the wrong way to audition. See the way that moron planted himself near the camera? When this happens at my apartment, I usher them out in two minutes. Never trust the boyfriends. Sometimes they bring a Negro, you never know if he's coming back to rob you. This was the biggest night of their year, those two from exit 39 on the Jersey Turnpike. They think they did a big New York audition, now they'll probably tell all their friends she's being considered for rock videos. Can you imagine the vile sex they have?"

"I'm here to do test shots for print work," said the next appointment, a tall blonde. There was a stark difference between what Sammy called "test shots" and what desperate hopefuls called "print work." Sometimes Sammy ran home from his instant black & white developer with these prized test shots, masturbating before the chemicals dried on the contact sheets. Here was Sammy juxtaposed against real-life female human beings seeking work.

But Sammy cuts this interview short also. The tall blonde wrote down her number on a fast food wrapper from her pocketbook. "Call if you need me," she said, with a needy wink.

"You're not going to call?" Sammy warned. "She's a horse. Maybe she's got huge tits, but after that, forget it. Her legs are like tree stumps, she's a horrible, sweating pig. If you don't believe me we can call her back for a test shoot, you can see her in a bathing suit."

A twinge of guilt occasionally came over Sammy. He felt a need to defend his actions: "Look, you're going to be dead and buried, you're nothing, you're not going to exist forever. Except for about seventy years. Now, during these seventy years, you're not going to have any sex with girls unless you resort to trickery, scams, deception. That's the only way you'll have sex. Otherwise you can be a good, decent guy, never have sex, then be six feet underground forever. What would be your choice?"

The third appointment was a winner. Jean Service was a pretty twenty-year-old blonde, presenting a whole different picture of womanhood from the toothy girl and the tree-stump one. She listed Danbury, Connecticut as home on the form. During her video Q&A, she acted like the Ivory Girl, presenting Miss America answers to Sammy's bland questions, with a full smile and bouncy hair. Sammy was most pleased. He then upped the ante, asking her to pose in a bathing suit and roll around a bit on the floor. Emerging from the changing room, she bent down, rolled over slowly as instructed, pushed out her little titties for as much cleavage as she could muster. A slutty move.

"Maybe we should take her to meet the *backers* at the Palladium," Sammy said aloud, baiting her gameness. He hesitated to ask if she'd "oil up," not wanting to scare away this potential Palladium date. Jean Service left The Exercise Tape optimistic.

"I'd have degraded her more during the test shoot," said Sammy, chewing his cud over a comforting plate of cow's muscles at Sun Lok Kee. "Except she was too nice."

Sammy loved slimy, off-the-menu dishes in Chinatown. Fish with their heads intact; tripe and mysterious concoctions of gruel, dishes only ordered by Chinese peasants off the boat. Whole shameful plates of tough sinews, which he gnawed at, hunched over, masticating in private disgrace in the backs of dumpy Chinatown restaurants. Here, Grubman was a throwback shtetle Jew, an inbred, an outcast, right out of a nineteenth-century Polish ghetto. This was his perfect night out. Could Jean Service possibly indulge him over a romantic candlelight dinner of livestock intestines?

And then he ruminated: "Imagine Jean Service going back to Connecticut, getting between some crisp, fresh sheets, clicking on her TV… thinking about the dirty New York Jews who taped her. Such a white girl. You could proudly take her on a date, always sweet, doesn't go insane… You'd probably have to go horseback riding, or some horrible thing she considers fun. Roller skating… she's probably got some disgusting yeast infection from rubbing up and down the horse all day. Her panties are shit-encrusted from sliding up her ass. Probably stinks like hell. Imagine the nightmare weekend you'd have up in Connecticut with her parents and the horses, the worst weekend of your life. Ugggh, forget her."

Hawaiian Tropics

A whole industry stalked the legions of blemished, fat-tushied teenybopper *gurls* wanting to break into glamour. Leading the charge were teenage fashion magazines, their back pages littered with model academy ads—institutions that used to be called "charm school" or "finishing school" in a more innocent era.

"You can't use the word Petites any more," bemoaned Shark. "The mob owns that word." The *Village Voice* had the corner on Petites Needed ads. This approach fed off the fact that all the major agencies rejected anyone under 5'8". As a result, thousands, maybe millions, of attractive girls felt hopeless. There were also ads seeking shoe and hand models. They told some prospect she'd make a great hand model, all she needed was a $500 portfolio. A cottage industry spun off each agency. There were requisite consultations with a hairstylist, photographer, makeup and fashion coordinator. The tri-state secretarial pool provided endless marks. Some agencies sent them on bullshit rounds. One ad had a talent search culminating in an appearance on the *Joe Franklin Show*.

"We pulled diz great scam," said an ecstatic Shark, the next time I came to his office. "Ads in the *New York Times* and everything." He proudly held open his ad in that week's *BackStage*:

MUSIC VIDEO: MADONNA & MODEL TYPES

Major video production company now in final casting stage seeking 22 Madonna prototypes for international label

> *music video. Time must be flexible, shooting to fit around schedules of recording artists. Also casting for fashion video. Fiorucci-type look needed for national runway show and department store designer. Auditions to be held at Marymount Manhattan College in the Mezzanine… .*

An old cunt-hound professor pal of Shark's at the prestigious feminist institution somehow secured the main auditorium at Marymount. Sammy looked over the mug shot of the Tops model Shark used in the ad.

"Some Bloomingdale's whore?" he asked, squinching his face.

"The criticizer," Shark came back. "Look, I make a living in this business. She's a very attractive girl. Don't get me wrong, I value your opinion dearly. But the proof is in the pudding, pal. She made $400 yesterday modeling at the fur show."

Shark had a particular fondness for furs and wore a full-length coat during the Superfly era. There were furry pictures of him in his "Russ Meyer stash," a cobwebbed shoebox storing old photos. In the '70s, Shark worked Vegas, where his sartorial taste ran to Wayne Newton outfits, now stored in the closet.

As a five-year-old boy in 1947, Shark's parents forced him into the illicit sport of kiddie boxing. It was an old Southern pastime. In his Alabama hometown, Fifty miles from the Florida border, he'd be thrust into a boxing ring with other five-year-old boys to slug it out. Spotlights hung over the ring at night. A crowd of revelers made bets, sort of like cockfighting. There was a whole backwoods Alabama circuit.

"Scary as hell," Shark remembered. "And real patriotic. This was right after the war. They'd blare records of 'The Star-Spangled Banner' and 'God Bless America' right before the bouts. Then you'd be pushed out into the ring, lights glaring. They didn't have headgear in those days, but we wore sixteen-ounce gloves with handwraps and shorts. Then, after the fights, they took me over the Florida state line at night. The guy who ran the fights and the races was diz big, scary-lookin' man. They'd drive the boys to this lagoon with the blackest water I've ever seen. They'd tie a rope around our waist. Then we'd race from one end to the other, about eighty yards, while all the men placed bets in a hat. The lagoon was filled with alligators. Whenever an alligator swam up close, the guys holding the ropes along the bank would lift you outta the water for a moment till the alligator swam past."

Shark had learned to swim with the alligators in the blackest lagoons of show business. One of those lagoons was the Hawaiian Tropic International Pageant. Many professional model chasers converged upon Daytona Beach, Florida for this perennial event. Sammy himself flew down. It's run by the fabulously rich suntan oil mogul, Ron Rice. Rice's oily empire also had humble beginnings, back in North Carolina. In high school, Rice dated and then married a girl who would go on to become Miss America 1963. As a young chemistry teacher and gym coach, Rice was fired for showing progressive sex education films to his junior high classes. He then became a lifeguard. Not satisfied with Coppertone or Sea 'n' Ski, Rice mixed his own batches of coconut oil, bananas and avocados in a garbage can. That garbage can was now silver-plated and resided on Rice's palatial estate in Daytona, with four pools and a disco. He was also a great white hunter of alligators, endangered ones at that. He was the only man to have allegedly fucked Meg Calendar, when she took the title in his contest.

"This slob is The King of Girls," said Sammy, breathless, on the phone from Daytona. "Ron Rice *owns* Daytona, everybody defers to him, the cops pay homage, high school girls run all his errands." Sammy met with Rice, trying to acquire rights for the first Hawaiian Tropic Model Agency in NYC. "He's got this insane trophy room with clippings of himself with Paul Newman and racing cars. He's got leopard skin rugs everywhere and sits on this huge polished wooden throne like some ancient Hawaiian king."

Sammy donned a rumpled Hawaiian shirt and Ray-Ban sunglasses. Three hundred incredible girls, ages eighteen to twenty-one, from all over heartland America were put up at some budget convention hotel. Sammy entered the main commissary.

"They're dressed worse than nude," moaned Sammy on the phone. "They look sweet at seventeen and everything that comes out of them is sweet—but come nineteen, they start to turn a tad overripe and begin to stink."

The girls were lined up at the cafeteria with pert nips, bubble butts, flesh so tantalizing. The air was electron-charged with teen hormones that nearly made him faint. To Sammy's great regret, each and every female prospect was accompanied by a father, or "total moron boyfriends in farmer hats and overalls." Or, worse yet, contingents of lady sponsors from their little hometowns. One of the events involved this million-gallon vat of coconut oil. Rice watched an assembly line of eighty gorgeous eighteen-year-olds in bathing suits dip in, one by one. And there sat Sammy, alone with his Nikon, the publisher of *Oui*, a porn rag that spelled poison to all present. Particularly in the recent wake of the Miss America scandal, where Vanessa Williams lost the title after her naked lesbo pix were unearthed in *Penthouse*. Sammy didn't have a prayer.

"All ya need down here is a hot car, and you can have all the blowjobs ya want," said Sammy. "Unfortunately, I don't drive." Ron Rice's personal Lamborghini cost a quarter-million and was featured in the Burt Reynolds *Cannonball Run* series. Rice sponsored NASCAR racers whose cars bore the logo *It ain't the motion, it's the lotion*. Paul Newman, whose motion moved to Rice's lotion, once drove the winning Hawaiian Tropic Porsche at LeMans, France. The prized celebrities young contestants "get to meet" included Donald Trump, Julio Iglesias and Burt Reynolds himself. For contestants who wanted to "go in that direction," as Rice put it, he "feeds" girls to the Playboy mansion. (Even with vats of oily girls in abundance, Rice would soon become embroiled for years in sexual harassment lawsuits from female employees.)

For Sammy, the whole trip provided another series of strike-outs. "This waitress I was pursuing at the commissary went off with a Negro at the end of her shift," Sammy sighed. "These girls are all gonna get AIDS, they experiment with Negroes and everything.

"Next year," said Sammy, debriefing in Chinatown, "maybe *I'll* be the King of Girls." Sammy was able to convince Ron Rice he was some important media kike from New York. If all went according to plan, next time he'd be flying down as publisher of a *Hawaiian Tropic Teen Model Magazine*, yet another brainstorm.

"These girls are total hicks. I overheard two at the commissary breakfast table talking about the great Chinese dinner they had last night. 'Ah *nevuh* did have Chinese.' Turns out they were speaking about McChicken Shanghai or some crap at McDonald's, a new test market item on the menu down there. 'Ah wish they had Chinese at mah McDonald's.'"

Sammy told me of his own entrepreneurial dreams for a future restaurant:

"It would be an expensive place for the rich. A dome surrounds the main dining area upstairs. Underneath the glass dome, on the ground below, is a clearly visible walk-in dirt grounds populated by derelicts, bag ladies, families on welfare. Clientele are invited to throw their leftovers over the dome and watch the starving grapple for it. Have a few niblets left on your corn on the cob? Toss the cob over. Leave a few bites on your lamb chop bone or a slice of your filet mignon—toss it over, and watch 'em scrapple. Oh, it would get a few bleeding heart protesters at first, but then things would settle down and it would be a big success."

This would have been the perfect restaurant for Mayor Koch's New York, a crumbling Roman Empire, where you had to step over the homeless on every block. Sammy's next horror restaurant would be a rib joint, where huge roast suckling pigs revolved around open spit ovens in view. A glassed-in mud patch would contain live pigs—which patrons could individually pick for the slaughter. And then, stuffed to the gills with hog, the slobs would be wheeled backward on chairs with coasters by their waiters to a scented lounge with soft music, where their dining seats would automatically recline so they could fall into satiated slumber.

Cast Party

While Sammy was in Daytona, I took Meg to the *SNL* cast party, our second date. Each week, *SNL* throws an after-show cast party at some unannounced locale. Two company limos dump off carloads of insiders, then return to 30 Rock for more.

My ever-lovin' darling fiancée down in Texas was still awaiting my long-postponed move there. The force was against me. I felt like Tom Ewell in *The Seven Year Itch*. If I were even briefly involved with a creature like Meg Calendar, I would dread a subway ride. Walking past a construction site would cause pandemonium. Could Meg ever wash dishes or do laundry? Could she found a leper colony on the streets of Calcutta like Mother Teresa? Would lepers and legless cripples start hooting and yelping like dingoes?

Meg struck out with Francis. He couldn't afford to be impressed with in-your-face beauty. The cycle of rejection came round. He was just as unattainable to Meg as she was to the model-chasers. Including suckers like me. Going home in the cab I entered some psychic condition beyond blue balls. I sensed these were to be my last minutes, my last shot with Meg Calendar.

"Want to come up for some herbal tea?" I asked, feeling pathetic.

"No way!" she snapped. Then she turned her head with a tight laugh of contempt.

But that wasn't quite the last I saw of her. A few nights later, Sammy and I were at the Palladium.

"There are seven females to every man in the world," claimed Sammy, watching all the girls go by. "Millions of women alone in the country, thousands of attractive ones, maybe thousands of beautiful ones. And not one for me. I get physically sick on the street, seeing legs, tits, wiggling asses that I can't have. I have to take codeine pills to sleep. It's amazing how miserable you are without a girl, how depressed and utterly ugly you feel every second. This craziness starts to feed on itself as the weeks go by. And then when you're with one, it's as if you've always been getting laid, you can't imagine otherwise, the world is right and normal. I'm amazed at these girls. They experiment with sub-racial, sexually ambiguous types, that's what they want. Not me. I might as well be that old fuck right there," said Grubman, pointing to a fat sixty-year-old bathroom attendant. "I look no different to these girls than him. Young models want rock stars with long hair, pro athletes. They want these heavy metal buffoons, idiotic baboons without a thought in their heads who mistreat them. They go for oily blue Negroes. But not me. I'm shocked every day."

One of the buffoons Sammy referred to was Damien. Damien was twenty-three, a suave, dark-skinned stud who performed at Show World. He high-stepped through the Palladium like a Puerto Rican peacock in a cheap zoot suit. He earned his living doing six-to-ten live sex shows on Show World's Triple Treat Stage. He scouted here and at Long Island discos. He laid romantic bullshit onto seventeen-year-old JAPs from Great Neck so thick, some actually followed him into New York afterward, fellating him onstage during the late show at Show World. Sometimes two at once. Just for kicks.

"Of course, I gotta lay some rock on 'em first, rocks this big," said Damien, holding his fists in circles of imaginary coke. "Then they start havin' fun and wanna get crazy in front of strange guys and freak 'em out. There were these twin sisters whose mother dropped 'em off in front of the disco in a Bentley, then waves bye bye, they'll be home at midnight. These girls live in Lake Success, Great Neck, their father is president of Ideal Toys, or Hasbro or some shit, and God forbid if he ever found out, he'd turn me into a Cabbage Patch Corpse. They don't just live in a mansion, they live on an estate. They bring me into their bathroom, it's got a marble bidet, a urinal, one regular toilet and one you can swim in.

"So I say, 'Wanna go to the Palladium, Studio 54? Come to the city with me, I'll take ya to a few parties.' Then I say, 'Oh, wait, I gotta stop over Show World a minute.'" Bring 'em up to the dressing room, say, 'Girls, may I ask this big favor of you?' There were 125 old guys out in the audience, and these two rich seventeen-year-old knockout twin bitches came out onstage and fucked like animals. With me and each other. I abused 'em with this under the spotlight," he said, clutching his unit. "Soon as we get offstage, I go 'So long, ladies,' and pretend I'm the janitor, don't know 'em from Adam. Bye, bye!

"I got this stage partner now, I don't know how old she is. My boss tells me sixteen, but I say, No way, get outta here. But he says if I tell anybody, the vice squad comes up and we're all out of biz. So the first time I screw her, I say, this chick's got a *cunt*, a woman's cunt, ain't no sixteen-year-old's cunt. So I feed her a lot of coke, a rock this big, that'll loosen her lips. And she tells me she's sixteen, I swear to God.

"So last night, she doesn't show up. So I gotta go grab some girl out of a booth downstairs at Show World. Those girls downstairs get forty percent of their booths—which could amount to two dollars or $300 in one night. Me, I get $60 a shift, I work five double shifts, that's a $600 paycheck. But whenever I ask a booth girl if she wants to do a live show with me, you can bet she'll say yeah. No one's ever turned me down. But for me to grab a girl out of the booth, ya gotta ask the manager first, clear it on the schedule. So I'm in my new Cerruti suit, decked out, strut into the boss' office, boy is he glad to see me. 'Damien,' he says, 'have I got a girl for you.' Yeah? 'A young blonde, white girl.' Yeah? 'And I want you to fuck her this show.' Do I ever wanna. I'm feelin' my oats. Where is she? 'Here,' he says, and out she walks."

Damien feigned a puke. "I brought her here tonight." Sure enough, out of the powder room she comes with a big smile. Sammy winces, muttering what a fat pig she is. Damien puts his arm around her. He turned as he left, with a humble bow. "Some things you gotta do for the company," he said. Off they went into the night.

Sammy and I entered the Mike Todd Room, and that's where I saw Meg for the last time. She walked past everyone in the crowd, oblivious to stares, and slid right up to me. Sammy said nothing, astonished. He automatically knew this was the one and only Meg. Her astonishing tits are practically bursting out of her bustier tonight. She seemed downright mischievous, a tattooed punk-rock model girlfriend at her side. She spoke. Words came out of her mouth.

Sammy leaned into me. "I can't believe she's talking to you," he whispered in my ear. "She likes you, she's confused, she never had anyone not call her back. Chase her."

"Shut up," I ordered Sammy. He continued whispering in my ear as though Meg and her girlfriend weren't there. This was the redwood tree of a girl that neither I or the Stud could chop down. The one Shark wouldn't even bother to fix Sammy up with.

"Seen Francis?" asked Meg.

"She's asking you questions," whispered Sammy in my ear.

"Francis Ford Coppola?" I asked.

Meg let out a huff of displeasure, but actually drew closer.

"Yeah, that Francis."

"Now she's rubbing into you," Sammy gasped. "I can't believe this is happening."

Meg and her friend decided not to notice Sammy. But they indicated they'd like drinks. Sammy dashed off to the line at the bar, usually a thirty-minute wait. "Oh my God, oh my God," he wheezed, cutting through the crowd like a linebacker. He was back in two minutes flat, drinks in hand. Each model accepted her glass from Grubman without acknowledgment. Sammy then went to grab us a table. This was heaven—a girl-less evening turned resplendent with hot, cleavaged Ford models. But the moment he returned, a table secured, Meg waved *ta-ta*. Then went off into the crowd, leaving Grubman and myself stranded like the idiots we were. We watched them take the drinks he'd bought and over-tipped for so they could sit with someone else.

"Oh, my God. So that's Meg Calendar," he calculated. "Her left tit sags."

Adding to Sammy's anguish, the dyke bartender was glaring at him. She held up a pair of scissors and pantomimed cutting off his dick. This would be the last time Sammy came to the Palladium.

Sammy imagined a noose tightening around his neck. He started removing his tie at the office. He had bad dreams. In one he envisioned a doomsday scenario at The Exercise Tape. A *New York Post* headline came to him that read: DEAD MINOR IN PORN KING'S BED. Then Sammy dreamed of himself in a tight jail cell with a Puerto Rican AIDS victim, one who sensually picked his nose in Sammy's face and lovingly offered him some.

Who could blame Sammy for his castration fears after becoming the poster-boy for Women Against Pornography? They had his mug shot pasted all over town in their recruitment literature, along with an editorial he wrote—in good humor, of course—for a certain men's publication. He's sorry his photo appeared in the editorial because it's now reprinted in Women Against Pornography's pamphlets. He has spawned a rallying cry. Amongst the thousands of WAP's, all it would take was one diesel dyke with a pair of garden shears. It could even happen at The Exercise Tape.

Sammy's regrettable editorial:

> *FACING UP TO THE PROBLEMS OF WOMEN*
>
> *Let's be reasonable and logical, and face up to facts. Women aren't human; they're not even like monkeys or orangutans. Those muddle-headed, pea-brained, waste-your-money liberals might want to brainwash you into thinking that girls are good for something other than sucking cock, but you and I and every other sensible man knows better. These sluts were put on earth to steal your money; be whining, complaining and arrogant; and to serve as reasonably comfortable holsters for your erections when one is aroused by the call of nature.*
>
> *First off, scientific research has it that women just aren't the same as men. They don't like things like cameras or computers or state-of-the-art stereos, simply because the higher centers of their brains aren't developed as well as*

> *a man's. Furthermore, according to a very fine article in* The National Enquirer, *it's been proven that women aren't as smart as men. It takes real guts to admit it, but women are mindless creatures... Don't let those detestable, ugly, disgusting, sour-pussed lesbian diesel-dyke Women's Libbers fool you, along with their cotillions of homo yes-men. Women are most happy when they are serving their twin gods of Mammon and King Cock...*
>
> *Men work hard, make money, grind the wheels of business, only to fall victim to early deaths dealt out by the insane caprices of vengeful sluts... They should be rounded up in a pen with pigs and fucked with sticks and forced to eat filthy offal, and maybe then they would appreciate a fine figure of a man who wants to own and take care of them, even if he is perhaps just a wee bit nervous and high-strung and suspicious of some people's motives ..."*

The editorial was reprinted in the brochures, though it faded out into broken type after a few paragraphs.

I asked Sammy, Was nothing about womanhood sacred? Had he a sister, a daughter, a wife? Well, he had a mother, but she never loved him. She fawned over his younger brother, Jonah.

"My younger brother, who I no longer talk to, married some ugly pig," said Sammy. "They're having a kid. He never cheats, stays home. When we were kids walking down the street, I'd see some girl and crane my neck 180 degrees, panting, Good God, did you see that? And he'd stand there going, 'Huh, huh?'"

Sammy felt some competitive pressure over his younger brother's marriage. So he decided to get him a wife, too. The lucky lady was a genteel Southern girl of twenty-two from Florida.

She came to interview for a job at Stephanie Mason's office. Sammy met her in the hallway, and for once, he didn't strike out. She agreed to a date. He phoned me afterward. "I just got reamed, steamed and dry cleaned," he said. "The girl blew me incredibly then fucked me twice. I'm happy."

Within two months of this date they were engaged. Sammy said her father owned a small oil company and was wealthy. "I'm thirty-four, desperate, and keep seeing myself in my forties, ugly, wrinkled, bent over, without a woman, and at that point with no chance. So I'm getting married."

After the engagement, Stephanie called, taking a pool of bets from everyone who knew Sammy. They were all placing $5 on when she'd dump him. Not particularly friends with any women in New York, Sammy made the bad call of asking Stephanie, his only female associate, to go out with his future wife, show her the city, take her shopping. So Stephanie, a worldly consumer, took the fiancée to the most expensive shops in Soho, encouraging her to break the bank with Sammy's credit cards. "These wives are expensive," he complained over the phone. "Mine's been spending $400 a shot on the card."

Unbeknownst to Sammy, his comrades at the office picked a week and bet $5. Stephanie felt Sammy's bride-to-be was terribly naive and latched onto him in a desperate moment. Her previous husband was an Iranian who worked in her father's oil business. Sammy proudly hoisted their Dade County divorce papers. She'd been treated so badly by men—she even had to make an appointment whenever she wanted to see her father—that Sammy's initial kindness was new to her. Of course, he would soon offer psychological torment, as opposed to the physical punishment inflicted by her former Iranian husband.

The girl had been raised with Southern table manners and she was offended when they walked into a restaurant. Only one chair was available; Sammy pulled it out, then sat down himself. She blew up over this delicate seating matter which left Sammy bewildered. He'd never held out a chair or opened a door for a woman in his life. He ate loudly with his mouth open making squishing, whistling noises. Whenever they reached a red light at the curb, Sammy took an extra step, crossing the street before her. Then he'd wait for her to catch up.

Sammy's fiancée was in for another shocker at the first meeting of his family. Seeing the whole clan of Grubmans threw the genteel lady from the South askew. They all ate with their mouths open, masticating.

Sammy arranged "How To Be A Jew" lessons from a cut-rate rabbi. He'd convert her in twelve easy lessons. Sammy insisted this was *her* idea, she wanted to convert. She may have harbored an exotic taste for deranged men, having run off to New York to marry a mockey pornographer, escaping her Iranian husband, a reputed terrorist. But she hadn't foreseen the degradation of a Jewish conversion and a wedding, à la Grubman.

"I'm going to introduce her to all the interesting men I can," said Stephanie, who began chumming up to Sammy. "I'll take her to the most expensive shops in Soho, even though the same stuff's available down the street on Orchard for half the price. I've taken out a bank account of the twenty bets in the pool so far about when she'll dump him. The winner gets interest."

Ultimately, what Stephanie was gifted at was turning girls out. She would introduce Sammy's wife to playboys and *playas*, dope kingpins and debonair blades with fancy cars and dubious backgrounds. She was dead set on turning Grubman's ever-suffering, Jewish-converted wife out as a call girl.

Sammy's marriage crashed on the rocks after a few miserable months. The ex-wife tried to ream, steam and dry-clean him in court. He faced further court battles as his jailbait lawsuit came to a head. The mother of the seventeen-year-old dildo model cost *Oui* a dainty dime, which prompted Sammy's departure from the sinking magazine.

But Sammy Grubman never went down like a captain with his ship. Whenever disaster lurked, Sammy was always able to crawl out of the bowl as troubled waters were about to swirl down the toilet. His attendance at beauty contests and discos began to wane. He kept to his apartment more, adding an extra lock or two and a security alarm. Flyers of his face were papered all over town like a Wanted Dead Or Alive poster. His waking moments became a brightly lit hell in which Sammy was convinced that members of the fairer sex were out hunting for his balls.

Postscript: Eighteen Years Later

Sometime after I left New York, Shark was run over by a truck. That's how he tells it. Whatever actually happened may never be established. The fact is, Shark is now a quadriplegic. He's hooked up to a high-tech wheelchair on the seventeenth floor of an East Side apartment building. Two gay assistants with Continental accents work for him. He is centrally positioned in the room.

"Diz operation is ten times bigger than when you last saw it," claims Shark. "This is my top girl," he says, gesturing to a swimsuit calendar on his desk. "She's gonna make a million dollars in diz business. I've got hundreds of girls. Showgirls fly in from Vegas every week with their managers."

Shark's ankles are turned out at a grotesque unnatural angle, secured by metal clamps. His midsection protrudes like Humpty Dumpty. He resembles something of the great British physicist, Stephen Hawkins, albeit now with a visible colostomy bag. His fingers are frozen in a spastic curl, each knuckle horribly bent. Yet his hands, though immobile, are able to hook a finger around the phone on his wheelchair to answer. A phone repairman is there. "If diz phone wasn't broken, you'd hear it ringing off the hook all day." And then it does.

"Tops Models," he answers. Some girl talk ensues. The walls are papered with model's promos, calendars, tearsheets. "We do some wonderful things here," Shark tells me. He has a relative who's a Brigadier General in the Army. Shark is fixing the General up with an Indian chief friend out West who's an expert tracker. "Diz guy can track anybody," says Shark. "So, I figure he's the only guy who can find Osama bin Laden. They've got a cave in Afghanistan that's thirty-one miles deep. That's nothin' to diz guy when he puts his ear to the ground. So he's flying in tomorrow to meet the General, I arranged a meeting here at Tops Models. The General has an appointment with President Bush the next day. If he likes what he sees in diz Indian, he'll bring him to meet Bush the next day, and then to Afghanistan."

His physical condition aside, Shark seems more successful and happy than ever. For all the scams and make-believe show-biz, he does scrounge out scraps of work here and there for his models. He sends them to some ninety-year-old retired theatrical agent who knows Joe Franklin. The old agent occasionally wangles a blowjob. All told, Shark provides cattle-call auditions for thousands of dreamers who'd otherwise never have such excitement in their lives.

Sammy Grubman moved to some high-rent real estate in lower Manhattan with a Hudson River view. When the World Trade Center was hit, his windows were blown out. Thousands of naked girl test shots scattered into oblivion. Emergency workers found body parts in his apartment. In the chaos that ensued, Sammy moved to Fort Greene, Brooklyn. Someone convinced him Fort Greene, a former ghetto, was becoming gentrified. But he found it wasn't.

"It takes three hours just to go to the supermarket," says Sammy. "The cashier doesn't know the prices, then goes back to check and disappears for thirty minutes. People wait on huge lines. It's bedlam. If these people didn't have managers or officials of some sort, it would be like Somalia."

Since leaving publishing, Grubman went into the business of "mail fraud." Fake ads for psychics, shenanigans with lottery tickets, various and sundry items where you mail in a dollar. The operation requires a "designated convict" to run his P.O. Box. This is a partner who picks up the mail: "Chances are nothing will happen, but there's also a chance you could get in a little trouble. Or a lot of trouble. If, say, an FBI stake-out decides to pick you up."

Sammy spent thousands on plastic surgery. There were complications, infections. After two years of repairs, his face settled down. He now has a strong jaw and clefted chin, like the young Kirk Douglas. He has a full head of hair, no bags under his eyes and taut, clear skin. He can easily pass himself off for a decade younger and gives his age to girls as thirty-eight. He had glamour shots of himself in a suit taken by noted girlie photographer Warren Tang.

"I had the photos retouched and airbrushed to perfection," says Sammy. "Then I put an ad in all the classifieds throughout Japan: 'Rich American businessman looking to introduce young women to New York.' I had it running like a well-oiled machine. I'd be dropping one off at JFK at the same time as picking up a new one, fresh from Tokyo. I had the flight schedules working like clockwork.

"These girls have no criteria whatsoever to judge American men, no point of reference, they know nothing. They have no idea of social strata, who to stay away from. This JAL flight attendant I have in the house now went out with Negroes before me. As far as they know, I'm the prime catch amongst American men. They never even heard of Pearl Harbor or Hiroshima, they've just heard that Americans did something bad to them a long time ago; they don't even know about World War II.

"But they like hip hop, that they've heard. So they all come over with the same guidebook. Each one says her favorite movie is *Titanic*, as if they're programmed. They all want to go shopping at the same stores for some stupid overpriced designer handbag and some jewelry. So I take them shopping, blow a few hundred. And they all want to go to the Met. I've taken dozens. They stand there before the same Dali exhibit. I ask them, 'What do you see in these paintings, what appeals to you?' And then they turn to a page in their guidebook, without a clue as to what they're looking at, then read some description and look up at me. 'Surreal, yes?'

"But they're incredibly proficient and dedicated when it comes to blowjobs. They'll spend hours diligently applying oil and working you up."

After redesigning his face, Sammy has now learned that "When it comes down to it, men's looks mean nothing to women. Oh, they might have some crush on poster-boy pop stars when they're teenagers, but after that, at bottom, they're all looking for two things: security and power.

"These Japanese girls who come to America are considered out of their minds back home. Total rebels. No respectable Japanese girl would ever fly to New York on her own to hook up with a strange man. But if it wasn't for them, I'd have no sex life whatsoever. If it wasn't for Asian girls, I'd have nothing."

The Stud did time in a mental hospital. He made a lot of enemies, just by nature of being the Stud. But he's no longer on a roll. He leads a quiet existence with one girlfriend in a place he once would have been embarrassed to be seen in—New Jersey.

Shark got Meg Calendar a double episode on some cop show from an old friend, an ex-NFL player who co-produced and appeared in the series. The football player took her on a weekend climbing excursion in the Valencia Mountains. The guy had a pet chimp who went everywhere with him, even mountain climbing. He was a well-behaved critter, cute as a kewpie doll. At the end of the trip, as Meg was leaving, she reached over to pat the chimp on the head and it bit off one of her nostrils. One savage crunch. She was rushed to the hospital and had several operations to fix her disfigured nose. Shark then lost touch with her. But he heard the former Ford model was now hooking out of Los Angeles. Ruined for modeling or even being an actress, she now possesses a new cavity on her face with unique possibilities in the hooking biz.

BABES ON BROADWAY

I always figured I'd lose my virginity on 8th Avenue. I was titillated over the idea that just forty blocks down the same avenue as my old Eldorado building was a shantytown of massage parlors. A sexual slum had risen out of Times Square that held strange mysteries of women, as if a hellish Land of Oz were in the city.

At this point in history, 8th Avenue became clogged with over a thousand hookers every night. They emerged like vampires after sunset. The white ones looked like little girls who snuck into their mommy's room and applied too much eyeliner and smeary lipstick, then stepped into klutzy high heels. They were lopsided, coulda-been cheerleaders in silver hot pants. Back home, they'd received their sexual initiations from colored boys on the wrong side of the tracks. Now, many had mulatto babies stashed away somewhere. Shunned in their hometowns, these hot young mamas migrated to New York in demented droves from California and the Midwest. They worked out of the parlors, they snagged customers into flophouses, they performed in cars, subway stairwells and parking lots of Times Square.

My very first morning living in New York, I felt the magnetic pull of Times Square. Within minutes after the moving trucks unloaded, I subwayed down to Child's Pancake House on 42nd and 8th for breakfast. Emerging from the recesses of the IND subway for the first time, I took a deep breath of crisp morning 42nd Street air. I must have been reincarnated from some show-biz personage who haunted the Square in the 1920s.

I discovered another dimension to the world of Broadway, which I'd known through my parents. Decrepit tenements hung storefront signs that said Hungry Hilda, Tina's Leisure Room, Christy's Mix and Mate, Rabbit Hutch, Psychedelic Grape, on and on, ad nauseam. I imagined all their customers were elevator men. Oh, lucky elevator men. Here was the last salvation of my virginity, which I didn't have the nerve to lose with some schoolgirl. It took me a year to build up the courage to call upon Times Square.

And so, with only Roy, one of my building's elevator men, briefed on my whereabouts, I was off to see the wizard, where females would serve up their naked bodies for the mere exchange of green paper. Sex with girls didn't seem like something that could be equated in financial terms then. No matter how you sliced it, I was certain, the man had a bargain.

At 10 P.M., I checked into the Sherman Hotel on 47th and 8th, a $10 room. It was the first time I'd ever checked into a hotel alone. I wanted my own safe room for the event, not some five-dollar roach trap, where the proverbial stick-up man might jump out of a closet. I bought my first Trojan for the occasion, a sly purchase, which gave me goosebumps.

An old man sat behind a sealed glass partition in the shabby lobby. He gave me the key to room 316. Then his sour breath came through the grill. "I just saw a pip run into the building next door. Big ruckus. Went upstairs to his whore, then cut the guy's balls off who was wit' her."

"You mean a pimp?" I asked, unsure now of whether to go through with the evening.

"Yeah, a pip. But it can't happen in here. We don't allow no prostitutes here."

I surveyed my room. The old black phone had a Circle-5 exchange. A huge toenail clipping was wedged into the carpet. I placed my rubber on the night table, proud of myself so far. Between the rubber and the room, I was halfway home.

It was a warm autumn night and 8th Avenue felt like another planet. There was an otherworldly fizz to the atmosphere, thick with prostitution, female hormones gone haywire. I stood on the strip at 47th Street. I would cruise down to 34th on 8th Avenue, then back up 9th Avenue to 50th Street. It was a thirty-block sweep. I'd make the trek several times, if necessary, until I found the most gorgeous whore in Times Square, one who would move the earth for me. I feared it would be so ecstatic an encounter that I might faint. But I was determined not to come home a virgin.

I peered into a storefront called Honey Hut, the windows boarded with plywood. Orange paint advertised "Lovely Exotics" waiting behind the gates offering "Body Rubs for $10 Complete." "Try Us," pleaded the sorry-looking scrawled letters. I opened the plywood door.

"What the fuck you want?" spat a bitter, leotarded black girl at the desk.

"Body rub?"

"I'll body rub yo' ass!" she said, reaching for a bat under the table. I meekly backpedaled out.

Thirty girls on each block stood at their designated posts. They beckoned to me, nodded out, ate pizza, scurried like minnows when the paddy wagon cruised by. Some were sloe-eyed, acned, welted, stoned and sick. Others had bright farm faces, not yet urbanized. Men trolled by in cars, as if it were an Arab trading post, haggling and bargaining. The prettiest white girls stood back in doorways, not having to exert salesmanship.

Seated behind the window at a Howard Johnson's was a bored pimp. He was treating four happy whores to banana splits—their reward for handing in over a thousand a week.

Below 42nd Street, I encountered 200-pound cleaning ladies in ten-dollar blonde beehive wigs from Woolworth's. They wore gold hot pants and beige hosiery, to make them seem racially ambiguous.

"Suck yo' dick, suck yo' dick," they chanted in taut vocal outbursts, as I walked by.

"Want some thex?" offered one buck-toothed, oh-so-sincere black girl. She kept knocking down her price. "I'll give you a *nice* suck and a fuck," she pleaded, going from $20 to $5. Then she offered for free—"C'mon, buckeroo, you cain't beat that." I was not about to perform the blessed event here, beside the 39th Street Rap Parlor, even if they paid me. But I felt honored.

My senses heightened after one thirty-block sweep, I paused to catch my breath. There were a half-dozen girls I would have chosen. Yet I just walked past them, afraid to make contact. Maybe I was kidding myself. The second time around, they would know I was hunting, not just on my way to Grandma's. Roy, the elevator man, and I, had taken indecisive treks like this. And Roy had surely embarked on self-pitying marches like this alone.

I walked further west to 11th Avenue, where the New York Central Railroad graveyard lay forgotten. I passed a plane hangar-sized Greyhound depot and the United Parcel Service warehouse. There were limousine companies in the area and taxi collision repair shops, all closed. I saw several maverick hookers, strayed far from the pack. Horse and buggy carriages returned to Centennial Stables at 38th Street, where the hookers stood outside petting filthy horses after their long shifts in Central Park. Both seemed like beasts of burden. I heard the patter of stiletto heels blend with the click-clack of horse's hooves on cobblestone. I imagined myself in the nineteenth century. Blonde heads bobbed up and down over laps in parked trucks.

"You for sale?" I inquired of a hard-faced 11th Avenue whore.

"I don't take walking gigs," she said. This was strictly car trade in the boondocks.

Whore faces kept spinning in my head as I crossed back to 8th Avenue. Each was a fiercely desirable virginity stopper. A new roster appeared on the streets, while some of the previous lineup were now occupied in hotel rooms. At 44th Street my eyes fixed upon the classiest-looking dame of the evening.

"Hey, you know it's good luck to give money to hookers," she said, the thinnest smile creeping through her lips. Heavenly cleavage in a black evening dress, milky complexion, full red lips and splendidly styled layers of black hair. She had curves from her hips to her stockinged legs that made me high. No platform-stilt heels, dime-store wigs or hokey hooker attire. I wondered whether she was padded up with foam rubber or Frederick's underthings, some kind of false advertising. How could she just stand there without being propositioned by fifty guys a minute?

A short Puerto Rican girl in polyester clothes stood at her side. "Whaddya think, should we give this guy a tumble?" asked the knockout to her sidekick, who shrugged. I had broken through the barrier. Like a trained athlete, some other part of me took over the motor functions.

"I got a room three blocks away," I said, breath shortening.

"Naw, that's too far. I like the Fulton, only one block away. Costs five bucks a room, not including me."

"… How do I know you won't rob me up there?" I asked.

"Believe me, honey, I'm more scared than you. You're a guy, and guys are ten times stronger than girls. Even if I had a knife, you'd just pull it away and cut me." She drew a finger across her throat and made a sound like a guillotine.

"But what if you have a gun?" I said.

"Here, you can check my pocketbook," offered the hooker, handing it over. I got goosebumps rummaging through the innards. It brought back an ancient memory of examining the pocketbook of a slumbering babysitter. Inside the bag was a mess of girlie goods—lipsticks, eyeliners, pancake pocket mirror, crumpled receipts, loose change and condoms. Of the many aromas that leaped out of the hooker's pocketbook, her Chiclets chewing gum hypnotized me.

"Looks safe," I shrugged, handing it back. "But can't we go to my hotel room? You'll love it, cost ten bucks, twice as much as yours."

"I don't go to nobody's room… Where'd you say it was?"

The hooker requested that Rosa, her partner, wait outside the door, and I agreed. Her name was Sherri and she was twenty-one—four whole years older than me, which made a hell of a difference. She was a woman, not a girl, like my schoolmates. As a matter of fact, she reminded me of Liz Taylor in *Suddenly Last Summer*, and I couldn't believe she was so casually walking with me into a sexual encounter. I snuck a look at her 'hind end, which jiggled right into my solar plexus. The two hookers and I strolled up 8th Avenue, all lighting up Marlboros. Then Sherri put her arm around my waist.

We all entered the Sherman Hotel, where my safe room awaited. As we reached the narrow staircase, a crude gate came crashing down, activated by the old man in the booth.

"What gives?" I asked.

"We don't allow no prostitutes in here. We respect the law."

"What?" I stammered, incredulously, while Sherri rolled her eyes. "You know, I travelled all the way in from Pittsburgh on business for a company meeting at your hotel. And you're saying we can't conduct the meeting here?"

"Chief, you cannot bring *any* women up to the rooms."

"My God, I'll lose the account." My voice jumped an octave.

"What type of account is that?" came the old man.

"Monsanto burlap and sorghum products." Pure nervous energy was running my show. I tugged at the anti-hooker gate, solid as a jail. I prayed the man would believe me. I didn't even know what burlap and sorghum were—just remembered them as national products of Third World nations in social studies reports. Now my virginity was on the line.

Sherri and her sidekick were giggling. She put in her two cents: "Look, we got a burlap buyers' conference in the morning. We need to go over the books ta-night!"

"You wanna go upstairs alone, fine, but no whores or pips," the man said straight to me.

Sherri turned to leave. "Why don't you come down the street to my hotel. It's okay, really." I was terrified of those fleabag joints, didn't know who would pop out of the closet. But I followed after Sherri, before my prize hooker disappeared into the sea after I'd spent three hours picking her out. I even felt romantic.

"You sure it's cool in there?" I asked.

"Christ, yeah, I'm there all the time... Listen, honey, I've spent a whole half-hour trying to settle down with you. I can't waste another minute." The honeymoon was over, her voice strictly business. "Follow me."

Five minutes later, we stepped up a flight of stairs where a long line of impatient hookers and dazed johns awaited the Fulton Hotel registration desk. The johns had to sign in as "Mrs. & Mrs.," Sherri explained, due to some quirk of the law. They were then issued five-dollar "honeymoon suites," where the clerk wished them a pleasant thirty-minute stay. My adrenaline activated, I began congratulating all the old gents ahead of me for getting married. The man in front accepted my handshake with a nod and thanks. I complimented the fellow behind for choosing one helluva bride.

When I reached the desk, I pulled out a wad of bills, which Sherri studied carefully. I had started with a hundred bucks, minus the ten for the Sherman room. Now I plucked out a five, then signed the register "Mr. & Mrs. Quickfuck." The register was thick, thousands of marriages puffing up the pages with ink.

Once this business was complete, I became withdrawn, following Sherri to room 27. Rosa stayed in the lobby. My next function—sticking it in for the first time in this 8th Avenue fleabag—now seemed like an unpleasant ritual I had to perform. I wasn't sure if I would have preferred to just talk.

The honeymoon suite was a stale-smelling cubicle. The window peered upon an enclosed, graying, brick-wall shaft. I locked the door with a tiny hook. The floor wasn't level, and the queen-size bed sagged with a terrible loneliness. Not one genuinely married couple had ever slept on it. Sherri pulled the bedspread down, something she did a dozen times a night.

"Wha'd you say yer name was?"

"George. George Disoto." Once, in high school, a kid named George Disoto had blurted out my name to the cops when he got busted for dealing hash. I decided I would thereafter summon forth Disoto's name when I needed an alias.

"Well, George, honey. What was it you were interested in?" Sherri seemed a bit tired and professional now, removing her pocketbook strap from around her shoulder. I suddenly noticed a nasal congestion in her voice, and a sloth-like droop to her eyelids. I checked her arms for needle marks, but they were smooth as Ivory Snow.

"You know. Just the regular stuff," I shrugged. Sex was no longer on my mind. "I'll congratulate you if you can get it up," I suddenly said, hoping she'd think I was an old hand who just happened to call on a pro tonight. She didn't seem to suspect I was a pathetic first-timer.

"Well, a *half-and-half* is fifty," she said. I was confused. "You know, that's where I blow ya first, then we fuck." I fumbled for my bills and counted out fifty for the hooker. This was twice the going rate for girls on 8th Avenue. She bagged the money quickly, then sat down on the bed, in no rush to get undressed. We only had a half-hour, and she'd stretch every minute she could doing nothing.

She casually walked to the bathroom, picking through her purse, adjusting her hair, while she told me to "get comfortable" on the bed.

"You know," I heard from the bathroom, "you're not so lively as a while ago. What happened?"

"Well, I guess I'm not in my usual hotel room," I said. I realized that if I was going to stick in in every hole she's got, as I'd boasted to Roy, I'd better get started.

"Do you have a girlfriend?" The bathroom door was open as she applied lipstick over a lumpy porcelain sink. The mirror was tilted and cracked.

"Not right now," I said. "They seem to be afraid of me."

"That's because you don't smile," said Sherri. "Square girls need to see a guy smile."

Her observation came as a blunt revelation. It was true that I had acquired the joyless poker face of an elevator man. "I can't just smile. You have to crack me up first."

"You really should be out there every night having fun at your age, ya only get older. You shouldn't hafta be here with me, a handsome guy like you. You should get over this problem with square girls. You definitely have a problem."

I had gotten down to my Jockey underwear and sat frozen on the bed. I admitted to seeing a psychiatrist occasionally.

"It could be the psychiatrist that's screwing you up. Maybe you should try prostitutes for a while until you gradually start to get better with square girls."

I suddenly imagined 8th Avenue prostitutes and Central Park West psychiatrists as natural enemies, competing for the same dollar. Their time cost about the same. Sherri walked out of the bathroom in a black bra and panties. Her face and her skin and her curves were breathtaking. If I had seen her in a men's magazine, it would be instant shoot-off. I imagined Dr. Greuland, my elderly psychiatrist, decked out in bra and panties, and what it might be like rolling around in the same bed at the Fulton with him.

"It's another twenty if you want the bra off," said Sherri, hesitating with her fingers at the back snap.

"What?" I asked, a victim of extortion.

"All I care about is money. You make me happy and I'll make you happy. I'll give ya a good time."

"What makes you think I'm having such a good time?" I asked. She went about arranging the bed as though it didn't matter to her one way or the other. I plucked out another twenty, which she dunked into her bag. Then she unhooked the bra. My eyes witnessed two heavenly white knockers unbound from their double C-cups with springing recoil. I had never really experienced live bosoms like these—only small, squirming ones, grappled for beneath sweaters of unendowed junior high girls.

Off with my underwear, she instructed, as she stretched her own panties off with an elastic swipe. She put a rubber in her mouth, and slickly applied it during the first half of the half-and-half. I was more preoccupied with flexing my arms, trying to look muscular. I cursed the rubber to myself.

"The reason you're not hard and excited is because you have no confidence. You're nervous with women, and it's impossible to get hard that way," she analysed. I took this as another fabulous revelation. I asked if we could start by kissing.

"I *hate* kissing," Sherri said, pulling back. "I don't do that for *no* price, with *no*body. If you're lookin' for love, honey, don't be comin' to a hooker. You won't find it there… But I like ya. You can suck my tits."

She fed me both of them. This turned out to be the highlight of the evening, so far. Her nipples were the best part, providing a rubbery tingle to my lips and tongue, which I'd only dreamed about. Then, gradually, the sensation lessened, and it felt like a mass of flesh with no sexual connotation. She seemed to be in a bored daze. I wondered whether I would be enjoying it more if she was responsive. But then, I knew from Roy to try not to take it personally. This whore wouldn't be turned on if Paul Newman and Robert Redford were suckling each one.

I mounted her on top. She was clean and fresh, the faintest perfume scent rising from her hairdo. I was awaiting some sort of magic, cruising through the atmosphere like an astronaut entering space for the first time. But I just sort of swished in, three-quarters erect, no friction, lots of spare room inside. No lust. Sherri still lay there nearly unconscious, with an occasional grunt of annoyance. Then she'd tug, try to milk it out of me fast, which I found hateful.

"Did you come yet?" she asked.

"No. Did you?" For a moment she snapped out of her daze and spoke to a childhood doll. She wrapped her legs around my back. "Baby, I don't get too many nice young boys like you."

I just wanted to keep my arms around her. "Hell, I know you don't particularly dig sex," I said. "But I hope you don't *hate* it. I hope it's at least as exciting as brushing your teeth."

She pulled her legs back down and became a zombie again.

"Look," she finally said, the businesswoman taking charge, "we're about to go overtime. You are gonna tip me ten?"

I believed she'd up and walk out before I finished. I agreed to give her another ten. But I had no sense of time, and there were no clocks in the room. A loud, abrupt knock at the door made me jump.

"Yeah, Joe, yeah!" screamed Sherri. She reassured me the management was just checking on her safety, and letting us know time was up. Even though she wore no watch, she was accustomed to the passage of thirty minutes the way a boxer was to three.

"You have to believe you can do it," coached Sherri. "Close your eyes and think of coming." I concentrated, and when I finally did, it was like a cap gun instead of the dynamite I'd expected. Miss 8th Avenue Hooker couldn't even tell, so I stayed in there an extra minute before she caught on.

Sherri was into her clothes in a jiffy. I mourned each body part that she covered. The bra was an especially sad sight to see go on. The panties went back over her rump, the stockings came over her legs, and all the things I'd paid $85 to spend a half-hour with, and would likely never lay my hands on again, were gone. The average rate outside was $20. Sherri stood before the bathroom mirror, picking her nose. I felt like I'd been in the room for hours.

Her Puerto Rican girlfriend was standing in the lobby, and I followed them past a line of other newlyweds waiting to sign the register. The act had felt mediocre, kind of like brushing your teeth. Yet I wished I could remain in that Times Square honeymoon suite another few hours, or that Sherri could become my girlfriend. I sensed that in time I'd be back on line, with the rest.

I JUST MET A GIRL NAMED MARIA

The hottest stripper of late to headline the Harmony Theatre (48th Street's "Home Away From Home") is Maria Krupa, the twenty-two-year-old daughter of Gene Krupa. She migrated up from the nightmare alley of 42nd Street's peeps to the relative sanctuary of the Harmony. Only the prettiest need apply, those with a modicum of ambition or stage presence.

The tall blonde worked onstage here for a year before revealing to Harmony owner Bob Anthony whose daughter she was. This news came like a battering ram. Anthony, as some of us remember, was a leading front man and vocalist throughout the big-band era. An old crony of Gene Krupa, Bob related all kinds of memories to Maria. The Harmony Burlesque video series titled Maria's segment "Dancing to the Beat of Her Own Drum."

The most famous drummer of the swing band era died when Maria was eleven, in 1973: "We were very close. I was his little girl. I was placed somewhere, but I made the decision to be on my own. I always got away and came back to New York, always, always. Me and my mother don't get along. She's a Jehovah's Witness. I tell her I'm bartending, but she knows what I'm doing. My parents were divorced when I was six and my father took custody. He used to show me off on tour, in Hawaii, California. He didn't want me to be in show business. I know he would turn over in his grave if he knew what I was doing. He was very religious; we used to go to church every Sunday. I'm not religious, but I feel he's my guardian angel."

Maria began on the ugly streets of 8th Avenue at the age of fourteen, as the prostitute boom began slowing down. "I had no other choice. I had to survive somehow," she says of her drug-addled teen years. She then spent four years working the champagne-hustle topless bars, then the peeps. A girlfriend of hers used to bring home a shopping bag of money earned at the Harmony. So now the leggy blonde dancer, after a hard youth in Times Square, has her name in lights at the Harmony, the only on-the-level joint left in the Square.

"I have fun onstage," she sighs, backstage, in what I assure her was once the headliner's dressing room at the old Melody Burlesk. "I like to dance. The money's not like it used to be, but it pays the bills. Sometimes it's good, they tip $30 or $40 during a set, but most of the time between $10 and $20. Either the crowd is gonna tip, or they're not gonna tip."

The Harmony offers an easier life than the lowly peeps and topless bars, where girls must beg for tips, then split commissions with management. Here, the hardest thing is killing two hours between each twenty-minute set (she does four shows daily). She briefly dated a gent whom she met during Mardi Gras. But now she becomes embarrassed when she encounters attractive guys in the audience and won't talk to them.

Though she leaves nothing to the imagination during her act, she scruples at posing for mags or doing porn flicks. *Playboy* or *Penthouse* maybe, but precious few Times Square maidens make that grade. "You've got to have a *body-body*," Maria says. Like other street-smart strippers here, she knows it won't advance her career in any way to do a third-rate layout for, say, *High Society* or *Swank*, which pay as low as $200 [half up front, half on publication (heh, heh)]. The only big payoffs come from *Playboy* or *Penthouse*, but even if you've got a body-body, you still need a face-face.

Gene Krupa used to headline the Metropole, now a Times Square topless bar, formerly a jazz club. "I danced there. Told 'em, 'My father used to work here.' But I didn't tell them who my father was."

Maria doesn't own any of his records, but wants to build a collection when she settles down someday. She plans to quit the biz when her trust fund arrives in several years. She kept secret about her father for over a year at the Harmony, until she found out that Bob Anthony, former big-band crooner, had worked with him. Now, Anthony is especially protective of Maria, keeps the guys off her.

She deflects many propositions and feels no sexual heat within when she performs. "I never get turned on, this is just a job. I'm in another world when I'm here—there's no feeling, just the money. You can't really dance, 'cause the music's too low. I'd like to do modern dance, like Solid Gold dancing! I wanna be some kind of star, I really do… but not a porno star."

She doesn't kiss during Mardi Gras, or allow patrons to paw anything other than her knockers. "I'm scared. I go to a gynecologist once a month. If customers look clean, during Mardi Gras, *sometimes* I'll let them suck my tits, but rarely. If they try to go underneath, I slap them. I don't know where their fingers have been. 'Just touch me here, that's it,'" she explains, mammary-wise, "and I don't even like that. Then they complain because they can't do anything else. I say, 'You can't even buy *Playboy* for a dollar, you spend three and all you get is pictures. Here you get to touch a girl for a lousy dollar.'

"When I'm sixty," says Maria, 'if I don't look good anymore, I'll pay money to get laid. I'll take a young guy out, think nothin' of it. As long as I'm not married... But now—I'm still just a baby."

—1985

(Not long after this interview, Maria Krupa died of a heroin overdose sitting on a barstool in Times Square. The other strippers at the bar immediately ran off so they wouldn't be questioned.)

MEMORIES OF *SCREW*

More than several milestones in my life occurred during my tenure at *Screw*. Some of these events may sound like a fairy tale, but they are true. First, I met my wife through the window of the eleventh floor, when she was staying at the Markle—run by the Salvation Army for young Southern women attending school in New York. Secondly, I met my best friend, Richard Jaccoma, at *Screw*. I published my first story there at age twenty, and soon after, the first comic strips with my brother Drew; the Friedman Bros. soon became the most feared cartoonists in New York. And finally, through the entrée of my *Screw* press pass, the hot gates of Times Square opened before me. This culminated in my 1986 book, *Tales of Times Square*.

My first month or two at *Screw* was miserable. I had vied for a writing job at *Saturday Night Live*, and attended their pre-season meetings. When it fell through, the opening at *Screw* (to replace the brilliant J.J. Kane—now reviewing movies for the *Daily News* as The Phantom of the Movies) seemed like a pitiful consolation. But I needed a job. Shortly after I arrived, John Lennon was assassinated. But when Richard Jaccoma appeared as Managing Editor things started to soar.

I was twenty-four, with privileged access to gorgeous, albeit demented, young porn starlets. There was no such thing as AIDS. *Saturday Night Live*, by comparison, went through its most disastrous season, its emasculated staff swamped in failure. But *Screw* offered a fascinating underworld, New York's avant-garde during those last few precious years of the great sexual revolution.

Our crack editorial team galvanized when Jaccoma hired Gil Reavill, who'd just arrived from the Midwest. How a corn-fed Midwesterner adopted the Goldstein persona, as his ghostwriter for fifteen years, was uncanny. Sydney, our editorial assistant, another Jaccoma hire, was a gorgeous Creole girl. She would brave catcalls and lewd propositions during her walk along 14th Street each morning, until she reached the sanctuary of *Screw*. After an afternoon he spent observing us, Philip Roth labeled us "nine-to-five anarchists."

The first time I entered the offices of *Screw* was in 1977. Oddly, the editors were all huddled around a telescope. There were stacks of hardcore stock shots, dildos littered about the floor, 8 mm porn loops and magazines piled everywhere. But the three editors paid me no mind as I walked in, and fought like schoolboys for the scope view. Fifty blocks away, a girl lay on a roof sunbathing topless.

Everything about *Screw* was the opposite of what outsiders might imagine. It was the only magazine out of dozens where I freelanced whose editors dealt straight, looked you in the eye and handled your work respectfully. It was the only men's magazine that paid like clockwork. The scale was low, but freelancers got paid from the same revolving two-week payroll as staffers.

Goldstein was the only man alive who could legitimately claim hookers as tax write-offs. Likewise, *Screw* reporters were reimbursed or fronted petty cash for research in the field, like peeps and whorehouses. Before I took over the Naked City listings, I was a stringer. *Screw*'s comptroller, Philip Eisenberg, was a Soviet bureaucrat who kept Goldstein's tax ledgers neat as a Torah scroll. He was also in charge of expenses. When someone needed petty cash for undercover reviews, Philip counted it out as if he were donating blood. "Nothing more than a handjob," he'd soberly remind you.

In the late '70s, however, New York boasted a dozen spectacular "leisure spas," which were theme park whorehouses, like Tahitia and Caesar's Retreat. The managers would routinely comp the guy from *Screw*. The girls were spectacular, about twenty lined up as you walked in. The boss would let you pick out any two you desired, each one of *Penthouse* caliber, then whisper instructions for them to give their best, he's the man from *Screw*. You were given a palatial suite for a few hours, a Vegas recreation of Caesar's bedroom or a Tahitian paradise.

When I was editing the Naked City listings, I farmed out a lot to other stringers. Believe it or not, you could even grow weary of sex joints. But the leisure spas were so much fun that the city of New York closed them all down.

Jaccoma and I were also responsible for overseeing *Midnight Blue*. We'd planned to shoot mock interview vignettes of Goldstein and budding starlet Veronica Hart, whose porno film acting remains unsurpassed to this day. I was smitten. I wrote some sketches and personally delivered them, along with flowers, to her loft, hoping to do a little "pre-production" work.

Veronica was new to Manhattan and had just returned from a tough day on the set. She sat down in the kitchen and began to luxuriously brush her hair and unwind. She began to blush while describing the leading man's attempt to keep his dick in her ass, but it kept popping out and they had to keep reshooting. Just another nine-to-five workday.

"Here, let me," I said, reaching for the brush.

She pulled back, slapping my hand. "What are you doing?" she said. "You know, I thought were friends." She could handle the task herself, thank you, and mentioned her fiancée, a cameraman whom I believe shot some of her films, would soon be home. This was a monogamous woman. Encountering porn actresses with prudish behavior was always jarring.

Most women were fascinated, after an obligatory snicker, to hear you were an editor at *Screw*. They would often confide something sexual. A whole courtroom would burst out laughing during jury duty, when you were asked what your job was. But not everybody approved.

A hardboiled newspaper reporter who'd gone to college with my father took me out to dinner. "I'm ashamed of you, Josh," he confided over drinks. "Aren't you ashamed to work there? You'll never be able to get a job at the *Daily News*. You need to do a few stories for *New York* or the *Voice*, sweep all that dirty crap away."

And then, out the side of his mouth: "Geeze, I bet you meet some broads there. Whaddya say, me and you, we take on a few of those porno broads one night? Geeze, that Goldstein must be rich. How much is he worth? Anyway, I'm ashamed of you. I'm tellin' ya, get outta there."

In the summer of 1981, when I was Senior Editor, I began to notice some interesting activity across the eleventh-floor art director's window. Ballerinas and cheerleader types scurried about in the windows of the building behind us. Incredibly, for twelve years, no other *Screw* staffer before me had ever noticed this phenomenon. I hollered out our window, about twenty yards, to a blonde knockout, for her phone number. Her roommates clasped their hands over her mouth, but not before she yelled back the downstairs phone exchange and their room. I dialed her up.

The girl who answered said it was her second day in New York from the Texas panhandle.

"Don't *ever* give out your phone number to strangers in this city," I advised.

"Well, just who are y'all?"

"We're *Screw* magazine," I said. "And thank God you gave your number to us. If you'd been across from Time-Life, you would have really fallen in with some perverts."

Within an hour, giddy college girls were hanging out of all the top floor dorm windows. I arranged dates for them with *Screw* personnel. It wasn't long before I became a regular "gentleman caller" at the waiting area in the quaint lobby of the Markle Evangeline Hall on 13th Street. Although men were strictly forbidden beyond this point, I was soon known by Major Anderson, the Salvation Army *commandant*. I enjoyed breakfast in the Markle cafeteria, just me and 500 nymphs in their morning bathrobes. In a *coup de grace*, the girls snuck me upstairs to the dorms, where I hid in their bunk beds. (Even the *Screw* press pass couldn't deliver like this!). The female hormones were so prevalent in these halls that hundreds of young ladies experienced their menstrual cycles simultaneously. When outside girlfriends visited at that time of the month, they too automatically began their periods. I dare say, the female hormones were so fragrant, I almost began to menstruate.

"It's the mother lode," gasped the editor of *High Society*, as word quickly spread throughout the men's magazine world. But I protected the girls from such swine: *Screw*, and only *Screw* would be the Markle Evangeline Hall's official male fraternity. Even the geeks from *Midnight Blue* on the fourth floor nearly ruined everything, exposing themselves like mongoloid idiots before our magic window.

Several elderly men also resided at the Markle. The qualifying age for men was a mere fifty-five. In the Salvation Army's world, gentlemen over fifty-five couldn't possibly be a threat to young girls, and indeed, the few living there were retired clergymen types, fuddy duds. The Markle was oblivious to the impending possibility that Al Goldstein himself would soon qualify (which I never told Al, for fear he *would* move in).

Larry Flynt's charades always seemed minuscule, pale imitations of the great Goldstein. Al feared no man alive (save for perhaps gangster John Gotti, and gay power broker/attorney Roy Cohn, who represented his third wife in their divorce). During a street confrontation one evening, as we led a Times Square tour for visiting ladies, Al cut down some porn store goons whom I thought were about to stomp us. Goldstein stood fearless before their threats, said he would see them dead first. They backed down, contritely apologizing. Though I witnessed some of Al's grand achievements, it's the little things that stand out. Like the time Annette Haven came up for her interview. She was in her prime and generated awe over the fact that such a stunning creature would actually do hardcore (and nothing but hardcore—she loathed "nudie-cutie" stuff). She was a woman of principle with a sexual mission. Goldstein had a mission too, and spent most of the interview whining for a blowjob.

"Oh, Al," she would say, bemused. But Goldstein wouldn't let up, as if begging for his life. If he landed a part in one of her movies, could he have one? No, she declared, that would be too contrived. And not for any amount of money. She liked Al but wouldn't do it as a matter of principle. I'd never seen a human being grovel to that degree. He followed her on his knees to the elevator, and onto 14th Street, until her limousine door slammed. He yelled after the limo for her to make an old Jewish man die happy. It was a heroic failure.

The Great Pornographer suffered grand excesses. Several donut shops along 14th Street were actually paid off to refuse Goldstein service. I believe one shop was bribed to lock their door, should Goldstein come a-knockin'. Sort of like the Wolfman begging his neighbors to keep their doors locked at night, no matter how much he howled. Al's four secretaries received calls from donut proprietors when Goldstein went off the deep end, swallowing donuts by the baker's dozen. All four secretaries from the fourth-floor business office at Milky Way would have to dash over and coax him out. Sort of like farm hands herding a berserk prize hog back into its corral.

We did theme issues with cover lines that screamed Armageddon & Dingleberries, or Voodoo & Vomit. Piled high at newsstands right alongside the *New York Post*, we knew millions of New Yorkers had a chance of at least *seeing* the cover lines. Goldstein might complain whenever we got too cerebral, like Gil Reavill's bogus Goldstein interview with Hitler's Third Reich architect, Albert Speer, which many people believed. "This is not a college paper!" bellowed Goldstein. "Get back to fuck shots!"

A particular brainchild of mine was our Sex and Diarrhea issue. Every page covered some form of shit. Goldstein was scheduled to appear on

BBC radio in London, where he hoped to score a distribution deal. As with any business trip, his secretary packed two dozen of that week's issue.

I heard the BBC radio tapes, one appalled British interviewer after another. "Mr. Goldstein, if this is a sex periodical, how come every single page has defecation, feces or diarrhea?"

Al grabbed the paper and was himself surprised to see the Sex & Diarrhea cover theme. BBC hosts raged on: "Mr. Goldstein, you are a revolting man. Get out of this studio! Get out of this country!" The business trip was cut short.

Though he was like a "Gandhi with his dick out," Goldstein liked to say that if he were assassinated, they could fill up Yankee Stadium with suspects. He even went on TV in Southern California, daring rednecks to get out their rifles and take their best shot. Californians were so inept, he said, they couldn't possibly shoot straight. There were alternate print crews at the plant where *Screw* was printed. When the Pope issue came out, Catholic pressmen walked off. But backup crews of blacks, Puerto Ricans, Polish, Italian or Jewish pressman stood at the ready, to fill in for any offended ethnic group.

I have but one remaining Times Square "mole," to this day. Uncle Lou, the beloved chauffeur, who's driven hundreds of porn stars to their club dates. He still calls me in Texas in the wee hours with news from Show World. Doesn't quite believe that I left the beat twelve years ago.

Lou befriends strippers for life, remaining loyal long after other fans have abandoned them. I once went to dinner in Times Square with Uncle Lou, who brought along a depressed, overweight ex-stripper. When she went for the powder room, he leaned over and said out the side of his mouth, "If you play your cards right, you got a shot with her."

"But I don't want a shot with her," I said.

"I think she likes ya," Lou continued, "she likes ya 'cause you don't come on like gangbusters."

Even if she'd been smashing, I've long since left the life. I married the girl who first answered the phone at the Markle. Followed her back to Texas, where we reside in a palace in Dallas.

—1998

THE RISE AND FALL OF AL GOLDSTEIN

Mr. Freedom of Speech

We called him The Great One. Every Friday afternoon he came up to the eleventh-floor editorial offices to check *Screw*'s bluelines before we went to press. Managing Editor Richard Jaccoma got the call from the fourth floor that he was on his way. Jaccoma would scurry from room to room like a headless chicken, trumpeting the emperor's arrival. He did this in the voice of Indian peasant boy Sabu, rolling his R's: "De Grrreat One, de Grrreat One is coming!"

They called John Gotti the Teflon Don when charges didn't stick. But Goldstein was the Teflon Pornographer. He weathered nineteen arrests in the late '60s, petty arrests, not righteous ones, when they busted blind news dealers for selling *Screw*. Weekends and overnighters in Riker's. The magazine debuted on newsstands the day after Nixon was elected President. It gave the world's oldest profession its first advertising medium and enabled the man on the street to get laid within an hour. It also made enemies fast. Goldstein was once arrested eight hours after grafting Mayor Lindsay's head on a naked photo composite. A typical 1970 trial concerned dildo ads. The State of New York argued in Superior Court that dildos could be used for criminally immoral purposes.

Screw was the first to call J. Edgar Hoover a faggot, when he was alive. Once dead, everybody called him a faggot. Finally, forces within the Nixon Administration initiated a mighty offensive to lock *Screw*'s publisher up for sixty years. Legend has it that Hoover's very last directive was, "Get Goldstein." A trial was held in Wichita, Kansas, a hamlet where the Federal government figured the local citizenry most likely to convict him for postal indecency. Postal inspectors in Kansas subscribed under fictitious names to entrap him. Nine of the jurors said *Screw* didn't arouse their prurient interest. After three years of trial and error, a hung jury exonerated him in 1978. Goldstein flew his Kansas jury to New York to celebrate at Plato's Retreat, and took them all out to dinner on the anniversary of his acquittal. This landmark victory thereafter insured the right of Americans to view buck-ass naked sex—with or without redeeming social value.

Al Goldstein is now an obese, diabetic, cigar-chomping trainwreck of sixty-six. He has faced down his own mortality many times. Goldstein has undergone more litigation than any publisher in America. He has endured fat farms, liposuctions, tummy tucks, gall-bladder removal and a tracheostomy while on trial in Kansas. He has enriched four ex-wives and put a son through Harvard Law School. He's taken enough medications to kill ten Elvises, for God knows how many personality disorders and imbalances. Downing pastrami sandwiches and pints of Häagen-Dazs ice cream, the Goldstein girth has fluctuated between a svelte 175 and an unsavory 350 pounds, which he is now.

But Al Goldstein's court battles could endow an entire law library. Leaf through the annals of *Screw*'s legal history and you will be amazed by the rogues' gallery of public puritans who tried to crush *Screw*—whose lives and careers then went down in flames or disgrace. These figures were branded with the "Goldstein Curse"—a dark omen bestowed by Goldstein in his weekly editorial. It works like Jewish voodoo.

It began with Mayor Lindsay, whose vice squad busted six blind news dealers for selling *Screw*, arresting Goldstein nineteen times on charges of second degree obscenity. Lindsay's presidential aspirations, star career and health fell into ruin after his last term. Nassau County D.A. Bill Cahn handcuffed Goldstein for obscenity, then ended up in Federal prison for tax fraud. Staten Island Congressman John Murphy was jailed in the Abscam investigation after he fought to remove Goldstein's cable-TV show *Midnight Blue* from the air. Even those who survived the Curse encountered misfortune of some kind. Mayor Giuliani's prostate cancer was announced soon after he received his Goldstein Curse for cleaning up Times Square.

Raving morality figures who aggressively targeted *Screw* include Charles Keating, founder of Citizens For Decent Literature. The same Charles

Keating later imprisoned for robbery in the multi-billion-dollar Lincoln Savings & Loan scandal. Televangelist Jim Bakker was ruined by fraud and sex scandal a month after Goldstein vacationed at Bakker's Heritage USA Christian theme park in South Carolina. Attorney General Ed Meese resigned over corruption charges after heading The Attorney General's Commission on Pornography. Among Meese's firebrand anti-smut Commissioners was Rev. Morton Hill, head of Morality in Media—who soon dropped dead. Also on the Reagan-era Commission was Times Square's most insidious anti-porn crusader. "Father" Bruce Ritter's career shattered when it was revealed he'd been molesting homeless boys in his care all along, while squandering Covenant House funds on male prostitutes.

Corporate raider Carl Icahn bankrupted TWA and lost his chairmanship in 1993. He too had been cursed after sparring with Goldstein. In 1996, Goldstein bested longtime foe Time-Warner Cable of New York in Federal court, for scrambling *Midnight Blue*'s cable signal. Even the *U.S.S. Intrepid* went into bankruptcy the moment it canceled a party they found out Goldstein had booked.

Goldstein's millions have gone into *Screw*'s Defense Department budget. It cost a dapper dime defending the right to degrade the high and mighty, and underwrite the First Amendment law firms of Herald Price Fahringer and Ken Norwick. A model named Angie Geary filed a $29-million defamation after *Midnight Blue* parodied her 1988 Wasa Crispbread commercial. It was eventually thrown out. During my own time at *Screw* there appeared a mild parody of the Poppin' Fresh doughboy humping the doughgirl while she had a yeast infection. Pillsbury responded with a $50-million lawsuit. Goldstein owned two shares of General Mills and flew to a stockholder's meeting in Minneapolis dressed as the doughboy. He reprimanded them for wasting shareholders' money on frivolous lawsuits. Once the suit was dismissed, Al co-opted the doughboy as *Screw*'s cover logo for a year. Japanese *Screw*, franchised at that time, was unfamiliar with American baking products. They assumed Poppin' Fresh was *Screw*'s cover logo. Though Japanese *Screw* was short-lived, Pillsbury's corporate symbol graced every cover.

Screw has prevailed in lawsuits leveled by ambitious D.A.'s trying to make their bones. But Goldstein barely escaped ruin after settling a lawsuit from the wife of an assistant D.A. Her phone number somehow penetrated *Screw*'s security check. She appeared in the hooker ads "Willing to Suck Nigger Cock Free."

Any major loss could have bankrupted *Screw* on the spot. But Goldstein prevailed. It seemed God himself was on the side of this fat, Hebrew action hero whose attackers lined up one by one, oblivious to each other's defeats, only to get chopped into herring.

He bested them all. Until now. The Great Pornographer has finally been brought down by a thirty-year-old former secretary, Jennifer Lozinski. This "filthy Jew whore," as she's described in *Screw*, has proven to be his most formidable enemy.

In July of 2002, Richard Jaccoma and I visit *Screw*, together there for the first time in twenty years. Goldstein hobbles in by cane, unseemly flesh billowing down from his waist. He has recently been bailed out from Riker's Island after "the worst nine days of my life." He owes Riker's another fifty days for harassing Lozinski.

"The Mafia said I'd be dead by this weekend," says Al.

"So what else is new?" I ask.

"If I get shot this weekend, you should be thrilled having my last interview."

Goldstein takes a load off his sockless, diabetic feet. "My life is not boring," he sighs, sinking into a chair. This week he's got a son who disowned him, he's taking over the Mafia's distribution of his paper, and he's been arrested for the *second* time in six weeks. His longtime distributor, Astro News, a Gambino Family newsstand supplier, threatened that he wouldn't live through the weekend if he switched distributors. Defiant, Goldstein will solidify the final switch today. The new distributors await in another room. Goldstein claims he lives for hate, and won't die because it would make too many people happy.

"I want you to hear this story," says Al, "it's un-fuckin' believable. I travel with Jean-Marc. Jean-Marc is a cigar buddy, 'cause I get lonely in the big castle in Florida. I date a little bit. But mostly I'm alone. So he and I, we smoke cigars, we go out, we go to Trapeze. Bottom line is, he's my buddy. His professional job is, I swear to God, he's a gigolo. He's a biker, he's got tattoos, he fucks older women. He's from Marseilles, living in America for twenty-two years, has his own home in Boca, a sports car and a Harley Davidson. He travels with me as my bodyguard."

Listening attentively in the office are the balding bon vivant Frenchman, Jean-Marc himself, and another finely tailored gent basking in Goldstein's presence.

"We get off the plane Wednesday, Jet Blue, and we arrive at a quarter to six. I'm comin' into town cause I'm takin' on the Mafia and going with a new distributor and I'm very excited. We've got four bags, we walk out to the taxi, and three guys in suits walk over, shake my hand. 'How are you, Al?' I said, 'Hi, how are you,' and they said, 'You're under arrest.'

"I thought it's a joke. I said, 'What, are you fuckin' guys kidding?' They said, 'No, we're sorry, Al, we've got to take you.' I explained I was already arrested three weeks ago, what's this about? I'm with my luggage, I said, 'C'mon, I wanna go home and take a shower.' They said, 'No, you're under arrest. Gina, your ex-wife, has brought charges against you for harassment.'"

The Great One revels in the daily melodrama of his life. Each incident is fodder for the inevitable Hollywood epic of his life story.

"Anyway, they all shake my hand, they're total gentlemen. So they let me bring the luggage upstairs where [*Screw* Art Director] Kevin's waiting for me. I'm more stunned than anything. They put me in the car without handcuffs. They bring me to the 67th precinct because that's where Gina lives and she's the one that brought the charges. The cops are all gentlemen, and this guy Joe here is saying, 'I'm the greatest fan of yours, read *Screw*, love your work. I'm just following orders. We're not gonna cuff you or put you in a cell. We'll put you in that room over there, we have to lock the door, we'll keep you here a few hours cause once you're in the Tombs you're gonna be with the animals.'

"It's now like 6:30, they keep me there till 10 o'clock. Then they bring me to the Tombs, I'm on the floor with fifteen people and 400 cockroaches. Then Joe here does something that makes me love him deeply."

The man in the expensive suit, sitting here as if we're huddled around a *shtetle* campfire being serenaded by the town's 350-pound rabbi, is Joe—one of the arresting officers. The detective now hangs with Al on off-duty hours.

"He says, 'Listen, I can get you a pastrami sandwich at the Stage Deli,' so he orders me a sandwich. And he knows every porno film, he's done 600 hookers, he loves Times Square. As any old hooker will tell you, cops are among the most frequent patrons. 90 percent of all gonorrhea and herpes cases come from women who've slept with cops.

"All the cops at the Tombs grew up with me. But I'm handcuffed and treated like shit. They take my medicine away, I'm a diabetic, I'm really sick, for ten hours I'm trying to get to Bellevue, no one cares, I'm having a diabetic attack, they don't care if you fuckin' die."

If convicted of these new charges for harassing Gina—his third wife and the mother of his son—Goldstein could get several years. The D.A. decided Goldstein was a flight risk and bail was set at $50,000. After thirty hours, he was released.

"So I took Joe and his wife to Katz's Saturday night to reciprocate for the pastrami sandwich. I invited him to an editorial meeting. He loves cigars, he loves his wife, loves pussy, loves to fuck. He loves pregnant women's milk. He's a great cop."

Mr. Freedom of Speech has always worn the First Amendment around his neck like a cross to ward off puritanical witch burners. He joined the ACLU when he was fifteen. His father denounced him as a Communist. The ACLU once told him he gave freedom of speech a bad name.

"But the issue here," insists Goldstein, "is that I never called Gina personally, like with Lozinski. The First Amendment. I have a better chance of winning on this second arrest because I did not make an actual phone call."

Goldstein didn't use the phone, but his readership did. A full-page photo of Gina ran in *Screw*, headlined "A World-Class Cunt." It was requested that readers phone her at the Allen Stevenson School and "ask her to stop being a cunt." Over a hundred people called. She became afraid. The Manhattan D.A.'s office issued an order of protection.

Gina was married to Goldstein for over a decade. Enacting the classic Madonna/whore mindset, Goldstein tried to separate his life in two—that of urbane businessman with family hearth in a five-story townhouse on the upper East Side, with a perfectly sane, upstanding wife. A school teacher whose husband just happened by day to be the clown prince of pornography. The most outrageous smut peddler in history. Like all close relationships in his life, romantic or business, it eventually went bad.

"She didn't like strangers phoning her business school to call her a cunt," shrugs Goldstein. "So she had me arrested."

Goldstein is particularly irritated about this because he thought she was well paid off in the divorce. "The reason Gina got $3 million is I wanted joint custody of Jordan. I knew no judge would give me joint custody, so I would have seen Jordan only two weeks a year. It was extortion, but I did it willingly. What more commitment can you make? He stayed with Gina half the time, we lived five blocks apart."

After twenty-four years of family calm, mother and son have teamed up against him. So he began running full-page spreads: "How America Got AIDS" depicts Gina naked, about to fellate a black witch doctor, accusing her of introducing the disease to America after a 1980 trip to Cuba. In another, his ex-wife rolls around naked with a hog, called "a dirty pig-fucker," whose "cunt ain't kosher." Goldstein pools his enemies together, printing mockups of Gina having sex with Manhattan D.A. Robert Morgenthau and Brooklyn D.A. Charlie Hynes.

It's as if Photoshop was created just for Goldstein. *Screw* has blossomed into an open book of Goldstein's failed relationships, lawsuits and personal hatreds. The magazine and *Midnight Blue* remain his salvation, his weekly therapy to vent frustration. Like Lenny Bruce, his life is degenerating into a series of arrests and trials. But they're becoming harder to categorize as trailblazing First Amendment issues.

When not the target of lawsuits, Goldstein is busy instigating his own. He is The Shopper from Hell. Mercedes, for instance, recently neglected to repair an electrical problem on his new Benz. Mock ads began appearing in *Screw* of the Benz USA president's head superimposed over a Nazi SS uniform:

"Buy a Benz—kill a Jew." Rather than even press the issue, they bought the car back and paid him thirty grand to just drop the whole matter. He did. "Nobody can fucking believe I got $30,000 from Mercedes," says Goldstein. "They told me I can't divulge the amount of the settlement. Fuck them."

Goldstein is usually right in his grievances. There is a sense he's striking a blow for all the Common Joe Screw readers who spend their miserable lives in a silent scream. Surly flight attendants, rude sales people or arrogant CEO's who cross Consumer Goldstein receive stiff public rebuke in a place they'd *really* rather not be mentioned—*Screw* and *Midnight Blue*. The Curse is rationed out to the worst of them. Citizen Al can smear political candidates by merely *endorsing* them.

Nine months ago in Brooklyn is where Goldstein was arrested on charges brought by Jennifer Lozinski. The incident: He cussed her out on the phone because he had to wait at LAX airport for a rental car. Cussing out secretaries was nothing new for Lovable Al. He would rain abuse into secretaries' answering machines in the wee hours. In the morning they soberly typed up his complaints into minutes. *Oh that Al*—it's just a routine part of the job.

But Lozinski, thirty, claimed to be unaccustomed to such foul language and quit. Goldstein then accused her of conspiring with a former *Screw* Ad Director who allegedly embezzled $130,000. He accused her of pilfering petty cash. He called her a "miserable lowlife" on *Midnight Blue*, flashing her address and number. And in the phone call that sealed his fate, Goldstein told her "I'm going to take you down." This phrase became the linchpin of debate in his misdemeanor trial. *Take her down* in the "Strawberry Fields" sense? In a sexual context? Lozinski feared he meant take down in a mob sense. Goldstein stood his ground under the mantle of Free Speech. His defense came up with a dozen definitions for the meaning of *take you down*. But this speech, for the first time in thirty years, didn't come free. The court found the threat a less than honorable extension of the First Amendment. Goldstein was convicted on six counts of misdemeanor harassment and given four concurrent sixty-day jail sentences.

Lozinski claimed she didn't know what *Screw* was, never saw explicit material during the eleven weeks she worked there. But it came out in court that she herself mailed vitriolic videos and copies of *Screw*, by Goldstein's directive, to friends and family of the very secretary who preceded her. Goldstein turned the trial into a circus. Dressed in prison stripes before sentencing, he told reporters outside Brooklyn Criminal Court that "Judge Chun makes a nice lo mein, but put too much starch in my shirt." He ran an editorial suggesting someone "slam a 747" into the office of Brooklyn D.A. Charles J. Hynes, complete with aerial directions to the building. As the trial progressed, *Screw* ran photos of the prosecutor being schtupped in the ass and blowing O.J. Simpson. He repeated these quips on the *Howard Stern Show*. Stern responded with a lecture on sanity.

When cross-examined by the assistant D.A. about his 747 editorial, Al went into a tirade about the First Amendment. Judge Daniel K. Chun—whom Goldstein addressed as "Judge Chopstick"—cleared the courtroom and charged him with contempt, setting bail at $100,000. But this order was rescinded when the shaken judge was reminded he couldn't charge Goldstein with contempt without a warning first. When the jury was led back in, ninety-one-year-old Al "Grandpa Munster" Lewis took the stand as Goldstein's character witness. In what was described by the *New York Post* as a "rambling discourse," Lewis was nearly ejected from court.

All four New York dailies gave him sympathetic coverage. Jimmy Breslin wrote two *Newsday* columns acknowledging Al as the media's foremost First Amendment martyr.

In his final address before sentencing, Goldstein told the judge, "You weren't in this country when I was out fighting for you—I'm a Korean War veteran… This is the proudest day of my life… Let's not forget that Lenny Bruce was not vindicated until five months after he was dead… When a movie is made about this trial, Richard Dreyfuss will play me and Howdy Doody will play you, your honor."

Judge Chopstick ordered him to start serving sixty days at Riker's.

"Jail means nothing to me," Goldstein trumpeted to *The New York Times* after sentencing, "because freedom means so much to me." He said he was intrigued by the prospect of having a big black boyfriend violate his love holes.

Herald Price Fahringer, who won for Goldstein in Kansas, is appealing. Goldstein has great hopes that the harassment statute he was convicted under will be declared unconstitutional.

Lozinski's Revenge

It had been over thirty years since Goldstein was at Riker's Island. He takes a long pause and the tone of his voice softens:

"You can't anticipate how horrible it is. Riker's is the vilest, it's gotten much worse. I was thirty-two then, now I'm sixty-six, I've got diabetes, I'm on fifteen medicines. So I was put in the methadone center. I'm with fifty *schvartzas*, all of them doing methadone in the bathroom. I'm with the Bloods, the Crips, I'm the only white person, the oldest there. Handcuffed all the time. There's no diabetic food. Breakfast, lunch and dinner is the same—pieces of bread and jelly. Like a third world country, everything at Riker's was broken—the toilets, the sinks, the copying machines. Nothing to do but stare at space. It's filthy, there are cockroaches, everyone hates you, it's a fuckin' horror."

Some corrections officers asked Goldstein for his autograph. But the twenty-year-old gangbangers had no idea who The Great Pornographer was. Even supporters within the NYPD were unable to sneak in pastrami sandwiches.

"I'm not some Mafia guy who can do time standing on my head. Theoretically, you're allowed to have visitors, but they wouldn't let me. I'm not talkin' theory, I'm talkin' truth. You can have *Penthouse*, *Playboy* and *Hustler*, but they wouldn't let me have *Screw*. They took *Newsweek*, *Time*, they took every magazine I had. They gave me only two—*Cigar Aficionado* just to aggravate me 'cause I can't smoke, and *Time Out*, the restaurant issue, since I wasn't allowed to eat. They're playing mind games, they're trying to break you." Lozinski got her revenge. In case there was a dearth of such creatures at Riker's, the guards got themselves one fat, angry, loudmouth New York Jew to aggravate. Not enjoying his stay, Goldstein was taken to the medical ward, where his *attitude* made him the ideal prisoner to torture. After seven hours waiting for permission to use a bathroom, Goldstein shit his pants. He refused to take a shower. "If I am to be in hell, I want to smell like hell," he told the guards. He began hallucinating, seeing double and hearing voices after being injected with God knows what.

"They performed surgery on me illegally. They put a catheter up my leg against my will in Riker's hospital. They stopped giving me my own diabetic medicine, they switched my anti-depressants to Zoloft, which I don't take. They injected insulin in my arm, which I don't take. It was Dr. Mengele. The corrections officer said I would leave in a pine box."

Watching CNN one night, an old man whose legs were amputated wheeled in and changed the channel over Goldstein's protest. "That was my one fight in prison and I yielded to a legless cripple," he says. "Let the cripple watch his nigger shows," Goldstein thought to himself, "I fucked Seka and Linda Lovelace. I'm sure the only girls this guy ever fucked were members of his own family."

Goldstein daydreamed of the steaks, lobsters and hookers he would ravish when he got out. He prayed for the first time in forty-two years—since he was jailed in Cuba for photographing Raul Castro and told he would be executed as an American spy. Fahringer's legal assistant, Tricia Dubnow, came to Goldstein's rescue. "She saw me laying on the floor shaking, puking, crying. She would not leave without me."

Tricia got locked up herself for twenty-five hours trying to bail Al out.

His bail was accepted after nine days in Riker's. He still owes them fifty more days. His passport confiscated, he can't travel a radius of more than twenty miles from his Florida home or his New York apartment.

"They won, they broke my spirit," Al told *The New York Times*, stumbling out of Riker's nearly comatose. It was the first time he ever cried during an interview.

Jordan

"The first arrest embarrassed my son, who graduated Harvard Law School," Goldstein continues. "Now that he's Mr. Harvard he's so ashamed. Two weeks ago he called me at eight o'clock in the morning and, are you ready for this, here's the message he personally delivered to me: he said, 'Dad, the reason I didn't invite you to Harvard Law School's graduation wasn't because of Mom—but because *I* did not want you there. I cannot wait for the day I read your *New York Times* obituary.' I said, Fuck you, and I hung up. That was worse than all the other shit. I wake up in the middle of the night crying."

Before Harvard, Jordan Goldstein finished first in his class of 781 students at Georgetown University. The chart is framed on Goldstein's office wall. Al's son was offered graduate scholarships to NYU and Oxford. But Al Goldstein—a fat, former bed-wetting stutterer from Williamsburg, Brooklyn—*lived* for the day he could send his son to Harvard.

Al's own father was a small timid fellow who said "sir" to elevator operators. His last years were spent with a job in the *Screw* mailroom. Rather than live in fear and resignation, Goldstein became the opposite of his father. And now his son Jordan has become a conservative beacon of respectability. They now hate each other as only family members can.

Immediately after their fallout, Goldstein declared his son dead in the pages of *Screw*. This is how Goldstein vents his rage, the only way he knows how, the way he is designed. The ads Proud Papa Goldstein has been running of his son and ex-wife are clearly the rantings of a divine madman. The *pièce de résistance* of his career. Jordan is surrounded by an In Loving Memory wreath with his 1996 Georgetown Summa Cum Laude report card: "His academic achievements will not be forgotten by his grieving former father—who'd like to remind you that Jordan's Ivy League education cost him nearly $700,000." *Screw*'s subscription ads feature a mockup of Jordan in the gym: "Order...today, or you might end up turning into a spoiled, thieving, faggot

Harvard boy..." Jordan's baby picture ("Wahhhh! I want my *Screw!*"). A "Who's Jordan's Dad?" contest to determine who knocked up Gina—with photos of possible impregnators Mike Tyson, Hitler, bin Laden, Nixon, Arafat and blind Egyptian cleric Omar Abdel-Rahman. A full-page Reward offer appears each week, seeking Jordan Ari Goldstein's current whereabouts and number. A mockup photo of Gina blowing Jordan; Jordan blowing the President of Georgetown University; and one mockup entitled "Nigger Lovin' Jews," showing Jordan and Gina copulating with Afro-Americans.

Gina may have once married The Great Pornographer, but Jordan didn't pick his dad.

"I was the greatest father, took him all over, filled him with love," says Goldstein, nearing tears. "I gave up my twenty-five-year friendship with Hefner 'cause he would not let Jordan come to movie night at the [Playboy] Mansion. On the radio I've mentioned my son graduated Harvard Law School and how proud I was. I said, Jordan, if I were a surgeon, an entrepreneur, if I worked for Enron, you wouldn't worry about me being proud of you. I *kvell* at your success. Most people graduate college and law school owing hundreds of thousands of dollars. You have $300,000 in the bank. I spent $700,000 on Georgetown, on your tutoring, on Horace Mann School in the Bronx. Aren't I entitled to be proud? I went to Georgetown, I met the president, Father Donovan. We shared Cuban cigars. I always acted appropriate for the moment. I'm not Larry Flynt. It's in my will, Jordan can never enter my business, my world."

Goldstein kept *Screw* out of Jordan's reach when he was a small child. I once saw Al hide a wayward copy of *Playboy* on the banister at his 61st Street townhouse when Jordan was a toddler. Al shows a photo of himself, the picture of propriety with Harvard officials and Jordan. The education was paid for through a million tricks by prostitutes who advertise in *Screw*.

"I am so proud that he would travel the high road. The road I traveled, people are always surprised I could string together a sentence. We're in the porno world, we're never taken seriously. But his turning on me, wishing me dead... I thought Gina was responsible for that, that's why I called her a cunt."

A loud, interruptive voice cuts through Goldstein's campfire story. Enter Professor Irwin Cory. The geriatric comedian was a master of malapropism and double talk. An old Lefty, he joins the meeting, fuming about being rejected by the Communist Party in 1941. He curses "those *rats*" Burl Ives, Karl Malden and Elia Kazan, who squealed to the House Committee on Un-American Activities. "Indians never went to war at the command of captains or kings," intones Corey. "There isn't the word war in their vocabulary, nor the word warrior, or brave or chief or squaw, which is a vulgar expression. It means cunt. The Idaho Indians wanted that word taken out of any place that's named like Squaw Valley—change it to Cunt Valley."

"You know why I love you, Irwin?" says Goldstein. "You make me look sane. Will you come to court as a character witness?"

"Oh, yeah, I'll be there," says Corey, composing himself. "I'm a character that cannot be improved upon."

"Good," says Goldstein. "Your fucking courage to talk about the Vietnam War that got you banned from Johnny Carson and Letterman is why I will always love you."

Corey's voice rises to an abrasive scream, oblivious to all in the room, as he rails against the Catholic Church owning Yankee Stadium.

"Irwin Corey, you are a fuckin' hero," interrupts Al, trying to shut him up. "Will you absorb the praise and leave? You can't."

Goldstein heads to his private office while Corey lectures out of control to the *Screw* art department. "He's too disruptive, I can't handle him." There's only one other man as crazy as Corey—Al "Grandpa Munster" Lewis. "When they're together I run out of the room," says Al.

A man of the people, Goldstein's New York taxi cab hack license is posted on his office wall. He's kept it up to date since the '60s. Now and then, Goldstein claims, he hits the streets behind the wheel of a cab when he feels a need to stay down to earth. Plato's Retreat founder Larry Levinson ended up driving one, and so have a few male porn stars past their prime.

Though he claims he's just an old Jew who smokes cigars, he's got girls waiting in every city. Recent snapshots on the wall attest to this.

He shares his primary residence in Florida with B-movie scream queen Linnea Quigley. An eleven-foot hand sculpture in the backyard gives the finger to passing boats on the intracoastal waterway there. In Amsterdam, there's "Happy Hooker" Xaviera Hollander ("She's too old to do much but eat gefilte fish and take drugs with me"). In L.A., there's Katherine, an alumnus of "Hollywood Madam" Heidi Fleiss. He's dated her for six years, "though I know she's still gonna hook." Here at the office, he's having an affair with a twenty-seven-year-old knockout East Indian chick.

But the shocking news is that his number one bitch has become Jean-Marc—who suddenly appears through a swinging trap window in the wall by Goldstein's desk—right there in case of trouble. The Frenchman is Goldstein's bodyguard, flunkie... and Gal Friday. Jean-Marc's loyalty to Al has nothing to do with money. Al has proclaimed himself bisexual, getting it on with the Frenchman. He prefers him to some women.

"My last wife, Patty, got a million," says Goldstein. "I have no money. I'm living on Social Security." Al tried to play Pygmalion to fourth wife Patty, "the Irish cleaning lady." She kept right on working even after marriage. Al's limousine took her to cleaning jobs, though the limo cost $40 an hour while she was making $8.

Goldstein's now down to one elderly, part-time Jewish lady at the reception desk. Before he ever dreamed he would someday rely on Social Security, he employed four full-time secretaries. One for business appointments, one to take abusive dictation, and two to fill out daily mail-order catalog whims. He circled electronic *chotchkas* by the hundred—VCRs, CD players, model trains, calculators, solar-powered cigar lighters. His gold Mickey Mouse watch was studded with diamonds. A storage room at *Screw*'s 14th Street headquarters was filled to capacity. His office still contains more gadgets than a gift shop. Only young girlfriends use the new $6,000 iPod at his desk. "I don't even know how to use a computer," he says. "I don't wanna learn at my age, my mind is filled."

Goldstein once published a magazine called *Gadget*, dedicated to his obsession with them (the party he was to throw at the *U.S.S. Intrepid* was for *Gadget*'s anniversary). For his sudden obsession with cigars, he created the first publication solely devoted to the subject. In 1981, he flew five members of the *Screw* staff down to Havana with him. The Ugly American personified, Al inquired toward every Cuban what he could buy or take. For the return trip, he stuffed each staffer's suitcase with contraband cigars. After they squeaked through customs, Goldstein rifled through staffers' luggage, scattering clothes at the baggage claim as he pulled out his precious cigars.

His humidor filled to capacity, Goldstein stuffed cigars into every crevice of his wine cellar. One weekend a white fungus attacked all of his Havanas. In a panic, he rushed in two specialists from Dunhill's, wondering whether he should post an armed guard at the humidor. At editorial meetings, Goldstein discussed the logistics of sending us—his editorial staff—back to Cuba in a dinghy to smuggle another 10,000 Havanas. It would be cheaper than hiring mercenaries. Goldstein would await us at the Miami docks.

Goldstein has declared all of his noble ventures outside of *Screw*—*Gadget*, *Cigar*, *National Screw*, *Screw West*, *Sex Sense*, *Bitch*, *Gay*, *Death* and *Smut*—to be publishing failures. Only *Screw* has prospered, not having missed a week since 1968. Nearing 1,800 issues, Goldstein now believes the whole operation is in jeopardy of folding. He can't meet the payroll for the first time, can't even buy Deer Park for the water coolers, which are dried out like a desert. He's given up space in the new offices on 24th Street.

"It's my fault," admits Goldstein, "I travel too much. I deserve everything I got, I didn't manage the company. Right now I'm doing everything I can to keep from going out of business. If I go, nobody else is gonna be able to do it. It would just die."

There is no contingency plan if Al dies. One idea is to pretend he's alive, a Colonel Sanders with his cock out. Or sell his DNA like Ted Williams. Goldstein's good friend Bob Guccione might have been interested in saving *Screw*, but he has throat cancer and his own magazine is sinking. There was once talk of Larry Flynt buying it. "But even Larry doesn't have the insanity needed to helm *Screw*," says Goldstein. "You need someone who's filled with hatred. It's not driven by love."

Astro News in Brooklyn reports *Screw* is now selling only two copies each on 600 newsstands in New York. "That's not possible," says Goldstein. The circulation, at one time over 40,000, has now fallen to 5,000. Robert

"DiBe" DiBernardo, the suave Gambino Family porn capo and Teamster liaison, was *Screw*'s longtime protector. Back in the day, nobody could muscle Goldstein. Then DiBe disappeared in 1986. Ten years later Sammy "The Bull" Gravano disclosed in his biography, *Underboss*, that his crew aced DiBe by order of John Gotti.

Mayor Giuliani closed all the whorehouses, once the bulk of *Screw*'s backpage ads. Free distribution of the *Village Voice* and *New York Press*, which began running the same ads once exclusive to *Screw*, cut deeply into circulation. And *Screw*, once piled high alongside the *New York Post* throughout the city, is now relegated to the back of the newsstand, due to Astro News.

But John Gotti has recently died in prison, and his son and his brother are in jail. "So now I'm making my move with a new distributor," Goldstein declares. "There's still the name *Screw* and the name Al Goldstein. I could go out of business quietly, or go fighting. So I made it clear I'm taking over distribution. This coming week is the first issue I take over. Another Family in Baltimore said they'd like to take over distribution. Astro News made it clear to me this can't happen, I'd be killed. I told Rick to go die. Rick left a message on my machine saying he'll destroy me and *Screw*. Rick basically wants to put *Screw* out of business and replace it with other papers he distributes."

The new distributor just paid twenty-five grand to take over distribution, and posted Al's $25,000 bail—an excellent show of faith. They got him a new apartment in Manhattan. The magazine will take on a glossy cover, rise to $3.95, run a minimum 150 fuck photos per issue, and give a hefty new cut to each newsstand.

"If I'm found dead, beaten up, crippled or maimed," Goldstein tells the detective at his side, "you go to Rick at Astro News. He's behind it."

Having cops as friends doesn't hurt. In the '70s and '80s, Al's full-time bodyguard was a former NYPD vice squad cop who once busted hookers, as well as news dealers that sold *Screw* in the '60s. If some rookie tried to ticket Al's limo while idling in a No Parking zone, Flynn would shove his bearded face into their squad car and give them hell. Whenever the big debonair Irishman accompanied Al to 42nd Street, the black streetwalkers had a field day. "Hey John Flynn, whatcha doin' John Flynn? You sho' is hot, John Flynn. Suck yo' dick, Officer Flynn?"

After years of faithful service to Milky Way Productions, the mother company of Goldstein's empire, John Flynn walked out of the limo to make a phone call. He left the keys inside. When he returned, the limo was gone. Goldstein gave him two weeks to find the car, or retire. The car was never found.

"If this experiment with *Screw* fails," says Goldstein, "I'm gonna try to kill myself in Pennsylvania. You don't wanna kill yourself in New York, L.A., Chicago or Florida. I have a girlfriend, she's thirty, a great cocksucker. She went to a nuthouse in Pennsylvania. She gets a dental plan, health insurance and $800 a month support there.

"But I can't kill myself because Jordan owns a $1.2-million insurance policy on me. I got it as a gift to him when he graduated Georgetown. I don't want him to have the joy of cashing in the policy."

Al always said they'd have to fill up Yankee Stadium with suspects if he were killed. But he hasn't been. Not yet. He's outlived the anti-porn crusaders, the "evil puritans who loathe pleasure and want to deny it to everybody else," as he's described them.

"I'm not going to be everyone's fucking piece of shit, I'm not everyone's buttboy. I believe in the next year I'll either die in the Tombs or Riker's, where they said I'd leave in a pine box, or by an assassin's bullet."

To all the D.A.'s and judges, his family that turned against him, the Mafia threats and the system that killed Lenny Bruce, Al says: "I fuck you all. I dare you to try and stop me. You may kill me, but I won't go quietly."

And so The Great One ends his campfire discourse to enter the next room, where the new distributors await. Serious muscle from out of town. Men he does not want anyone at the office to meet. If it is to be his last weekend on earth, he will not go quietly.

(Screw *ceased publication as such in October 2003, after thirty-five years.*)

AFTERWORD

I Gave My Regards To Broadway

Grand Luncheonette was condemned in 1997. This humble hot-grease frankfurter counter with a bullet-hole ridden window was the last 42nd Street storefront to close. You can still see it in movies like *Taxi Driver*. Metal gates shuttered every entrance on the Deuce. Grand's owner, grilling hot dogs there for fifty-eight years, told reporters, "The oddest thing is when people come here to ask: 'Where's Times Square?'"

It may be an urban theme park fit for a eunuch, but Times Square is still astonishing. My six-year-old daughter, with little prompting from me, is awestruck. On every trip from Texas, she sits transfixed on my shoulders as we hit the old stomping grounds. She doesn't feel nostalgia for bygone Playland arcades, nor does she mourn the Melody Burlesk. Toys 'R Us, Hello Kitty and *The Lion King* suffice.

The last few porn stores on the Deuce—that's 42nd Street between 7th and 8th Avenues—were evicted in 1996. This block, where the dirtiest sex known to man was depicted, was finally castrated. "The symbolism cannot be underestimated," said the president of the Times Square Business Improvement District, to the *Times*. "This sea change marks the end of a long, sad chapter."

The neighborhood has seen over $4 billion in private redevelopment. Rescuing the New Amsterdam Theater, where *The Lion*

King played, was an epic achievement. *Mary Poppins* plays there now. Not even a real Phantom could have survived in its basement catacombs sprouting huge mushrooms in a stagnant pond with fifty feral cats. Disney anted up $8 million, prompting the State of New York to put up another $34 million for rehabilitation. The New Amsterdam regained its virginity, looking finer than it did on opening night in 1903. (The befuddled Disney guide who led my tour announced that "the theater began showing kung-fu movies in 1936.")

The final exhibit in Madame Tussaud's new wax museum on 42nd is a solemn World Trade Center tribute—firemen hoisting the American flag. The old Times Square would have featured jumpers splattering onto the sidewalk. Madame Tussaud's is pitifully out of touch with the old Times Square's zeitgeist. Madame makes an attempt at good taste with excruciatingly inappropriate wax celebrities, like TV weatherman Al Roker, Ru Paul and Donald Trump. Now that's bad taste.

In contrast to the $22 wax ticket, 42nd Street enjoyed a brief appearance by the Chashama arts complex, a non-profit performance art organization. This stretch of reincarnated $4 sideshows put the block to good use. Real estate baron Douglas Durst lent the four storefronts to his producer daughter Anita. It was an altruistic experiment for the public good, a rare gesture amongst developers. Anchored by the Bindlestiff Cirkus and Palace of Variety, vaudeville-burlesque returned briefly to Times Square.

A national renaissance in burlesque was predicted by Morton Minsky in *Tales* (Chapter 2) and it's happening now. This neo-burlesque, sans gynecology, *is* for your aunt from Dubuque. Especially if she's a lesbian. But Times Square always belonged to the Common Man. Lord only knows who that is today. Outside of Sardi's, there are no more cozy private phone booths—occupied by what A.J. Liebling coined "telephone booth Indians"—the once-ubiquitous Bud Abbott types who operated around Broadway.

After Mayor Giuliani left office, a lunatic's soapbox reopened on one of Broadway's traffic islands. The deranged "lost tribe" of black Hebrews, for instance, in robes and combat boots, once again harangued the white man that the day was coming when he will be chained in slavery. These *shvartzim* were ordered to take a hike during the Giuliani years, but reemerged with Bloomberg.

Since the Cold War began, Times Square has figured in the collective imagination as the nuclear bullseye for Armageddon. (By my figuring, only Show World, cockroaches and Keith Richards will survive.) Only a mayoral fanatic of such conflicted moral fiber as Giuliani could make the city this safe. The fact that decent Americans like your aunt from Dubuque can once again stroll safely down 42nd Street is a miracle. Women, children and callow fellows are no longer assaulted by disembowelment show cards, fuck holes and Riker's Island inmates on 42nd Street. Sex is no longer cheap and dirty. New York is no longer a town without foreplay. High life and low life do not co-exist in corporate America.

"Retailtainment"—*see the show, buy the crap*—is the new pornography of Times Square. Times Square refuses to become fossilized, but it no longer boasts the virility of Satan. There's no good reason a designated red-light district couldn't have remained behind subdued storefronts on at least one block, say 42nd between 6th and 7th.

But Giuliani's zoning restrictions were enacted in 1995. Hundreds of Russian, Polish and Slavic Live Nude Girls born behind the Iron Curtain were suddenly liberated from behind the peep show curtain. The notorious "60/40" law went into effect, all but crushing the porn right out of Times Square. "Adult-use" establishments had to stock at least sixty percent non-sexual filler. And the more patriotic the better: I ♥ NY tees, statues of Liberty, Empire State Buildings, cut-out Popeye and Erik Estrada videos in Spanish, and other clearance-item tourist crap.

Times Square also saw the demise of two-fisted 8th Avenue Irish bars. Downey's and Jimmy Ray's—gone. No more steaming corned beef & cabbage plates for the working man at Blarney Stone or Shandon Star. Smith's on 45th Street became a white-collar shrine just by nature of its being the last blue-collar holdout of its kind. The last Howard Johnson's on 46th & Broadway ("the new Algonquin roundtable," according to magician Penn Gillette, who presided over fried-clam dinner parties there) was shut in 2006. Brave octogenarians, Jack and Morris Rubenstein, held out as long as they could, proclaiming that Times Square still needed its last Howard Johnson's (there once were five).

Joe Franklin's 8th Avenue restaurant proved that TV's very first talk-show host was still alive. Broadway hadn't had a greeter of that caliber since Jack Dempsey's closed at the Brill Building. Apparently, Joe rushed about wearing a raincoat, as if perennially late for appointments. "Gotta go, gotta go," he greeted patrons.

For those few of us who cared about the fate of 42nd Street's golden age theaters, there were positive results. The exterior of the New Victory Theater now resembles its 1899 façade as Hammerstein's Victoria. The New Vic is now a 499-seat (one seat less than B'way minimum) cutting-edge children's vaudeville theater. The Vic and the New Amsterdam are the two greatest saves on the block. The Ford Center for the Performing Arts combined locations of the Lyric (opened in 1903) and the Apollo (1920) into one giant new theater. The Ford, like its namesake in Detroit, can only accommodate mass-market blockbusters. The 43rd Street side restored the lovely façade of the Lyric. The Apollo's boxes, ceiling dome and proscenium were restored to the Ford. The Ford Center is run with cold auto-industry efficiency.

More amazing was the transfer of the Empire Theater, which opened in 1912 as the Eltinge, later to become Times Square's beloved Laffmovie house in 1942. The 3,700-ton Empire was literally rolled on rails 170 feet west to become reincarnated as the lobby and mezzanine for the AMC 25 cinema. Its terra-cotta exterior, plaster ceilings and proscenium survive. The same ceilings under which Clark Gable, Laurence Olivier, Abbott & Costello and Jackie Gleason debuted on 42nd Street.

But each era in Times Square reflects its own time. Rest assured, 42nd Street will return to a futuristic squalor for our descendants to enjoy. Some apocalyptic, Disneyfied world of sleaze and pornography and blight and ruin lurks in the future. It's genetically encoded into the urban ecosystem called Times Square.

Josh Alan Friedman
Dallas, Texas
2007